Find "arguments"
replace with "param

See "review" sections at
end of each chapter for functions
that Max can call (obv).

An Introduction to

Programming in Emacs Lisp

An Introduction to

Programming in Emacs Lisp

Revised Third Edition

by Robert J. Chassell

This is an *Introduction to Programming in Emacs Lisp*, for people who are not programmers.

Edition 3.10, 28 October 2009

Published by the:

GNU Press,
a division of the
Free Software Foundation, Inc.
51 Franklin Street, Fifth Floor
Boston, MA 02110-1301 USA

http://www.fsf.org/licensing/gnu-press/
email: sales@fsf.org
Tel: +1 (617) 542-5942
Fax: +1 (617) 542-2652

ISBN 1-882114-43-4

Short Contents

Table of Contents

Preface

Most of the GNU Emacs integrated environment is written in the programming language called Emacs Lisp. The code written in this programming language is the software—the sets of instructions—that tell the computer what to do when you give it commands. Emacs is designed so that you can write new code in Emacs Lisp and easily install it as an extension to the editor.

(GNU Emacs is sometimes called an "extensible editor", but it does much more than provide editing capabilities. It is better to refer to Emacs as an "extensible computing environment". However, that phrase is quite a mouthful. It is easier to refer to Emacs simply as an editor. Moreover, everything you do in Emacs—find the Mayan date and phases of the moon, simplify polynomials, debug code, manage files, read letters, write books—all these activities are kinds of editing in the most general sense of the word.)

Although Emacs Lisp is usually thought of in association only with Emacs, it is a full computer programming language. You can use Emacs Lisp as you would any other programming language.

Perhaps you want to understand programming; perhaps you want to extend Emacs; or perhaps you want to become a programmer. This introduction to Emacs Lisp is designed to get you started: to guide you in learning the fundamentals of programming, and more importantly, to show you how you can teach yourself to go further.

On Reading this Text

All through this document, you will see little sample programs you can run inside of Emacs. If you read this document in Info inside of GNU Emacs, you can run the programs as they appear. (This is easy to do and is explained when the examples are presented.) Alternatively, you can read this introduction as a printed book while sitting beside a computer running Emacs. (This is what I like to do; I like printed books.) If you don't have a running Emacs beside you, you can still read this book, but in this case, it is best to treat it as a novel or as a travel guide to a country not yet visited: interesting, but not the same as being there.

Much of this introduction is dedicated to walkthroughs or guided tours of code used in GNU Emacs. These tours are designed for two purposes: first, to give you familiarity with real, working code (code you use every day); and, second, to give you familiarity with the way Emacs works. It is interesting to see how a working environment is implemented. Also, I hope that you will pick up the habit of browsing through source code. You can learn from it and mine it for ideas. Having GNU Emacs is like having a dragon's cave of treasures.

In addition to learning about Emacs as an editor and Emacs Lisp as a programming language, the examples and guided tours will give you an opportunity to get acquainted with Emacs as a Lisp programming environment. GNU Emacs supports programming and provides tools that you will want to become comfortable using, such as `M-.` (the key which invokes the `find-tag` command). You will also learn about buffers and other objects that are part of the environment. Learning about these features of Emacs is like learning new routes around your home town.

Finally, I hope to convey some of the skills for using Emacs to learn aspects of programming that you don't know. You can often use Emacs to help you understand what puzzles you or to find out how to do something new. This self-reliance is not only a pleasure, but an advantage.

For Whom This is Written

This text is written as an elementary introduction for people who are not programmers. If you are a programmer, you may not be satisfied with this primer. The reason is that you may have become expert at reading reference manuals and be put off by the way this text is organized.

An expert programmer who reviewed this text said to me:

> I prefer to learn from reference manuals. I "dive into" each paragraph, and "come up for air" between paragraphs.

> When I get to the end of a paragraph, I assume that that subject is done, finished, that I know everything I need (with the possible exception of the case when the next paragraph starts talking about it in more detail). I expect that a well written reference manual will not have a lot of redundancy, and that it will have excellent pointers to the (one) place where the information I want is.

This introduction is not written for this person!

Firstly, I try to say everything at least three times: first, to introduce it; second, to show it in context; and third, to show it in a different context, or to review it.

Secondly, I hardly ever put all the information about a subject in one place, much less in one paragraph. To my way of thinking, that imposes too heavy a burden on the reader. Instead I try to explain only what you need to know at the time. (Sometimes I include a little extra information so you won't be surprised later when the additional information is formally introduced.)

When you read this text, you are not expected to learn everything the first time. Frequently, you need make only a nodding acquaintance with some of the items mentioned. My hope is that I have structured the text and given you enough hints that you will be alert to what is important, and concentrate on it.

You will need to dive into some paragraphs; there is no other way to read them. But I have tried to keep down the number of such paragraphs. This book is intended as an approachable hill, rather than as a daunting mountain.

This introduction to *Programming in Emacs Lisp* has a companion document, *The GNU Emacs Lisp Reference Manual*. The reference manual has more detail than this introduction. In the reference manual, all the information about one topic is concentrated in one place. You should turn to it if you are like the programmer quoted above. And, of course, after you have read this *Introduction*, you will find the *Reference Manual* useful when you are writing your own programs.

Lisp History

Lisp was first developed in the late 1950s at the Massachusetts Institute of Technology for research in artificial intelligence. The great power of the Lisp language makes it superior for other purposes as well, such as writing editor commands and integrated environments.

GNU Emacs Lisp is largely inspired by Maclisp, which was written at MIT in the 1960s. It is somewhat inspired by Common Lisp, which became a standard in the 1980s. However, Emacs Lisp is much simpler than Common Lisp. (The standard Emacs distribution contains an optional extensions file, `cl.el`, that adds many Common Lisp features to Emacs Lisp.)

A Note for Novices

If you don't know GNU Emacs, you can still read this document profitably. However, I recommend you learn Emacs, if only to learn to move around your computer screen. You can teach yourself how to use Emacs with the built-in tutorial. To use it, type `C-h t`. (This means you press and release the `CTRL` key and the `h` at the same time, and then press and release `t`.)

Also, I often refer to one of Emacs's standard commands by listing the keys which you press to invoke the command and then giving the name of the command in parentheses, like this: `M-C-\` (`indent-region`). What this means is that the `indent-region` command is customarily invoked by typing `M-C-\`. (You can, if you wish, change the keys that are typed to invoke the command; this is called *rebinding*. See Section 16.8 "Keymaps", page 189.) The abbreviation `M-C-\` means that you type your `META` key, `CTRL` key and `\` key all at the same time. (On many modern keyboards the `META` key is labeled `ALT`.) Sometimes a combination like this is called a keychord, since it is similar to the way you play a chord on a piano. If your keyboard does not have a `META` key, the `ESC` key prefix is used in place of it. In this case, `M-C-\` means that you press and release your `ESC` key and then type the `CTRL` key and the `\` key at the same time. But usually `M-C-\` means press the `CTRL` key along with the key that is labeled `ALT` and, at the same time, press the `\` key.

In addition to typing a lone keychord, you can prefix what you type with `C-u`, which is called the *universal argument*. The `C-u` keychord passes an argument to the subsequent command. Thus, to indent a region of plain text by 6 spaces, mark the region, and then type `C-u 6 M-C-\`. (If you do not specify a number, Emacs either passes the number 4 to the command or otherwise runs the command differently than it would otherwise.) See Section "Numeric Arguments" in *The GNU Emacs Manual*.

If you are reading this in Info using GNU Emacs, you can read through this whole document just by pressing the space bar, `SPC`. (To learn about Info, type `C-h i` and then select Info.)

A note on terminology: when I use the word Lisp alone, I often am referring to the various dialects of Lisp in general, but when I speak of Emacs Lisp, I am referring to GNU Emacs Lisp in particular.

Thank You

My thanks to all who helped me with this book. My especial thanks to
Jim Blandy, Noah Friedman, Jim Kingdon, Roland McGrath, Frank Ritter,
Randy Smith, Richard M. Stallman, and Melissa Weisshaus. My thanks also go
to both Philip Johnson and David Stampe for their patient encouragement. My
mistakes are my own.

Robert J. Chassell

`bob@gnu.org`

1 List Processing

To the untutored eye, Lisp is a strange programming language. In Lisp code there are parentheses everywhere. Some people even claim that the name stands for "Lots of Isolated Silly Parentheses". But the claim is unwarranted. Lisp stands for LISt Processing, and the programming language handles *lists* (and lists of lists) by putting them between parentheses. The parentheses mark the boundaries of the list. Sometimes a list is preceded by an apostrophe "'", called a *single-quote* in Lisp.[1] Lists are the basis of Lisp.

1.1 Lisp Lists

In Lisp, a list looks like this: `'(rose violet daisy buttercup)`. This list is preceded by a single apostrophe. It could just as well be written as follows, which looks more like the kind of list you are likely to be familiar with:

```
'(rose
  violet
  daisy
  buttercup)
```

The elements of this list are the names of the four different flowers, separated from each other by whitespace and surrounded by parentheses, like flowers in a field with a stone wall around them.

Lists can also have numbers in them, as in this list: `(+ 2 2)`. This list has a plus-sign, '+', followed by two '2's, each separated by whitespace.

In Lisp, both data and programs are represented the same way; that is, they are both lists of words, numbers, or other lists, separated by whitespace and surrounded by parentheses. (Since a program looks like data, one program may easily serve as data for another; this is a very powerful feature of Lisp.) (Incidentally, these two parenthetical remarks are *not* Lisp lists, because they contain ';' and '.' as punctuation marks.)

Here is another list, this time with a list inside of it:

```
'(this list has (a list inside of it))
```

The components of this list are the words 'this', 'list', 'has', and the list '(a list inside of it)'. The interior list is made up of the words 'a', 'list', 'inside', 'of', 'it'.

1.1.1 Lisp Atoms

In Lisp, what we have been calling words are called *atoms*. This term comes from the historical meaning of the word atom, which means "indivisible". As far as Lisp is concerned, the words we have been using in the lists cannot be divided into any smaller parts and still mean the same thing as part of a program; likewise with numbers and single character symbols like '+'. On the other hand, unlike an ancient

---

[1] A single-quote is an abbreviation for the special form `quote`; you need not think about special forms now. See ⟨undefined⟩ "Complications", page ⟨undefined⟩.

atom, a list can be split into parts. (See Chapter 7 "`car cdr` & `cons` Fundamental Functions", page 71.)

In a list, atoms are separated from each other by whitespace. They can be right next to a parenthesis.

Technically speaking, a list in Lisp consists of parentheses surrounding atoms separated by whitespace or surrounding other lists or surrounding both atoms and other lists. A list can have just one atom in it or have nothing in it at all. A list with nothing in it looks like this: (), and is called the *empty list*. Unlike anything else, an empty list is considered both an atom and a list at the same time.

The printed representation of both atoms and lists are called *symbolic expressions* or, more concisely, *s-expressions*. The word *expression* by itself can refer to either the printed representation, or to the atom or list as it is held internally in the computer. Often, people use the term *expression* indiscriminately. (Also, in many texts, the word *form* is used as a synonym for expression.)

Incidentally, the atoms that make up our universe were named such when they were thought to be indivisible; but it has been found that physical atoms are not indivisible. Parts can split off an atom or it can fission into two parts of roughly equal size. Physical atoms were named prematurely, before their truer nature was found. In Lisp, certain kinds of atom, such as an array, can be separated into parts; but the mechanism for doing this is different from the mechanism for splitting a list. As far as list operations are concerned, the atoms of a list are unsplittable.

As in English, the meanings of the component letters of a Lisp atom are different from the meaning the letters make as a word. For example, the word for the South American sloth, the '`ai`', is completely different from the two words, '`a`', and '`i`'.

There are many kinds of atom in nature but only a few in Lisp: for example, *numbers*, such as 37, 511, or 1729, and *symbols*, such as '`+`', '`foo`', or '`forward-line`'. The words we have listed in the examples above are all symbols. In everyday Lisp conversation, the word "atom" is not often used, because programmers usually try to be more specific about what kind of atom they are dealing with. Lisp programming is mostly about symbols (and sometimes numbers) within lists. (Incidentally, the preceding three word parenthetical remark is a proper list in Lisp, since it consists of atoms, which in this case are symbols, separated by whitespace and enclosed by parentheses, without any non-Lisp punctuation.)

Text between double quotation marks—even sentences or paragraphs—is also an atom. Here is an example:

```
'(this list includes "text between quotation marks.")
```

In Lisp, all of the quoted text including the punctuation mark and the blank spaces is a single atom. This kind of atom is called a *string* (for "string of characters") and is the sort of thing that is used for messages that a computer can print for a human to read. Strings are a different kind of atom than numbers or symbols and are used differently.

1.1.2 Whitespace in Lists

The amount of whitespace in a list does not matter. From the point of view of the Lisp language,

```
'(this list
   looks like this)
```

is exactly the same as this:

```
'(this list looks like this)
```

Both examples show what to Lisp is the same list, the list made up of the symbols 'this', 'list', 'looks', 'like', and 'this' in that order.

Extra whitespace and newlines are designed to make a list more readable by humans. When Lisp reads the expression, it gets rid of all the extra whitespace (but it needs to have at least one space between atoms in order to tell them apart.)

Odd as it seems, the examples we have seen cover almost all of what Lisp lists look like! Every other list in Lisp looks more or less like one of these examples, except that the list may be longer and more complex. In brief, a list is between parentheses, a string is between quotation marks, a symbol looks like a word, and a number looks like a number. (For certain situations, square brackets, dots and a few other special characters may be used; however, we will go quite far without them.)

1.1.3 GNU Emacs Helps You Type Lists

When you type a Lisp expression in GNU Emacs using either Lisp Interaction mode or Emacs Lisp mode, you have available to you several commands to format the Lisp expression so it is easy to read. For example, pressing the `TAB` key automatically indents the line the cursor is on by the right amount. A command to properly indent the code in a region is customarily bound to `M-C-\`. Indentation is designed so that you can see which elements of a list belong to which list—elements of a sub-list are indented more than the elements of the enclosing list.

In addition, when you type a closing parenthesis, Emacs momentarily jumps the cursor back to the matching opening parenthesis, so you can see which one it is. This is very useful, since every list you type in Lisp must have its closing parenthesis match its opening parenthesis. (See Section "Major Modes" in *The GNU Emacs Manual*, for more information about Emacs's modes.)

1.2 Run a Program

A list in Lisp—any list—is a program ready to run. If you run it (for which the Lisp jargon is *evaluate*), the computer will do one of three things: do nothing except return to you the list itself; send you an error message; or, treat the first symbol in the list as a command to do something. (Usually, of course, it is the last of these three things that you really want!)

The single apostrophe, `'`, that I put in front of some of the example lists in preceding sections is called a *quote*; when it precedes a list, it tells Lisp to do nothing with the list, other than take it as it is written. But if there is no quote preceding a list, the first item of the list is special: it is a command for the computer to obey. (In Lisp, these commands are called *functions*.) The list (+ 2 2) shown above did not have a quote in front of it, so Lisp understands that the + is an instruction to do something with the rest of the list: add the numbers that follow.

If you are reading this inside of GNU Emacs in Info, here is how you can evaluate such a list: place your cursor immediately after the right hand parenthesis of the following list and then type C-x C-e:

    (+ 2 2)

You will see the number 4 appear in the echo area. (What you have just done is evaluate the list. The echo area is the line at the bottom of the screen that displays or echoes text.) Now try the same thing with a quoted list: place the cursor right after the following list and type C-x C-e:

    '(this is a quoted list)

You will see (this is a quoted list) appear in the echo area.

In both cases, what you are doing is giving a command to the program inside of GNU Emacs called the *Lisp interpreter*—giving the interpreter a command to evaluate the expression. The name of the Lisp interpreter comes from the word for the task done by a human who comes up with the meaning of an expression—who interprets it.

You can also evaluate an atom that is not part of a list—one that is not surrounded by parentheses; again, the Lisp interpreter translates from the humanly readable expression to the language of the computer. But before discussing this (see Section 1.7 "Variables", page 9), we will discuss what the Lisp interpreter does when you make an error.

1.3 Generate an Error Message

Partly so you won't worry if you do it accidentally, we will now give a command to the Lisp interpreter that generates an error message. This is a harmless activity; and indeed, we will often try to generate error messages intentionally. Once you understand the jargon, error messages can be informative. Instead of being called "error" messages, they should be called "help" messages. They are like signposts to a traveler in a strange country; deciphering them can be hard, but once understood, they can point the way.

The error message is generated by a built-in GNU Emacs debugger. We will enter the debugger. You get out of the debugger by typing q.

What we will do is evaluate a list that is not quoted and does not have a meaningful command as its first element. Here is a list almost exactly the same as the one we just used, but without the single-quote in front of it. Position the cursor right after it and type C-x C-e:

    (this is an unquoted list)

A *Backtrace* window will open up and you should see the following in it:

```
---------- Buffer: *Backtrace* ----------
Debugger entered--Lisp error: (void-function this)
  (this is an unquoted list)
  eval((this is an unquoted list))
  eval-last-sexp-1(nil)
  eval-last-sexp(nil)
  call-interactively(eval-last-sexp)
---------- Buffer: *Backtrace* ----------
```

Your cursor will be in this window (you may have to wait a few seconds before it becomes visible). To quit the debugger and make the debugger window go away, type:

```
q
```

Please type `q` right now, so you become confident that you can get out of the debugger. Then, type `C-x C-e` again to re-enter it.

Based on what we already know, we can almost read this error message.

You read the `*Backtrace*` buffer from the bottom up; it tells you what Emacs did. When you typed `C-x C-e`, you made an interactive call to the command `eval-last-sexp`. `eval` is an abbreviation for "evaluate" and `sexp` is an abbreviation for "symbolic expression". The command means "evaluate last symbolic expression", which is the expression just before your cursor.

Each line above tells you what the Lisp interpreter evaluated next. The most recent action is at the top. The buffer is called the `*Backtrace*` buffer because it enables you to track Emacs backwards.

At the top of the `*Backtrace*` buffer, you see the line:

```
Debugger entered--Lisp error: (void-function this)
```

The Lisp interpreter tried to evaluate the first atom of the list, the word 'this'. It is this action that generated the error message 'void-function this'.

The message contains the words 'void-function' and 'this'.

The word 'function' was mentioned once before. It is a very important word. For our purposes, we can define it by saying that a *function* is a set of instructions to the computer that tell the computer to do something.

Now we can begin to understand the error message: 'void-function this'. The function (that is, the word 'this') does not have a definition of any set of instructions for the computer to carry out.

The slightly odd word, 'void-function', is designed to cover the way Emacs Lisp is implemented, which is that when a symbol does not have a function definition attached to it, the place that should contain the instructions is void.

On the other hand, since we were able to add 2 plus 2 successfully, by evaluating (+ 2 2), we can infer that the symbol + must have a set of instructions for the computer to obey and those instructions must be to add the numbers that follow the +.

It is possible to prevent Emacs entering the debugger in cases like this. We do not explain how to do that here, but we will mention what the result looks like, because you may encounter a similar situation if there is a bug in some Emacs code that you are using. In such cases, you will see only one line of error message; it will appear in the echo area and look like this:

```
Symbol's function definition is void: this
```
The message goes away as soon as you type a key, even just to move the cursor.

We know the meaning of the word 'Symbol'. It refers to the first atom of the list, the word 'this'. The word 'function' refers to the instructions that tell the computer what to do. (Technically, the symbol tells the computer where to find the instructions, but this is a complication we can ignore for the moment.)

The error message can be understood: 'Symbol's function definition is void: this'. The symbol (that is, the word 'this') lacks instructions for the computer to carry out.

1.4 Symbol Names and Function Definitions

We can articulate another characteristic of Lisp based on what we have discussed so far—an important characteristic: a symbol, like +, is not itself the set of instructions for the computer to carry out. Instead, the symbol is used, perhaps temporarily, as a way of locating the definition or set of instructions. What we see is the name through which the instructions can be found. Names of people work the same way. I can be referred to as 'Bob'; however, I am not the letters 'B', 'o', 'b' but am, or was, the consciousness consistently associated with a particular life-form. The name is not me, but it can be used to refer to me.

In Lisp, one set of instructions can be attached to several names. For example, the computer instructions for adding numbers can be linked to the symbol plus as well as to the symbol + (and are in some dialects of Lisp). Among humans, I can be referred to as 'Robert' as well as 'Bob' and by other words as well.

On the other hand, a symbol can have only one function definition attached to it at a time. Otherwise, the computer would be confused as to which definition to use. If this were the case among people, only one person in the world could be named 'Bob'. However, the function definition to which the name refers can be changed readily. (See Section 3.2 "Install a Function Definition", page 28.)

Since Emacs Lisp is large, it is customary to name symbols in a way that identifies the part of Emacs to which the function belongs. Thus, all the names for functions that deal with Texinfo start with 'texinfo-' and those for functions that deal with reading mail start with 'rmail-'.

1.5 The Lisp Interpreter

Based on what we have seen, we can now start to figure out what the Lisp interpreter does when we command it to evaluate a list. First, it looks to see whether there is a quote before the list; if there is, the interpreter just gives us the list. On the other hand, if there is no quote, the interpreter looks at the first element in the list and sees whether it has a function definition. If it does, the interpreter carries out the instructions in the function definition. Otherwise, the interpreter prints an error message.

This is how Lisp works. Simple. There are added complications which we will get to in a minute, but these are the fundamentals. Of course, to write Lisp programs, you need to know how to write function definitions and attach them to names, and how to do this without confusing either yourself or the computer.

Now, for the first complication. In addition to lists, the Lisp interpreter can evaluate a symbol that is not quoted and does not have parentheses around it. The Lisp interpreter will attempt to determine the symbol's value as a *variable*. This situation is described in the section on variables. (See Section 1.7 "Variables", page 9.)

The second complication occurs because some functions are unusual and do not work in the usual manner. Those that don't are called *special forms*. They are used for special jobs, like defining a function, and there are not many of them. In the next few chapters, you will be introduced to several of the more important special forms.

As well as special forms, there are also *macros*. A macro is a construct defined in Lisp, which differs from a function in that it translates a Lisp expression into another expression that is to be evaluated in place of the original expression. (See Section 8.2.2 "Lisp macro", page 85.)

For the purposes of this introduction, you do not need to worry too much about whether something is a special form, macro, or ordinary function. For example, `if` is a special form (see Section 3.7 "if", page 35), but `when` is a macro (see Section 8.2.2 "Lisp macro", page 85). In earlier versions of Emacs, `defun` was a special form, but now it is a macro (see Section 3.1 "defun", page 26). It still behaves in the same way.

The final complication is this: if the function that the Lisp interpreter is looking at is not a special form, and if it is part of a list, the Lisp interpreter looks to see whether the list has a list inside of it. If there is an inner list, the Lisp interpreter first figures out what it should do with the inside list, and then it works on the outside list. If there is yet another list embedded inside the inner list, it works on that one first, and so on. It always works on the innermost list first. The interpreter works on the innermost list first, to evaluate the result of that list. The result may be used by the enclosing expression.

Otherwise, the interpreter works left to right, from one expression to the next.

1.5.1 Byte Compiling

One other aspect of interpreting: the Lisp interpreter is able to interpret two kinds of entity: humanly readable code, on which we will focus exclusively, and specially processed code, called *byte compiled* code, which is not humanly readable. Byte compiled code runs faster than humanly readable code.

You can transform humanly readable code into byte compiled code by running one of the compile commands such as `byte-compile-file`. Byte compiled code is usually stored in a file that ends with a `.elc` extension rather than a `.el` extension. You will see both kinds of file in the `emacs/lisp` directory; the files to read are those with `.el` extensions.

As a practical matter, for most things you might do to customize or extend Emacs, you do not need to byte compile; and I will not discuss the topic here. See

Section "Byte Compilation" in *The GNU Emacs Lisp Reference Manual*, for a full description of byte compilation.

1.6 Evaluation

When the Lisp interpreter works on an expression, the term for the activity is called *evaluation*. We say that the interpreter "evaluates the expression". I've used this term several times before. The word comes from its use in everyday language, "to ascertain the value or amount of; to appraise", according to *Webster's New Collegiate Dictionary*.

After evaluating an expression, the Lisp interpreter will most likely *return* the value that the computer produces by carrying out the instructions it found in the function definition, or perhaps it will give up on that function and produce an error message. (The interpreter may also find itself tossed, so to speak, to a different function or it may attempt to repeat continually what it is doing for ever and ever in an infinite loop. These actions are less common; and we can ignore them.) Most frequently, the interpreter returns a value.

At the same time the interpreter returns a value, it may do something else as well, such as move a cursor or copy a file; this other kind of action is called a *side effect*. Actions that we humans think are important, such as printing results, are often side effects to the Lisp interpreter. It is fairly easy to learn to use side effects.

In summary, evaluating a symbolic expression most commonly causes the Lisp interpreter to return a value and perhaps carry out a side effect; or else produce an error.

1.6.1 Evaluating Inner Lists

If evaluation applies to a list that is inside another list, the outer list may use the value returned by the first evaluation as information when the outer list is evaluated. This explains why inner expressions are evaluated first: the values they return are used by the outer expressions.

We can investigate this process by evaluating another addition example. Place your cursor after the following expression and type `C-x C-e`:

```
(+ 2 (+ 3 3))
```

The number 8 will appear in the echo area.

What happens is that the Lisp interpreter first evaluates the inner expression, `(+ 3 3)`, for which the value 6 is returned; then it evaluates the outer expression as if it were written `(+ 2 6)`, which returns the value 8. Since there are no more enclosing expressions to evaluate, the interpreter prints that value in the echo area.

Now it is easy to understand the name of the command invoked by the keystrokes `C-x C-e`: the name is `eval-last-sexp`. The letters `sexp` are an abbreviation for "symbolic expression", and `eval` is an abbreviation for "evaluate". The command evaluates the last symbolic expression.

As an experiment, you can try evaluating the expression by putting the cursor at the beginning of the next line immediately following the expression, or inside the expression.

Here is another copy of the expression:

```
(+ 2 (+ 3 3))
```

If you place the cursor at the beginning of the blank line that immediately follows the expression and type `C-x C-e`, you will still get the value 8 printed in the echo area. Now try putting the cursor inside the expression. If you put it right after the next to last parenthesis (so it appears to sit on top of the last parenthesis), you will get a 6 printed in the echo area! This is because the command evaluates the expression `(+ 3 3)`.

Now put the cursor immediately after a number. Type `C-x C-e` and you will get the number itself. In Lisp, if you evaluate a number, you get the number itself—this is how numbers differ from symbols. If you evaluate a list starting with a symbol like `+`, you will get a value returned that is the result of the computer carrying out the instructions in the function definition attached to that name. If a symbol by itself is evaluated, something different happens, as we will see in the next section.

1.7 Variables

In Emacs Lisp, a symbol can have a value attached to it just as it can have a function definition attached to it. The two are different. The function definition is a set of instructions that a computer will obey. A value, on the other hand, is something, such as number or a name, that can vary (which is why such a symbol is called a variable). The value of a symbol can be any expression in Lisp, such as a symbol, number, list, or string. A symbol that has a value is often called a *variable*.

A symbol can have both a function definition and a value attached to it at the same time. Or it can have just one or the other. The two are separate. This is somewhat similar to the way the name Cambridge can refer to the city in Massachusetts and have some information attached to the name as well, such as "great programming center".

Another way to think about this is to imagine a symbol as being a chest of drawers. The function definition is put in one drawer, the value in another, and so on. What is put in the drawer holding the value can be changed without affecting the contents of the drawer holding the function definition, and vice versa.

The variable `fill-column` illustrates a symbol with a value attached to it: in every GNU Emacs buffer, this symbol is set to some value, usually 72 or 70, but sometimes to some other value. To find the value of this symbol, evaluate it by itself. If you are reading this in Info inside of GNU Emacs, you can do this by putting the cursor after the symbol and typing `C-x C-e`:

```
fill-column
```

After I typed `C-x C-e`, Emacs printed the number 72 in my echo area. This is the value for which `fill-column` is set for me as I write this. It may be different for you in your Info buffer. Notice that the value returned as a variable is printed in exactly the same way as the value returned by a function carrying out its instructions. From the point of view of the Lisp interpreter, a value returned is a value returned. What kind of expression it came from ceases to matter once the value is known.

A symbol can have any value attached to it or, to use the jargon, we can *bind* the variable to a value: to a number, such as 72; to a string, `"such as this"`; to a list, such as (`spruce pine oak`); we can even bind a variable to a function definition.

A symbol can be bound to a value in several ways. See Section 1.9 "Setting the Value of a Variable", page 16, for information about one way to do this.

1.7.1 Error Message for a Symbol Without a Function

When we evaluated `fill-column` to find its value as a variable, we did not place parentheses around the word. This is because we did not intend to use it as a function name.

If `fill-column` were the first or only element of a list, the Lisp interpreter would attempt to find the function definition attached to it. But `fill-column` has no function definition. Try evaluating this:

```
(fill-column)
```

You will create a `*Backtrace*` buffer that says:

```
---------- Buffer: *Backtrace* ----------
Debugger entered--Lisp error: (void-function fill-column)
  (fill-column)
  eval((fill-column))
  eval-last-sexp-1(nil)
  eval-last-sexp(nil)
  call-interactively(eval-last-sexp)
---------- Buffer: *Backtrace* ----------
```

(Remember, to quit the debugger and make the debugger window go away, type *q* in the `*Backtrace*` buffer.)

1.7.2 Error Message for a Symbol Without a Value

If you attempt to evaluate a symbol that does not have a value bound to it, you will receive an error message. You can see this by experimenting with our 2 plus 2 addition. In the following expression, put your cursor right after the +, before the first number 2, type *C-x C-e*:

```
(+ 2 2)
```

In GNU Emacs 22, you will create a `*Backtrace*` buffer that says:

```
---------- Buffer: *Backtrace* ----------
Debugger entered--Lisp error: (void-variable +)
  eval(+)
  eval-last-sexp-1(nil)
  eval-last-sexp(nil)
  call-interactively(eval-last-sexp)
---------- Buffer: *Backtrace* ----------
```

(Again, you can quit the debugger by typing *q* in the `*Backtrace*` buffer.)

This backtrace is different from the very first error message we saw, which said, '`Debugger entered--Lisp error: (void-function this)`'. In this case, the function does not have a value as a variable; while in the other error message, the function (the word '`this`') did not have a definition.

In this experiment with the +, what we did was cause the Lisp interpreter to evaluate the + and look for the value of the variable instead of the function definition. We did this by placing the cursor right after the symbol rather than after the parenthesis of the enclosing list as we did before. As a consequence, the Lisp interpreter evaluated the preceding s-expression, which in this case was + by itself.

Since + does not have a value bound to it, just the function definition, the error message reported that the symbol's value as a variable was void.

1.8 Arguments

To see how information is passed to functions, let's look again at our old standby, the addition of two plus two. In Lisp, this is written as follows:

```
(+ 2 2)
```

If you evaluate this expression, the number 4 will appear in your echo area. What the Lisp interpreter does is add the numbers that follow the +.

The numbers added by + are called the *arguments* of the function +. These numbers are the information that is given to or *passed* to the function.

The word "argument" comes from the way it is used in mathematics and does not refer to a disputation between two people; instead it refers to the information presented to the function, in this case, to the +. In Lisp, the arguments to a function are the atoms or lists that follow the function. The values returned by the evaluation of these atoms or lists are passed to the function. Different functions require different numbers of arguments; some functions require none at all.[2]

1.8.1 Arguments' Data Types

The type of data that should be passed to a function depends on what kind of information it uses. The arguments to a function such as + must have values that are numbers, since + adds numbers. Other functions use different kinds of data for their arguments.

---

[2] It is curious to track the path by which the word "argument" came to have two different meanings, one in mathematics and the other in everyday English. According to the *Oxford English Dictionary*, the word derives from the Latin for '`to make clear, prove`'; thus it came to mean, by one thread of derivation, "the evidence offered as proof", which is to say, "the information offered", which led to its meaning in Lisp. But in the other thread of derivation, it came to mean "to assert in a manner against which others may make counter assertions", which led to the meaning of the word as a disputation. (Note here that the English word has two different definitions attached to it at the same time. By contrast, in Emacs Lisp, a symbol cannot have two different function definitions at the same time.)

For example, the `concat` function links together or unites two or more strings of text to produce a string. The arguments are strings. Concatenating the two character strings `abc`, `def` produces the single string `abcdef`. This can be seen by evaluating the following:

```
(concat "abc" "def")
```

The value produced by evaluating this expression is `"abcdef"`.

A function such as `substring` uses both a string and numbers as arguments. The function returns a part of the string, a *substring* of the first argument. This function takes three arguments. Its first argument is the string of characters, the second and third arguments are numbers that indicate the beginning (inclusive) and end (exclusive) of the substring. The numbers are a count of the number of characters (including spaces and punctuation) from the beginning of the string. Note that the characters in a string are numbered from zero, not one.

For example, if you evaluate the following:

```
(substring "The quick brown fox jumped." 16 19)
```

you will see `"fox"` appear in the echo area. The arguments are the string and the two numbers.

Note that the string passed to `substring` is a single atom even though it is made up of several words separated by spaces. Lisp counts everything between the two quotation marks as part of the string, including the spaces. You can think of the `substring` function as a kind of atom smasher since it takes an otherwise indivisible atom and extracts a part. However, `substring` is only able to extract a substring from an argument that is a string, not from another type of atom such as a number or symbol.

1.8.2 An Argument as the Value of a Variable or List

An argument can be a symbol that returns a value when it is evaluated. For example, when the symbol `fill-column` by itself is evaluated, it returns a number. This number can be used in an addition.

Position the cursor after the following expression and type *C-x C-e*:

```
(+ 2 fill-column)
```

The value will be a number two more than what you get by evaluating `fill-column` alone. For me, this is 74, because my value of `fill-column` is 72.

As we have just seen, an argument can be a symbol that returns a value when evaluated. In addition, an argument can be a list that returns a value when it is evaluated. For example, in the following expression, the arguments to the function `concat` are the strings `"The "` and `" red foxes."` and the list `(number-to-string (+ 2 fill-column))`.

```
(concat "The " (number-to-string (+ 2 fill-column)) " red foxes.")
```

If you evaluate this expression—and if, as with my Emacs, `fill-column` evaluates to 72—`"The 74 red foxes."` will appear in the echo area. (Note that you must put spaces after the word 'The' and before the word 'red' so they will appear in the final string. The function `number-to-string` converts the integer that the addition function returns to a string. `number-to-string` is also known as `int-to-string`.)

1.8.3 Variable Number of Arguments

Some functions, such as `concat`, `+` or `*`, take any number of arguments. (The `*` is the symbol for multiplication.) This can be seen by evaluating each of the following expressions in the usual way. What you will see in the echo area is printed in this text after '⇒', which you may read as "evaluates to".

In the first set, the functions have no arguments:

```
(+)        ⇒ 0

(*)        ⇒ 1
```

In this set, the functions have one argument each:

```
(+ 3)      ⇒ 3

(* 3)      ⇒ 3
```

In this set, the functions have three arguments each:

```
(+ 3 4 5) ⇒ 12

(* 3 4 5) ⇒ 60
```

1.8.4 Using the Wrong Type Object as an Argument

When a function is passed an argument of the wrong type, the Lisp interpreter produces an error message. For example, the `+` function expects the values of its arguments to be numbers. As an experiment we can pass it the quoted symbol `hello` instead of a number. Position the cursor after the following expression and type *C-x C-e*:

```
(+ 2 'hello)
```

When you do this you will generate an error message. What has happened is that `+` has tried to add the 2 to the value returned by `'hello`, but the value returned by `'hello` is the symbol `hello`, not a number. Only numbers can be added. So `+` could not carry out its addition.

You will create and enter a `*Backtrace*` buffer that says:

```
---------- Buffer: *Backtrace* ----------
Debugger entered--Lisp error:
        (wrong-type-argument number-or-marker-p hello)
  +(2 hello)
  eval((+ 2 (quote hello)))
  eval-last-sexp-1(nil)
  eval-last-sexp(nil)
  call-interactively(eval-last-sexp)
---------- Buffer: *Backtrace* ----------
```

As usual, the error message tries to be helpful and makes sense after you learn how to read it.[3]

The first part of the error message is straightforward; it says 'wrong type argument'. Next comes the mysterious jargon word 'number-or-marker-p'. This word is trying to tell you what kind of argument the `+` expected.

---

[3] `(quote hello)` is an expansion of the abbreviation `'hello`.

The symbol `number-or-marker-p` says that the Lisp interpreter is trying to determine whether the information presented it (the value of the argument) is a number or a marker (a special object representing a buffer position). What it does is test to see whether the `+` is being given numbers to add. It also tests to see whether the argument is something called a marker, which is a specific feature of Emacs Lisp. (In Emacs, locations in a buffer are recorded as markers. When the mark is set with the `C-@` or `C-SPC` command, its position is kept as a marker. The mark can be considered a number—the number of characters the location is from the beginning of the buffer.) In Emacs Lisp, `+` can be used to add the numeric value of marker positions as numbers.

The 'p' of `number-or-marker-p` is the embodiment of a practice started in the early days of Lisp programming. The 'p' stands for "predicate". In the jargon used by the early Lisp researchers, a predicate refers to a function to determine whether some property is true or false. So the 'p' tells us that `number-or-marker-p` is the name of a function that determines whether it is true or false that the argument supplied is a number or a marker. Other Lisp symbols that end in 'p' include `zerop`, a function that tests whether its argument has the value of zero, and `listp`, a function that tests whether its argument is a list.

Finally, the last part of the error message is the symbol `hello`. This is the value of the argument that was passed to `+`. If the addition had been passed the correct type of object, the value passed would have been a number, such as 37, rather than a symbol like `hello`. But then you would not have got the error message.

1.8.5 The `message` Function

Like `+`, the `message` function takes a variable number of arguments. It is used to send messages to the user and is so useful that we will describe it here.

A message is printed in the echo area. For example, you can print a message in your echo area by evaluating the following list:

```
(message "This message appears in the echo area!")
```

The whole string between double quotation marks is a single argument and is printed *in toto*. (Note that in this example, the message itself will appear in the echo area within double quotes; that is because you see the value returned by the `message` function. In most uses of `message` in programs that you write, the text will be printed in the echo area as a side-effect, without the quotes. See Section 3.3.1 "`multiply-by-seven` in detail", page 30, for an example of this.)

However, if there is a '`%s`' in the quoted string of characters, the `message` function does not print the '`%s`' as such, but looks to the argument that follows the string. It evaluates the second argument and prints the value at the location in the string where the '`%s`' is.

You can see this by positioning the cursor after the following expression and typing *C-x C-e*:

```
(message "The name of this buffer is: %s." (buffer-name))
```

In Info, `"The name of this buffer is: *info*."` will appear in the echo area. The function `buffer-name` returns the name of the buffer as a string, which the `message` function inserts in place of `%s`.

To print a value as an integer, use '`%d`' in the same way as '`%s`'. For example, to print a message in the echo area that states the value of the `fill-column`, evaluate the following:

```
(message "The value of fill-column is %d." fill-column)
```

On my system, when I evaluate this list, `"The value of fill-column is 72."` appears in my echo area[4].

If there is more than one '`%s`' in the quoted string, the value of the first argument following the quoted string is printed at the location of the first '`%s`' and the value of the second argument is printed at the location of the second '`%s`', and so on.

For example, if you evaluate the following,

```
(message "There are %d %s in the office!"
         (- fill-column 14) "pink elephants")
```

a rather whimsical message will appear in your echo area. On my system it says, `"There are 58 pink elephants in the office!"`.

The expression `(- fill-column 14)` is evaluated and the resulting number is inserted in place of the '`%d`'; and the string in double quotes, `"pink elephants"`, is treated as a single argument and inserted in place of the '`%s`'. (That is to say, a string between double quotes evaluates to itself, like a number.)

Finally, here is a somewhat complex example that not only illustrates the computation of a number, but also shows how you can use an expression within an expression to generate the text that is substituted for '`%s`':

```
(message "He saw %d %s"
         (- fill-column 32)
         (concat "red "
                 (substring
                  "The quick brown foxes jumped." 16 21)
                 " leaping."))
```

In this example, `message` has three arguments: the string, `"He saw %d %s"`, the expression, `(- fill-column 32)`, and the expression beginning with the function `concat`. The value resulting from the evaluation of `(- fill-column 32)` is inserted in place of the '`%d`'; and the value returned by the expression beginning with `concat` is inserted in place of the '`%s`'.

When your fill column is 70 and you evaluate the expression, the message `"He saw 38 red foxes leaping."` appears in your echo area.

---

[4] Actually, you can use `%s` to print a number. It is non-specific. `%d` prints only the part of a number left of a decimal point, and not anything that is not a number.

1.9 Setting the Value of a Variable

There are several ways by which a variable can be given a value. One of the ways is to use either the function `set` or the function `setq`. Another way is to use `let` (see Section 3.6 "let", page 33). (The jargon for this process is to *bind* a variable to a value.)

The following sections not only describe how `set` and `setq` work but also illustrate how arguments are passed.

1.9.1 Using `set`

To set the value of the symbol `flowers` to the list `'(rose violet daisy buttercup)`, evaluate the following expression by positioning the cursor after the expression and typing *C-x C-e*.

```
(set 'flowers '(rose violet daisy buttercup))
```

The list (`rose violet daisy buttercup`) will appear in the echo area. This is what is *returned* by the `set` function. As a side effect, the symbol `flowers` is bound to the list; that is, the symbol `flowers`, which can be viewed as a variable, is given the list as its value. (This process, by the way, illustrates how a side effect to the Lisp interpreter, setting the value, can be the primary effect that we humans are interested in. This is because every Lisp function must return a value if it does not get an error, but it will only have a side effect if it is designed to have one.)

After evaluating the `set` expression, you can evaluate the symbol `flowers` and it will return the value you just set. Here is the symbol. Place your cursor after it and type *C-x C-e*.

```
flowers
```

When you evaluate `flowers`, the list (`rose violet daisy buttercup`) appears in the echo area.

Incidentally, if you evaluate `'flowers`, the variable with a quote in front of it, what you will see in the echo area is the symbol itself, `flowers`. Here is the quoted symbol, so you can try this:

```
'flowers
```

Note also, that when you use `set`, you need to quote both arguments to `set`, unless you want them evaluated. Since we do not want either argument evaluated, neither the variable `flowers` nor the list (`rose violet daisy buttercup`), both are quoted. (When you use `set` without quoting its first argument, the first argument is evaluated before anything else is done. If you did this and `flowers` did not have a value already, you would get an error message that the '`Symbol's value as variable is void`'; on the other hand, if `flowers` did return a value after it was evaluated, the `set` would attempt to set the value that was returned. There are situations where this is the right thing for the function to do; but such situations are rare.)

1.9.2 Using `setq`

As a practical matter, you almost always quote the first argument to `set`. The combination of `set` and a quoted first argument is so common that it has its own name: the special form `setq`. This special form is just like `set` except that the first argument is quoted automatically, so you don't need to type the quote mark yourself. Also, as an added convenience, `setq` permits you to set several different variables to different values, all in one expression.

To set the value of the variable `carnivores` to the list `'(lion tiger leopard)` using `setq`, the following expression is used:

```
(setq carnivores '(lion tiger leopard))
```

This is exactly the same as using `set` except the first argument is automatically quoted by `setq`. (The 'q' in `setq` means `quote`.)

With `set`, the expression would look like this:

```
(set 'carnivores '(lion tiger leopard))
```

Also, `setq` can be used to assign different values to different variables. The first argument is bound to the value of the second argument, the third argument is bound to the value of the fourth argument, and so on. For example, you could use the following to assign a list of trees to the symbol `trees` and a list of herbivores to the symbol `herbivores`:

```
(setq trees '(pine fir oak maple)
      herbivores '(gazelle antelope zebra))
```

(The expression could just as well have been on one line, but it might not have fit on a page; and humans find it easier to read nicely formatted lists.)

Although I have been using the term "assign", there is another way of thinking about the workings of `set` and `setq`; and that is to say that `set` and `setq` make the symbol *point* to the list. This latter way of thinking is very common and in forthcoming chapters we shall come upon at least one symbol that has "pointer" as part of its name. The name is chosen because the symbol has a value, specifically a list, attached to it; or, expressed another way, the symbol is set to point to the list.

1.9.3 Counting

Here is an example that shows how to use `setq` in a counter. You might use this to count how many times a part of your program repeats itself. First set a variable to zero; then add one to the number each time the program repeats itself. To do this, you need a variable that serves as a counter, and two expressions: an initial `setq` expression that sets the counter variable to zero; and a second `setq` expression that increments the counter each time it is evaluated.

```
(setq counter 0)                ; Letfls call this the initializer.

(setq counter (+ counter 1))    ; This is the incrementer.

counter                         ; This is the counter.
```

(The text following the ';' are comments. See Section 3.2.1 "Change a Function Definition", page 29.)

If you evaluate the first of these expressions, the initializer, `(setq counter 0)`, and then evaluate the third expression, `counter`, the number 0 will appear in the echo area. If you then evaluate the second expression, the incrementer, `(setq counter (+ counter 1))`, the counter will get the value 1. So if you again evaluate counter, the number 1 will appear in the echo area. Each time you evaluate the second expression, the value of the counter will be incremented.

When you evaluate the incrementer, (setq counter (+ counter 1)), the Lisp interpreter first evaluates the innermost list; this is the addition. In order to evaluate this list, it must evaluate the variable counter and the number 1. When it evaluates the variable counter, it receives its current value. It passes this value and the number 1 to the + which adds them together. The sum is then returned as the value of the inner list and passed to the setq which sets the variable counter to this new value. Thus, the value of the variable, counter, is changed.

1.10 Summary

Learning Lisp is like climbing a hill in which the first part is the steepest. You have now climbed the most difficult part; what remains becomes easier as you progress onwards.

In summary,

- Lisp programs are made up of expressions, which are lists or single atoms.

- Lists are made up of zero or more atoms or inner lists, separated by whitespace and surrounded by parentheses. A list can be empty.

- Atoms are multi-character symbols, like forward-paragraph, single character symbols like +, strings of characters between double quotation marks, or numbers.

- A number evaluates to itself.

- A string between double quotes also evaluates to itself.

- When you evaluate a symbol by itself, its value is returned.

- When you evaluate a list, the Lisp interpreter looks at the first symbol in the list and then at the function definition bound to that symbol. Then the instructions in the function definition are carried out.

- A single-quote ' ' tells the Lisp interpreter that it should return the following expression as written, and not evaluate it as it would if the quote were not there.

- Arguments are the information passed to a function. The arguments to a function are computed by evaluating the rest of the elements of the list of which the function is the first element.

- A function always returns a value when it is evaluated (unless it gets an error); in addition, it may also carry out some action that is a side effect. In many cases, a function's primary purpose is to create a side effect.

1.11 Exercises

A few simple exercises:

- Generate an error message by evaluating an appropriate symbol that is not within parentheses.

- Generate an error message by evaluating an appropriate symbol that is between parentheses.

- Create a counter that increments by two rather than one.

- Write an expression that prints a message in the echo area when evaluated.

2 Practicing Evaluation

Before learning how to write a function definition in Emacs Lisp, it is useful to spend a little time evaluating various expressions that have already been written. These expressions will be lists with the functions as their first (and often only) element. Since some of the functions associated with buffers are both simple and interesting, we will start with those. In this section, we will evaluate a few of these. In another section, we will study the code of several other buffer-related functions, to see how they were written.

Whenever you give an editing command to Emacs Lisp, such as the command to move the cursor or to scroll the screen, *you are evaluating an expression,* the first element of which is a function. *This is how Emacs works.*

When you type keys, you cause the Lisp interpreter to evaluate an expression and that is how you get your results. Even typing plain text involves evaluating an Emacs Lisp function, in this case, one that uses `self-insert-command`, which simply inserts the character you typed. The functions you evaluate by typing keystrokes are called *interactive* functions, or *commands*; how you make a function interactive will be illustrated in the chapter on how to write function definitions. See Section 3.3 "Making a Function Interactive", page 29.

In addition to typing keyboard commands, we have seen a second way to evaluate an expression: by positioning the cursor after a list and typing *C-x C-e*. This is what we will do in the rest of this section. There are other ways to evaluate an expression as well; these will be described as we come to them.

Besides being used for practicing evaluation, the functions shown in the next few sections are important in their own right. A study of these functions makes clear the distinction between buffers and files, how to switch to a buffer, and how to determine a location within it.

2.1 Buffer Names

The two functions, `buffer-name` and `buffer-file-name`, show the difference between a file and a buffer. When you evaluate the following expression, (`buffer-name`), the name of the buffer appears in the echo area. When you evaluate (`buffer-file-name`), the name of the file to which the buffer refers appears in the echo area. Usually, the name returned by (`buffer-name`) is the same as the name of the file to which it refers, and the name returned by (`buffer-file-name`) is the full path-name of the file.

A file and a buffer are two different entities. A file is information recorded permanently in the computer (unless you delete it). A buffer, on the other hand, is information inside of Emacs that will vanish at the end of the editing session (or when you kill the buffer). Usually, a buffer contains information that you have copied from a file; we say the buffer is *visiting* that file. This copy is what you work on and modify. Changes to the buffer do not change the file, until you save the buffer. When you save the buffer, the buffer is copied to the file and is thus saved permanently.

If you are reading this in Info inside of GNU Emacs, you can evaluate each of
the following expressions by positioning the cursor after it and typing *C-x C-e*.

    (buffer-name)

    (buffer-file-name)

When I do this in Info, the value returned by evaluating (buffer-name) is
"*info*", and the value returned by evaluating (buffer-file-name) is nil.

On the other hand, while I am writing this document, the value returned by
evaluating (buffer-name) is "introduction.texinfo", and the value returned by
evaluating (buffer-file-name) is "/gnu/work/intro/introduction.texinfo".

The former is the name of the buffer and the latter is the name of the file. In
Info, the buffer name is "*info*". Info does not point to any file, so the result of
evaluating (buffer-file-name) is nil. The symbol nil is from the Latin word
for "nothing"; in this case, it means that the buffer is not associated with any file.
(In Lisp, nil is also used to mean "false" and is a synonym for the empty list, ().)

When I am writing, the name of my buffer is "introduction.texinfo". The
name of the file to which it points is "/gnu/work/intro/introduction.texinfo".

(In the expressions, the parentheses tell the Lisp interpreter to treat
buffer-name and buffer-file-name as functions; without the parentheses, the
interpreter would attempt to evaluate the symbols as variables. See Section 1.7
"Variables", page 9.)

In spite of the distinction between files and buffers, you will often find that
people refer to a file when they mean a buffer and vice versa. Indeed, most people
say, "I am editing a file," rather than saying, "I am editing a buffer which I will
soon save to a file." It is almost always clear from context what people mean. When
dealing with computer programs, however, it is important to keep the distinction
in mind, since the computer is not as smart as a person.

The word "buffer", by the way, comes from the meaning of the word as a cushion
that deadens the force of a collision. In early computers, a buffer cushioned the
interaction between files and the computer's central processing unit. The drums or
tapes that held a file and the central processing unit were pieces of equipment that
were very different from each other, working at their own speeds, in spurts. The
buffer made it possible for them to work together effectively. Eventually, the buffer
grew from being an intermediary, a temporary holding place, to being the place
where work is done. This transformation is rather like that of a small seaport that
grew into a great city: once it was merely the place where cargo was warehoused
temporarily before being loaded onto ships; then it became a business and cultural
center in its own right.

Not all buffers are associated with files. For example, a *scratch* buffer does
not visit any file. Similarly, a *Help* buffer is not associated with any file.

In the old days, when you lacked a ~/.emacs file and started an Emacs session
by typing the command emacs alone, without naming any files, Emacs started with
the *scratch* buffer visible. Nowadays, you will see a splash screen. You can
follow one of the commands suggested on the splash screen, visit a file, or press the
spacebar to reach the *scratch* buffer.

If you switch to the *scratch* buffer, type (buffer-name), position the cursor after it, and then type *C-x C-e* to evaluate the expression. The name "*scratch*" will be returned and will appear in the echo area. "*scratch*" is the name of the buffer. When you type (buffer-file-name) in the *scratch* buffer and evaluate that, nil will appear in the echo area, just as it does when you evaluate (buffer-file-name) in Info.

Incidentally, if you are in the *scratch* buffer and want the value returned by an expression to appear in the *scratch* buffer itself rather than in the echo area, type *C-u C-x C-e* instead of *C-x C-e*. This causes the value returned to appear after the expression. The buffer will look like this:

```
(buffer-name)"*scratch*"
```

You cannot do this in Info since Info is read-only and it will not allow you to change the contents of the buffer. But you can do this in any buffer you can edit; and when you write code or documentation (such as this book), this feature is very useful.

2.2 Getting Buffers

The buffer-name function returns the *name* of the buffer; to get the buffer *itself*, a different function is needed: the current-buffer function. If you use this function in code, what you get is the buffer itself.

A name and the object or entity to which the name refers are different from each other. You are not your name. You are a person to whom others refer by name. If you ask to speak to George and someone hands you a card with the letters 'G', 'e', 'o', 'r', 'g', and 'e' written on it, you might be amused, but you would not be satisfied. You do not want to speak to the name, but to the person to whom the name refers. A buffer is similar: the name of the scratch buffer is *scratch*, but the name is not the buffer. To get a buffer itself, you need to use a function such as current-buffer.

However, there is a slight complication: if you evaluate current-buffer in an expression on its own, as we will do here, what you see is a printed representation of the name of the buffer without the contents of the buffer. Emacs works this way for two reasons: the buffer may be thousands of lines long—too long to be conveniently displayed; and, another buffer may have the same contents but a different name, and it is important to distinguish between them.

Here is an expression containing the function:

```
(current-buffer)
```

If you evaluate this expression in Info in Emacs in the usual way, #<buffer *info*> will appear in the echo area. The special format indicates that the buffer itself is being returned, rather than just its name.

Incidentally, while you can type a number or symbol into a program, you cannot do that with the printed representation of a buffer: the only way to get a buffer itself is with a function such as current-buffer.

A related function is other-buffer. This returns the most recently selected buffer other than the one you are in currently, not a printed representation of its name. If you have recently switched back and forth from the `*scratch*` buffer, `other-buffer` will return that buffer.

You can see this by evaluating the expression:

```
(other-buffer)
```

You should see `#<buffer *scratch*>` appear in the echo area, or the name of whatever other buffer you switched back from most recently[1].

2.3 Switching Buffers

The `other-buffer` function actually provides a buffer when it is used as an argument to a function that requires one. We can see this by using `other-buffer` and `switch-to-buffer` to switch to a different buffer.

But first, a brief introduction to the `switch-to-buffer` function. When you switched back and forth from Info to the `*scratch*` buffer to evaluate `(buffer-name)`, you most likely typed *C-x b* and then typed `*scratch*`[2] when prompted in the minibuffer for the name of the buffer to which you wanted to switch. The keystrokes, *C-x b*, cause the Lisp interpreter to evaluate the interactive function `switch-to-buffer`. As we said before, this is how Emacs works: different keystrokes call or run different functions. For example, *C-f* calls `forward-char`, *M-e* calls `forward-sentence`, and so on.

By writing `switch-to-buffer` in an expression, and giving it a buffer to switch to, we can switch buffers just the way *C-x b* does:

```
(switch-to-buffer (other-buffer))
```

The symbol `switch-to-buffer` is the first element of the list, so the Lisp interpreter will treat it as a function and carry out the instructions that are attached to it. But before doing that, the interpreter will note that `other-buffer` is inside parentheses and work on that symbol first. `other-buffer` is the first (and in this case, the only) element of this list, so the Lisp interpreter calls or runs the function. It returns another buffer. Next, the interpreter runs `switch-to-buffer`, passing to it, as an argument, the other buffer, which is what Emacs will switch to. If you are reading this in Info, try this now. Evaluate the expression. (To get back, type *C-x b RET*.)[3]

---

[1] Actually, by default, if the buffer from which you just switched is visible to you in another window, `other-buffer` will choose the most recent buffer that you cannot see; this is a subtlety that I often forget.

[2] Or rather, to save typing, you probably only typed *RET* if the default buffer was `*scratch*`, or if it was different, then you typed just part of the name, such as `*sc`, pressed your *TAB* key to cause it to expand to the full name, and then typed *RET*.

[3] Remember, this expression will move you to your most recent other buffer that you cannot see. If you really want to go to your most recently selected buffer, even if you can still see it, you need to evaluate the following more complex expression:

```
(switch-to-buffer (other-buffer (current-buffer) t))
```

In this case, the first argument to `other-buffer` tells it which buffer to skip—the current one—and the second argument tells `other-buffer` it is OK to switch to a visible buffer. In regular use, `switch-to-buffer` takes you to a buffer not visible in

In the programming examples in later sections of this document, you will see the function `set-buffer` more often than `switch-to-buffer`. This is because of a difference between computer programs and humans: humans have eyes and expect to see the buffer on which they are working on their computer terminals. This is so obvious, it almost goes without saying. However, programs do not have eyes. When a computer program works on a buffer, that buffer does not need to be visible on the screen.

`switch-to-buffer` is designed for humans and does two different things: it switches the buffer to which Emacs's attention is directed; and it switches the buffer displayed in the window to the new buffer. `set-buffer`, on the other hand, does only one thing: it switches the attention of the computer program to a different buffer. The buffer on the screen remains unchanged (of course, normally nothing happens there until the command finishes running).

Also, we have just introduced another jargon term, the word *call*. When you evaluate a list in which the first symbol is a function, you are calling that function. The use of the term comes from the notion of the function as an entity that can do something for you if you call it—just as a plumber is an entity who can fix a leak if you call him or her.

2.4 Buffer Size and the Location of Point

Finally, let's look at several rather simple functions, `buffer-size`, `point`, `point-min`, and `point-max`. These give information about the size of a buffer and the location of point within it.

The function `buffer-size` tells you the size of the current buffer; that is, the function returns a count of the number of characters in the buffer.

```
(buffer-size)
```

You can evaluate this in the usual way, by positioning the cursor after the expression and typing *C-x C-e*.

In Emacs, the current position of the cursor is called *point*. The expression `(point)` returns a number that tells you where the cursor is located as a count of the number of characters from the beginning of the buffer up to point.

---

windows since you would most likely use *C-x o* (`other-window`) to go to another visible buffer.

You can see the character count for point in this buffer by evaluating the following expression in the usual way:

```
(point)
```

As I write this, the value of point is 65724. The `point` function is frequently used in some of the examples later in this book.

The value of point depends, of course, on its location within the buffer. If you evaluate point in this spot, the number will be larger:

```
(point)
```

For me, the value of point in this location is 66043, which means that there are 319 characters (including spaces) between the two expressions. (Doubtless, you will see different numbers, since I will have edited this since I first evaluated point.)

The function `point-min` is somewhat similar to `point`, but it returns the value of the minimum permissible value of point in the current buffer. This is the number 1 unless *narrowing* is in effect. (Narrowing is a mechanism whereby you can restrict yourself, or a program, to operations on just a part of a buffer. See Chapter 6 "Narrowing and Widening", page 67.) Likewise, the function `point-max` returns the value of the maximum permissible value of point in the current buffer.

2.5 Exercise

Find a file with which you are working and move towards its middle. Find its buffer name, file name, length, and your position in the file.

3 How To Write Function Definitions

When the Lisp interpreter evaluates a list, it looks to see whether the first symbol on the list has a function definition attached to it; or, put another way, whether the symbol points to a function definition. If it does, the computer carries out the instructions in the definition. A symbol that has a function definition is called, simply, a function (although, properly speaking, the definition is the function and the symbol refers to it.)

All functions are defined in terms of other functions, except for a few *primitive* functions that are written in the C programming language. When you write functions' definitions, you will write them in Emacs Lisp and use other functions as your building blocks. Some of the functions you will use will themselves be written in Emacs Lisp (perhaps by you) and some will be primitives written in C. The primitive functions are used exactly like those written in Emacs Lisp and behave like them. They are written in C so we can easily run GNU Emacs on any computer that has sufficient power and can run C.

Let me re-emphasize this: when you write code in Emacs Lisp, you do not distinguish between the use of functions written in C and the use of functions written in Emacs Lisp. The difference is irrelevant. I mention the distinction only because it is interesting to know. Indeed, unless you investigate, you won't know whether an already-written function is written in Emacs Lisp or C.

3.1 The `defun` Macro

In Lisp, a symbol such as `mark-whole-buffer` has code attached to it that tells the computer what to do when the function is called. This code is called the *function definition* and is created by evaluating a Lisp expression that starts with the symbol `defun` (which is an abbreviation for *define function*).

In subsequent sections, we will look at function definitions from the Emacs source code, such as `mark-whole-buffer`. In this section, we will describe a simple function definition so you can see how it looks. This function definition uses arithmetic because it makes for a simple example. Some people dislike examples using arithmetic; however, if you are such a person, do not despair. Hardly any of the code we will study in the remainder of this introduction involves arithmetic or mathematics. The examples mostly involve text in one way or another.

A function definition has up to five parts following the word `defun`:

1. The name of the symbol to which the function definition should be attached.

2. A list of the arguments that will be passed to the function. If no arguments will be passed to the function, this is an empty list, `()`.

3. Documentation describing the function. (Technically optional, but strongly recommended.)

4. Optionally, an expression to make the function interactive so you can use it by typing `M-x` and then the name of the function; or by typing an appropriate key or keychord.

5. The code that instructs the computer what to do: the *body* of the function definition.

It is helpful to think of the five parts of a function definition as being organized in a template, with slots for each part:

```
(defun function-name (arguments...)
  "optional-documentation..."
  (interactive argument-passing-info)    ; optional
  body...)
```

As an example, here is the code for a function that multiplies its argument by 7. (This example is not interactive. See Section 3.3 "Making a Function Interactive", page 29, for that information.)

```
(defun multiply-by-seven (number)
  "Multiply NUMBER by seven."
  (* 7 number))
```

This definition begins with a parenthesis and the symbol `defun`, followed by the name of the function.

The name of the function is followed by a list that contains the arguments that will be passed to the function. This list is called the *argument list*. In this example, the list has only one element, the symbol, `number`. When the function is used, the symbol will be bound to the value that is used as the argument to the function.

Instead of choosing the word `number` for the name of the argument, I could have picked any other name. For example, I could have chosen the word `multiplicand`. I picked the word "number" because it tells what kind of value is intended for this slot; but I could just as well have chosen the word "multiplicand" to indicate the role that the value placed in this slot will play in the workings of the function. I could have called it `foogle`, but that would have been a bad choice because it would not tell humans what it means. The choice of name is up to the programmer and should be chosen to make the meaning of the function clear.

Indeed, you can choose any name you wish for a symbol in an argument list, even the name of a symbol used in some other function: the name you use in an argument list is private to that particular definition. In that definition, the name refers to a different entity than any use of the same name outside the function definition. Suppose you have a nick-name "Shorty" in your family; when your family members refer to "Shorty", they mean you. But outside your family, in a movie, for example, the name "Shorty" refers to someone else. Because a name in an argument list is private to the function definition, you can change the value of such a symbol inside the body of a function without changing its value outside the function. The effect is similar to that produced by a `let` expression. (See Section 3.6 "let", page 33.)

The argument list is followed by the documentation string that describes the function. This is what you see when you type *C-h f* and the name of a function. Incidentally, when you write a documentation string like this, you should make the first line a complete sentence since some commands, such as `apropos`, print only the first line of a multi-line documentation string. Also, you should not indent the second line of a documentation string, if you have one, because that looks odd when you use *C-h f* (`describe-function`). The documentation string is optional, but it is so useful, it should be included in almost every function you write.

The third line of the example consists of the body of the function definition. (Most functions' definitions, of course, are longer than this.) In this function, the body is the list, `(* 7 number)`, which says to multiply the value of *number* by 7. (In Emacs Lisp, `*` is the function for multiplication, just as `+` is the function for addition.)

When you use the `multiply-by-seven` function, the argument `number` evaluates to the actual number you want used. Here is an example that shows how `multiply-by-seven` is used; but don't try to evaluate this yet!

```
(multiply-by-seven 3)
```

The symbol `number`, specified in the function definition in the next section, is bound to the value 3 in the actual use of the function. Note that although `number` was inside parentheses in the function definition, the argument passed to the `multiply-by-seven` function is not in parentheses. The parentheses are written in the function definition so the computer can figure out where the argument list ends and the rest of the function definition begins.

If you evaluate this example, you are likely to get an error message. (Go ahead, try it!) This is because we have written the function definition, but not yet told the computer about the definition—we have not yet loaded the function definition in Emacs. Installing a function is the process that tells the Lisp interpreter the definition of the function. Installation is described in the next section.

3.2 Install a Function Definition

If you are reading this inside of Info in Emacs, you can try out the `multiply-by-seven` function by first evaluating the function definition and then evaluating (`multiply-by-seven 3`). A copy of the function definition follows. Place the cursor after the last parenthesis of the function definition and type *C-x C-e*. When you do this, `multiply-by-seven` will appear in the echo area. (What this means is that when a function definition is evaluated, the value it returns is the name of the defined function.) At the same time, this action installs the function definition.

```
(defun multiply-by-seven (number)
  "Multiply NUMBER by seven."
  (* 7 number))
```

By evaluating this `defun`, you have just installed `multiply-by-seven` in Emacs. The function is now just as much a part of Emacs as `forward-word` or any other editing function you use. (`multiply-by-seven` will stay installed until you quit Emacs. To reload code automatically whenever you start Emacs, see Section 3.5 "Installing Code Permanently", page 32.)

You can see the effect of installing `multiply-by-seven` by evaluating the following sample. Place the cursor after the following expression and type *C-x C-e*. The number 21 will appear in the echo area.

```
(multiply-by-seven 3)
```

If you wish, you can read the documentation for the function by typing *C-h f* (`describe-function`) and then the name of the function, `multiply-by-seven`. When you do this, a `*Help*` window will appear on your screen that says:

```
multiply-by-seven is a Lisp function.

(multiply-by-seven NUMBER)

Multiply NUMBER by seven.
```
(To return to a single window on your screen, type *C-x 1*.)

3.2.1 Change a Function Definition

If you want to change the code in `multiply-by-seven`, just rewrite it. To install the new version in place of the old one, evaluate the function definition again. This is how you modify code in Emacs. It is very simple.

As an example, you can change the `multiply-by-seven` function to add the number to itself seven times instead of multiplying the number by seven. It produces the same answer, but by a different path. At the same time, we will add a comment to the code; a comment is text that the Lisp interpreter ignores, but that a human reader may find useful or enlightening. The comment is that this is the second version.

```
(defun multiply-by-seven (number)      ; Second version.
  "Multiply NUMBER by seven."
  (+ number number number number number number number))
```

The comment follows a semicolon, ';'. In Lisp, everything on a line that follows a semicolon is a comment. The end of the line is the end of the comment. To stretch a comment over two or more lines, begin each line with a semicolon.

See Section 16.3 "Beginning a `.emacs` File", page 185, and Section "Comments" in *The GNU Emacs Lisp Reference Manual*, for more about comments.

You can install this version of the `multiply-by-seven` function by evaluating it in the same way you evaluated the first function: place the cursor after the last parenthesis and type *C-x C-e*.

In summary, this is how you write code in Emacs Lisp: you write a function; install it; test it; and then make fixes or enhancements and install it again.

3.3 Make a Function Interactive

You make a function interactive by placing a list that begins with the special form `interactive` immediately after the documentation. A user can invoke an interactive function by typing *M-x* and then the name of the function; or by typing the keys to which it is bound, for example, by typing *C-n* for `next-line` or *C-x h* for `mark-whole-buffer`.

Interestingly, when you call an interactive function interactively, the value returned is not automatically displayed in the echo area. This is because you often call an interactive function for its side effects, such as moving forward by a word or line, and not for the value returned. If the returned value were displayed in the echo area each time you typed a key, it would be very distracting.

Both the use of the special form `interactive` and one way to display a value in the echo area can be illustrated by creating an interactive version of `multiply-by-seven`.

Here is the code:

```
(defun multiply-by-seven (number)        ; Interactive version.
  "Multiply NUMBER by seven."
  (interactive "p")
  (message "The result is %d" (* 7 number)))
```

You can install this code by placing your cursor after it and typing *C-x C-e*. The name of the function will appear in your echo area. Then, you can use this code by typing *C-u* and a number and then typing *M-x multiply-by-seven* and pressing RET. The phrase 'The result is ...' followed by the product will appear in the echo area.

Speaking more generally, you invoke a function like this in either of two ways:

1. By typing a prefix argument that contains the number to be passed, and then typing *M-x* and the name of the function, as with *C-u 3 M-x forward-sentence*; or,

2. By typing whatever key or keychord the function is bound to, as with *C-u 3 M-e*.

Both the examples just mentioned work identically to move point forward three sentences. (Since multiply-by-seven is not bound to a key, it could not be used as an example of key binding.)

(See Section 16.7 "Some Keybindings", page 188, to learn how to bind a command to a key.)

A *prefix argument* is passed to an interactive function by typing the META key followed by a number, for example, *M-3 M-e*, or by typing *C-u* and then a number, for example, *C-u 3 M-e* (if you type *C-u* without a number, it defaults to 4).

3.3.1 An Interactive multiply-by-seven

Let's look at the use of the special form `interactive` and then at the function `message` in the interactive version of multiply-by-seven. You will recall that the function definition looks like this:

```
(defun multiply-by-seven (number)        ; Interactive version.
  "Multiply NUMBER by seven."
  (interactive "p")
  (message "The result is %d" (* 7 number)))
```

In this function, the expression, (interactive "p"), is a list of two elements. The "p" tells Emacs to pass the prefix argument to the function and use its value for the argument of the function.

The argument will be a number. This means that the symbol `number` will be bound to a number in the line:

```
(message "The result is %d" (* 7 number))
```

For example, if your prefix argument is 5, the Lisp interpreter will evaluate the line as if it were:

```
(message "The result is %d" (* 7 5))
```

(If you are reading this in GNU Emacs, you can evaluate this expression yourself.) First, the interpreter will evaluate the inner list, which is `(* 7 5)`. This returns a value of 35. Next, it will evaluate the outer list, passing the values of the second and subsequent elements of the list to the function `message`.

As we have seen, `message` is an Emacs Lisp function especially designed for sending a one line message to a user. (See Section 1.8.5 "The `message` function", page 14.) In summary, the `message` function prints its first argument in the echo area as is, except for occurrences of '%d' or '%s' (and various other %-sequences which we have not mentioned). When it sees a control sequence, the function looks to the second or subsequent arguments and prints the value of the argument in the location in the string where the control sequence is located.

In the interactive `multiply-by-seven` function, the control string is '%d', which requires a number, and the value returned by evaluating `(* 7 5)` is the number 35. Consequently, the number 35 is printed in place of the '%d' and the message is 'The result is 35'.

(Note that when you call the function `multiply-by-seven`, the message is printed without quotes, but when you call `message`, the text is printed in double quotes. This is because the value returned by `message` is what appears in the echo area when you evaluate an expression whose first element is `message`; but when embedded in a function, `message` prints the text as a side effect without quotes.)

3.4 Different Options for `interactive`

In the example, `multiply-by-seven` used `"p"` as the argument to `interactive`. This argument told Emacs to interpret your typing either *C-u* followed by a number or `META` followed by a number as a command to pass that number to the function as its argument. Emacs has more than twenty characters predefined for use with `interactive`. In almost every case, one of these options will enable you to pass the right information interactively to a function. (See Section "Code Characters for `interactive`" in *The GNU Emacs Lisp Reference Manual*.)

Consider the function `zap-to-char`. Its interactive expression is

```
(interactive "p\ncZap to char: ")
```

The first part of the argument to `interactive` is 'p', with which you are already familiar. This argument tells Emacs to interpret a prefix, as a number to be passed to the function. You can specify a prefix either by typing *C-u* followed by a number or by typing `META` followed by a number. The prefix is the number of specified characters. Thus, if your prefix is three and the specified character is 'x', then you will delete all the text up to and including the third next 'x'. If you do not set a prefix, then you delete all the text up to and including the specified character, but no more.

The 'c' tells the function the name of the character to which to delete.

More formally, a function with two or more arguments can have information passed to each argument by adding parts to the string that follows `interactive`. When you do this, the information is passed to each argument in the same order it is specified in the `interactive` list. In the string, each part is separated from the next part by a '\n', which is a newline. For example, you can follow 'p' with a '\n' and an 'cZap to char: '. This causes Emacs to pass the value of the prefix argument (if there is one) and the character.

In this case, the function definition looks like the following, where `arg` and `char` are the symbols to which `interactive` binds the prefix argument and the specified character:

```
(defun name-of-function (arg char)
  "documentation..."
  (interactive "p\ncZap to char: ")
  body-of-function...)
```

(The space after the colon in the prompt makes it look better when you are prompted. See Section 5.1 "The Definition of `copy-to-buffer`", page 55, for an example.)

When a function does not take arguments, `interactive` does not require any. Such a function contains the simple expression (`interactive`). The `mark-whole-buffer` function is like this.

Alternatively, if the special letter-codes are not right for your application, you can pass your own arguments to `interactive` as a list.

See Section 4.4 "The Definition of `append-to-buffer`", page 49, for an example. See Section "Using `Interactive`" in *The GNU Emacs Lisp Reference Manual*, for a more complete explanation about this technique.

3.5 Install Code Permanently

When you install a function definition by evaluating it, it will stay installed until you quit Emacs. The next time you start a new session of Emacs, the function will not be installed unless you evaluate the function definition again.

At some point, you may want to have code installed automatically whenever you start a new session of Emacs. There are several ways of doing this:

- If you have code that is just for yourself, you can put the code for the function definition in your `.emacs` initialization file. When you start Emacs, your `.emacs` file is automatically evaluated and all the function definitions within it are installed. See Chapter 16 "Your `.emacs` File", page 182.

- Alternatively, you can put the function definitions that you want installed in one or more files of their own and use the `load` function to cause Emacs to evaluate and thereby install each of the functions in the files. See Section 16.9 "Loading Files", page 190.

- Thirdly, if you have code that your whole site will use, it is usual to put it in a file called `site-init.el` that is loaded when Emacs is built. This makes the code available to everyone who uses your machine. (See the `INSTALL` file that is part of the Emacs distribution.)

Finally, if you have code that everyone who uses Emacs may want, you can post it on a computer network or send a copy to the Free Software Foundation. (When you do this, please license the code and its documentation under a license that permits other people to run, copy, study, modify, and redistribute the code and which protects you from having your work taken from you.) If you send a copy of your code to the Free Software Foundation, and properly protect yourself and others, it may be included in the next release of Emacs. In large part, this is how Emacs has grown over the past years, by donations.

3.6 `let`

The `let` expression is a special form in Lisp that you will need to use in most function definitions.

`let` is used to attach or bind a symbol to a value in such a way that the Lisp interpreter will not confuse the variable with a variable of the same name that is not part of the function.

To understand why the `let` special form is necessary, consider the situation in which you own a home that you generally refer to as "the house", as in the sentence, "The house needs painting." If you are visiting a friend and your host refers to "the house", he is likely to be referring to *his* house, not yours, that is, to a different house.

If your friend is referring to his house and you think he is referring to your house, you may be in for some confusion. The same thing could happen in Lisp if a variable that is used inside of one function has the same name as a variable that is used inside of another function, and the two are not intended to refer to the same value. The `let` special form prevents this kind of confusion.

The `let` special form prevents confusion. `let` creates a name for a *local variable* that overshadows any use of the same name outside the `let` expression. This is like understanding that whenever your host refers to "the house", he means his house, not yours. (Symbols used in argument lists work the same way. See Section 3.1 "The `defun` Macro", page 26.)

Local variables created by a `let` expression retain their value *only* within the `let` expression itself (and within expressions called within the `let` expression); the local variables have no effect outside the `let` expression.

Another way to think about `let` is that it is like a `setq` that is temporary and local. The values set by `let` are automatically undone when the `let` is finished. The setting only affects expressions that are inside the bounds of the `let` expression. In computer science jargon, we would say the binding of a symbol is visible only in functions called in the `let` form; in Emacs Lisp, scoping is dynamic, not lexical.

`let` can create more than one variable at once. Also, `let` gives each variable it creates an initial value, either a value specified by you, or `nil`. (In the jargon, this is binding the variable to the value.) After `let` has created and bound the variables, it executes the code in the body of the `let`, and returns the value of the last expression in the body, as the value of the whole `let` expression. ("Execute" is a jargon term that means to evaluate a list; it comes from the use of the word meaning "to give practical effect to" (*Oxford English Dictionary*). Since you evaluate an expression to perform an action, "execute" has evolved as a synonym to "evaluate".)

3.6.1 The Parts of a `let` Expression

A `let` expression is a list of three parts. The first part is the symbol `let`. The second part is a list, called a *varlist*, each element of which is either a symbol by itself or a two-element list, the first element of which is a symbol. The third part of the `let` expression is the body of the `let`. The body usually consists of one or more lists.

A template for a `let` expression looks like this:

```
(let varlist body...)
```

The symbols in the varlist are the variables that are given initial values by the `let` special form. Symbols by themselves are given the initial value of `nil`; and each symbol that is the first element of a two-element list is bound to the value that is returned when the Lisp interpreter evaluates the second element.

Thus, a varlist might look like this: `(thread (needles 3))`. In this case, in a `let` expression, Emacs binds the symbol `thread` to an initial value of `nil`, and binds the symbol `needles` to an initial value of 3.

When you write a `let` expression, what you do is put the appropriate expressions in the slots of the `let` expression template.

If the varlist is composed of two-element lists, as is often the case, the template for the `let` expression looks like this:

```
(let ((variable value)
      (variable value)
      ...)
  body...)
```

3.6.2 Sample `let` Expression

The following expression creates and gives initial values to the two variables `zebra` and `tiger`. The body of the `let` expression is a list which calls the `message` function.

```
(let ((zebra "stripes")
      (tiger "fierce"))
  (message "One kind of animal has %s and another is %s."
           zebra tiger))
```

Here, the varlist is `((zebra "stripes") (tiger "fierce"))`.

The two variables are `zebra` and `tiger`. Each variable is the first element of a two-element list and each value is the second element of its two-element list. In the varlist, Emacs binds the variable `zebra` to the value `"stripes"`[1], and binds the variable `tiger` to the value `"fierce"`. In this example, both values are strings. The values could just as well have been another list or a symbol. The body of the

---

[1] According to Jared Diamond in *Guns, Germs, and Steel*, "... zebras become impossibly dangerous as they grow older" but the claim here is that they do not become fierce like a tiger. (1997, W. W. Norton and Co., ISBN 0-393-03894-2, page 171)

`let` follows after the list holding the variables. In this example, the body is a list that uses the `message` function to print a string in the echo area.

You may evaluate the example in the usual fashion, by placing the cursor after the last parenthesis and typing *C-x C-e*. When you do this, the following will appear in the echo area:

```
"One kind of animal has stripes and another is fierce."
```

As we have seen before, the `message` function prints its first argument, except for '%s'. In this example, the value of the variable `zebra` is printed at the location of the first '%s' and the value of the variable `tiger` is printed at the location of the second '%s'.

3.6.3 Uninitialized Variables in a `let` Statement

If you do not bind the variables in a `let` statement to specific initial values, they will automatically be bound to an initial value of `nil`, as in the following expression:

```
(let ((birch 3)
      pine
      fir
      (oak 'some))
  (message
   "Here are %d variables with %s, %s, and %s value."
   birch pine fir oak))
```

Here, the varlist is `((birch 3) pine fir (oak 'some))`.

If you evaluate this expression in the usual way, the following will appear in your echo area:

```
"Here are 3 variables with nil, nil, and some value."
```

In this example, Emacs binds the symbol `birch` to the number 3, binds the symbols `pine` and `fir` to `nil`, and binds the symbol `oak` to the value `some`.

Note that in the first part of the `let`, the variables `pine` and `fir` stand alone as atoms that are not surrounded by parentheses; this is because they are being bound to `nil`, the empty list. But `oak` is bound to `some` and so is a part of the list `(oak 'some)`. Similarly, `birch` is bound to the number 3 and so is in a list with that number. (Since a number evaluates to itself, the number does not need to be quoted. Also, the number is printed in the message using a '%d' rather than a '%s'.) The four variables as a group are put into a list to delimit them from the body of the `let`.

3.7 The `if` Special Form

A third special form, in addition to `defun` and `let`, is the conditional `if`. This form is used to instruct the computer to make decisions. You can write function definitions without using `if`, but it is used often enough, and is important enough, to be included here. It is used, for example, in the code for the function `beginning-of-buffer`.

The basic idea behind an `if`, is that *if* a test is true, *then* an expression is evaluated. If the test is not true, the expression is not evaluated. For example, you might make a decision such as, "if it is warm and sunny, then go to the beach!"

An `if` expression written in Lisp does not use the word "then"; the test and the action are the second and third elements of the list whose first element is `if`. Nonetheless, the test part of an `if` expression is often called the *if-part* and the second argument is often called the *then-part*.

Also, when an `if` expression is written, the true-or-false-test is usually written on the same line as the symbol `if`, but the action to carry out if the test is true, the then-part, is written on the second and subsequent lines. This makes the `if` expression easier to read.

```
(if true-or-false-test
    action-to-carry-out-if-test-is-true)
```

The true-or-false-test will be an expression that is evaluated by the Lisp interpreter.

Here is an example that you can evaluate in the usual manner. The test is whether the number 5 is greater than the number 4. Since it is, the message '5 is greater than 4!' will be printed.

```
(if (> 5 4)                              ; if-part
    (message "5 is greater than 4!"))    ; then-part
```

(The function > tests whether its first argument is greater than its second argument and returns true if it is.)

Of course, in actual use, the test in an `if` expression will not be fixed for all time as it is by the expression (> 5 4). Instead, at least one of the variables used in the test will be bound to a value that is not known ahead of time. (If the value were known ahead of time, we would not need to run the test!)

For example, the value may be bound to an argument of a function definition. In the following function definition, the character of the animal is a value that is passed to the function. If the value bound to `characteristic` is "fierce", then the message, 'It is a tiger!' will be printed; otherwise, `nil` will be returned.

```
(defun type-of-animal (characteristic)
  "Print message in echo area depending on CHARACTERISTIC.
If the CHARACTERISTIC is the string \"fierce\",
then warn of a tiger."
  (if (equal characteristic "fierce")
      (message "It is a tiger!")))
```

If you are reading this inside of GNU Emacs, you can evaluate the function definition in the usual way to install it in Emacs, and then you can evaluate the following two expressions to see the results:

```
(type-of-animal "fierce")

(type-of-animal "striped")
```

When you evaluate (`type-of-animal "fierce"`), you will see the following message printed in the echo area: "It is a tiger!"; and when you evaluate (`type-of-animal "striped"`) you will see `nil` printed in the echo area.

3.7.1 The `type-of-animal` Function in Detail

Let's look at the `type-of-animal` function in detail.

The function definition for `type-of-animal` was written by filling the slots of two templates, one for a function definition as a whole, and a second for an `if` expression.

The template for every function that is not interactive is:

```
(defun name-of-function (argument-list)
  "documentation..."
  body...)
```

The parts of the function that match this template look like this:

```
(defun type-of-animal (characteristic)
  "Print message in echo area depending on CHARACTERISTIC.
 If the CHARACTERISTIC is the string \"fierce\",
 then warn of a tiger."
  body: the if expression)
```

The name of function is `type-of-animal`; it is passed the value of one argument. The argument list is followed by a multi-line documentation string. The documentation string is included in the example because it is a good habit to write documentation string for every function definition. The body of the function definition consists of the `if` expression.

The template for an `if` expression looks like this:

```
(if true-or-false-test
    action-to-carry-out-if-the-test-returns-true)
```

In the `type-of-animal` function, the code for the `if` looks like this:

```
(if (equal characteristic "fierce")
    (message "It is a tiger!")))
```

Here, the true-or-false-test is the expression:

```
(equal characteristic "fierce")
```

In Lisp, `equal` is a function that determines whether its first argument is equal to its second argument. The second argument is the string `"fierce"` and the first argument is the value of the symbol `characteristic`—in other words, the argument passed to this function.

In the first exercise of `type-of-animal`, the argument `"fierce"` is passed to `type-of-animal`. Since `"fierce"` is equal to `"fierce"`, the expression, (equal characteristic "fierce"), returns a value of true. When this happens, the `if` evaluates the second argument or then-part of the `if`: (message "It is a tiger!").

On the other hand, in the second exercise of `type-of-animal`, the argument `"striped"` is passed to `type-of-animal`. `"striped"` is not equal to `"fierce"`, so the then-part is not evaluated and `nil` is returned by the `if` expression.

3.8 If–then–else Expressions

An `if` expression may have an optional third argument, called the *else-part*, for the case when the true-or-false-test returns false. When this happens, the second argument or then-part of the overall `if` expression is *not* evaluated, but the third or else-part *is* evaluated. You might think of this as the cloudy day alternative for the decision "if it is warm and sunny, then go to the beach, else read a book!".

The word "else" is not written in the Lisp code; the else-part of an `if` expression comes after the then-part. In the written Lisp, the else-part is usually written to start on a line of its own and is indented less than the then-part:

```
(if true-or-false-test
    action-to-carry-out-if-the-test-returns-true
  action-to-carry-out-if-the-test-returns-false)
```

For example, the following `if` expression prints the message '`4 is not greater than 5!`' when you evaluate it in the usual way:

```
(if (> 4 5)                                 ; if-part
    (message "4 falsely greater than 5!") ; then-part
  (message "4 is not greater than 5!"))   ; else-part
```

Note that the different levels of indentation make it easy to distinguish the then-part from the else-part. (GNU Emacs has several commands that automatically indent `if` expressions correctly. See Section 1.1.3 "GNU Emacs Helps You Type Lists", page 3.)

We can extend the `type-of-animal` function to include an else-part by simply incorporating an additional part to the `if` expression.

You can see the consequences of doing this if you evaluate the following version of the `type-of-animal` function definition to install it and then evaluate the two subsequent expressions to pass different arguments to the function.

```
(defun type-of-animal (characteristic)  ; Second version.
  "Print message in echo area depending on CHARACTERISTIC.
If the CHARACTERISTIC is the string \"fierce\",
then warn of a tiger; else say it is not fierce."
  (if (equal characteristic "fierce")
      (message "It is a tiger!")
    (message "It is not fierce!")))


(type-of-animal "fierce")

(type-of-animal "striped")
```

When you evaluate (`type-of-animal "fierce"`), you will see the following message printed in the echo area: `"It is a tiger!"`; but when you evaluate (`type-of-animal "striped"`), you will see `"It is not fierce!"`.

(Of course, if the *characteristic* were `"ferocious"`, the message `"It is not fierce!"` would be printed; and it would be misleading! When you write code, you need to take into account the possibility that some such argument will be tested by the `if` and write your program accordingly.)

3.9 Truth and Falsehood in Emacs Lisp

There is an important aspect to the truth test in an `if` expression. So far, we have spoken of "true" and "false" as values of predicates as if they were new kinds of Emacs Lisp objects. In fact, "false" is just our old friend `nil`. Anything else—anything at all—is "true".

The expression that tests for truth is interpreted as *true* if the result of evaluating it is a value that is not `nil`. In other words, the result of the test is considered true if the value returned is a number such as 47, a string such as `"hello"`, or a symbol (other than `nil`) such as `flowers`, or a list (so long as it is not empty), or even a buffer!

Before illustrating a test for truth, we need an explanation of `nil`.

In Emacs Lisp, the symbol `nil` has two meanings. First, it means the empty list. Second, it means false and is the value returned when a true-or-false-test tests false. `nil` can be written as an empty list, `()`, or as `nil`. As far as the Lisp interpreter is concerned, `()` and `nil` are the same. Humans, however, tend to use `nil` for false and `()` for the empty list.

In Emacs Lisp, any value that is not `nil`—is not the empty list—is considered true. This means that if an evaluation returns something that is not an empty list, an `if` expression will test true. For example, if a number is put in the slot for the test, it will be evaluated and will return itself, since that is what numbers do when evaluated. In this conditional, the `if` expression will test true. The expression tests false only when `nil`, an empty list, is returned by evaluating the expression.

You can see this by evaluating the two expressions in the following examples.

In the first example, the number 4 is evaluated as the test in the `if` expression and returns itself; consequently, the then-part of the expression is evaluated and returned: '`true`' appears in the echo area. In the second example, the `nil` indicates false; consequently, the else-part of the expression is evaluated and returned: '`false`' appears in the echo area.

```
(if 4
    'true
  'false)
```

```
(if nil
    'true
  'false)
```

Incidentally, if some other useful value is not available for a test that returns true, then the Lisp interpreter will return the symbol `t` for true. For example, the expression `(> 5 4)` returns `t` when evaluated, as you can see by evaluating it in the usual way:

```
(> 5 4)
```

On the other hand, this function returns `nil` if the test is false.

```
(> 4 5)
```

3.10 `save-excursion`

The `save-excursion` function is the third and final special form that we will discuss in this chapter.

In Emacs Lisp programs used for editing, the `save-excursion` function is very common. It saves the location of point, executes the body of the function, and then restores point to its previous position if its location was changed. Its primary purpose is to keep the user from being surprised and disturbed by unexpected movement of point.

Before discussing `save-excursion`, however, it may be useful first to review what point and mark are in GNU Emacs. *Point* is the current location of the cursor. Wherever the cursor is, that is point. More precisely, on terminals where the cursor appears to be on top of a character, point is immediately before the character. In Emacs Lisp, point is an integer. The first character in a buffer is number one, the second is number two, and so on. The function `point` returns the current position of the cursor as a number. Each buffer has its own value for point.

The *mark* is another position in the buffer; its value can be set with a command such as *C-SPC* (`set-mark-command`). If a mark has been set, you can use the command *C-x C-x* (`exchange-point-and-mark`) to cause the cursor to jump to the mark and set the mark to be the previous position of point. In addition, if you set another mark, the position of the previous mark is saved in the mark ring. Many mark positions can be saved this way. You can jump the cursor to a saved mark by typing *C-u C-SPC* one or more times.

The part of the buffer between point and mark is called *the region*. Numerous commands work on the region, including `center-region`, `count-lines-region`, `kill-region`, and `print-region`.

The `save-excursion` special form saves the location of point and restores this position after the code within the body of the special form is evaluated by the Lisp interpreter. Thus, if point were in the beginning of a piece of text and some code moved point to the end of the buffer, the `save-excursion` would put point back to where it was before, after the expressions in the body of the function were evaluated.

In Emacs, a function frequently moves point as part of its internal workings even though a user would not expect this. For example, `count-lines-region` moves point. To prevent the user from being bothered by jumps that are both unexpected and (from the user's point of view) unnecessary, `save-excursion` is often used to keep point in the location expected by the user. The use of `save-excursion` is good housekeeping.

To make sure the house stays clean, `save-excursion` restores the value of point even if something goes wrong in the code inside of it (or, to be more precise and to use the proper jargon, "in case of abnormal exit"). This feature is very helpful.

In addition to recording the value of point, `save-excursion` keeps track of the current buffer, and restores it, too. This means you can write code that will change the buffer and have `save-excursion` switch you back to the original buffer. This is how `save-excursion` is used in `append-to-buffer`. (See Section 4.4 "The Definition of `append-to-buffer`", page 49.)

3.10.1 Template for a `save-excursion` Expression

The template for code using `save-excursion` is simple:

```
(save-excursion
  body...)
```

The body of the function is one or more expressions that will be evaluated in sequence by the Lisp interpreter. If there is more than one expression in the body, the value of the last one will be returned as the value of the `save-excursion` function. The other expressions in the body are evaluated only for their side effects; and `save-excursion` itself is used only for its side effect (which is restoring the position of point).

In more detail, the template for a `save-excursion` expression looks like this:

```
(save-excursion
  first-expression-in-body
  second-expression-in-body
  third-expression-in-body
    ...
  last-expression-in-body)
```

An expression, of course, may be a symbol on its own or a list.

In Emacs Lisp code, a `save-excursion` expression often occurs within the body of a `let` expression. It looks like this:

```
(let varlist
  (save-excursion
    body...))
```

3.11 Review

In the last few chapters we have introduced a macro and a fair number of functions and special forms. Here they are described in brief, along with a few similar functions that have not been mentioned yet.

`eval-last-sexp`

Evaluate the last symbolic expression before the current location of point. The value is printed in the echo area unless the function is invoked with an argument; in that case, the output is printed in the current buffer. This command is normally bound to `C-x C-e`.

`defun`

Define function. This macro has up to five parts: the name, a template for the arguments that will be passed to the function, documentation, an optional interactive declaration, and the body of the definition.

For example, in Emacs the function definition of `dired-unmark-all-marks` is as follows.

```
(defun dired-unmark-all-marks ()
  "Remove all marks from all files in the Dired buffer."
  (interactive)
  (dired-unmark-all-files ?\r))
```

`interactive`

Declare to the interpreter that the function can be used interactively. This special form may be followed by a string with one or more parts that pass the information to the arguments of the function, in sequence. These parts may also tell the interpreter to prompt for information. Parts of the string are separated by newlines, '\n'.

Common code characters are:

b   The name of an existing buffer.

f   The name of an existing file.

p   The numeric prefix argument. (Note that this p is lower case.)

r   Point and the mark, as two numeric arguments, smallest first. This is the only code letter that specifies two successive arguments rather than one.

See Section "Code Characters for 'interactive'" in *The GNU Emacs Lisp Reference Manual*, for a complete list of code characters.

let   Declare that a list of variables is for use within the body of the let and give them an initial value, either nil or a specified value; then evaluate the rest of the expressions in the body of the let and return the value of the last one. Inside the body of the let, the Lisp interpreter does not see the values of the variables of the same names that are bound outside of the let.

For example,

```
(let ((foo (buffer-name))
      (bar (buffer-size)))
  (message
   "This buffer is %s and has %d characters."
   foo bar))
```

save-excursion
             Record the values of point and the current buffer before evaluating the body of this special form. Restore the value of point and buffer afterward.

For example,

```
(message "We are %d characters into this buffer."
         (- (point)
            (save-excursion
              (goto-char (point-min)) (point))))
```

if   Evaluate the first argument to the function; if it is true, evaluate the second argument; else evaluate the third argument, if there is one.

The if special form is called a *conditional*. There are other conditionals in Emacs Lisp, but if is perhaps the most commonly used.

For example,

```
(if (= 22 emacs-major-version)
    (message "This is version 22 Emacs")
  (message "This is not version 22 Emacs"))
```

```
<
>
<=
>=
```
The < function tests whether its first argument is smaller than its second argument. A corresponding function, >, tests whether the first argument is greater than the second. Likewise, <= tests whether the first argument is less than or equal to the second and >= tests whether the first argument is greater than or equal to the second. In all cases, both arguments must be numbers or markers (markers indicate positions in buffers).

`=`   The = function tests whether two arguments, both numbers or markers, are equal.

```
equal
eq
```
Test whether two objects are the same. `equal` uses one meaning of the word "same" and `eq` uses another: `equal` returns true if the two objects have a similar structure and contents, such as two copies of the same book. On the other hand, `eq`, returns true if both arguments are actually the same object.

```
string<
string-lessp
string=
string-equal
```
The `string-lessp` function tests whether its first argument is smaller than the second argument. A shorter, alternative name for the same function (a `defalias`) is `string<`.

The arguments to `string-lessp` must be strings or symbols; the ordering is lexicographic, so case is significant. The print names of symbols are used instead of the symbols themselves.

An empty string, '`""`', a string with no characters in it, is smaller than any string of characters.

`string-equal` provides the corresponding test for equality. Its shorter, alternative name is `string=`. There are no string test functions that correspond to >, >=, or <=.

`message`   Print a message in the echo area. The first argument is a string that can contain '`%s`', '`%d`', or '`%c`' to print the value of arguments that follow the string. The argument used by '`%s`' must be a string or a symbol; the argument used by '`%d`' must be a number. The argument used by '`%c`' must be an ASCII code number; it will be printed as the character with that ASCII code. (Various other %-sequences have not been mentioned.)

```
setq
set
```
The `setq` function sets the value of its first argument to the value of the second argument. The first argument is automatically quoted by `setq`. It does the same for succeeding pairs of arguments. Another

function, `set`, takes only two arguments and evaluates both of them before setting the value returned by its first argument to the value returned by its second argument.

`buffer-name`
> Without an argument, return the name of the buffer, as a string.

`buffer-file-name`
> Without an argument, return the name of the file the buffer is visiting.

`current-buffer`
> Return the buffer in which Emacs is active; it may not be the buffer that is visible on the screen.

`other-buffer`
> Return the most recently selected buffer (other than the buffer passed to `other-buffer` as an argument and other than the current buffer).

`switch-to-buffer`
> Select a buffer for Emacs to be active in and display it in the current window so users can look at it. Usually bound to *C-x b*.

`set-buffer`
> Switch Emacs's attention to a buffer on which programs will run. Don't alter what the window is showing.

`buffer-size`
> Return the number of characters in the current buffer.

`point`   Return the value of the current position of the cursor, as an integer counting the number of characters from the beginning of the buffer.

`point-min` Return the minimum permissible value of point in the current buffer. This is 1, unless narrowing is in effect.

`point-max` Return the value of the maximum permissible value of point in the current buffer. This is the end of the buffer, unless narrowing is in effect.

3.12 Exercises

- Write a non-interactive function that doubles the value of its argument, a number. Make that function interactive.
- Write a function that tests whether the current value of `fill-column` is greater than the argument passed to the function, and if so, prints an appropriate message.

4 A Few Buffer-Related Functions

In this chapter we study in detail several of the functions used in GNU Emacs. This is called a "walk-through". These functions are used as examples of Lisp code, but are not imaginary examples; with the exception of the first, simplified function definition, these functions show the actual code used in GNU Emacs. You can learn a great deal from these definitions. The functions described here are all related to buffers. Later, we will study other functions.

4.1 Finding More Information

In this walk-through, I will describe each new function as we come to it, sometimes in detail and sometimes briefly. If you are interested, you can get the full documentation of any Emacs Lisp function at any time by typing *C-h f* and then the name of the function (and then RET). Similarly, you can get the full documentation for a variable by typing *C-h v* and then the name of the variable (and then RET).

Also, `describe-function` will tell you the location of the function definition.

Put point into the name of the file that contains the function and press the RET key. In this case, RET means `push-button` rather than "return" or "enter". Emacs will take you directly to the function definition.

More generally, if you want to see a function in its original source file, you can use the `xref-find-definitions` function to jump to it. `xref-find-definitions` works with a wide variety of languages, not just Lisp, and C, and it works with non-programming text as well. For example, `xref-find-definitions` will jump to the various nodes in the Texinfo source file of this document.

To use the `xref-find-definitions` command, type *M-.* (i.e., press the period key while holding down the META key, or else type the ESC key and then type the period key), and then, at the prompt, type in the name of the function whose source code you want to see, such as `mark-whole-buffer`, and then type RET. Emacs will switch buffers and display the source code for the function on your screen. To switch back to your current buffer, type *C-x b RET*. (On some keyboards, the META key is labeled ALT.)

Incidentally, the files that contain Lisp code are conventionally called *libraries*. The metaphor is derived from that of a specialized library, such as a law library or an engineering library, rather than a general library. Each library, or file, contains functions that relate to a particular topic or activity, such as `abbrev.el` for handling abbreviations and other typing shortcuts, and `help.el` for help. (Sometimes several libraries provide code for a single activity, as the various `rmail...` files provide code for reading electronic mail.) In *The GNU Emacs Manual*, you will see sentences such as "The *C-h p* command lets you search the standard Emacs Lisp libraries by topic keywords."

4.2 A Simplified `beginning-of-buffer` Definition

The `beginning-of-buffer` command is a good function to start with since you are likely to be familiar with it and it is easy to understand. Used as an interactive command, `beginning-of-buffer` moves the cursor to the beginning of the buffer, leaving the mark at the previous position. It is generally bound to *M-<*.

In this section, we will discuss a shortened version of the function that shows how it is most frequently used. This shortened function works as written, but it does not contain the code for a complex option. In another section, we will describe the entire function. (See Section 5.3 "Complete Definition of `beginning-of-buffer`", page 61.)

Before looking at the code, let's consider what the function definition has to contain: it must include an expression that makes the function interactive so it can be called by typing *M-x beginning-of-buffer* or by typing a keychord such as *M-<*; it must include code to leave a mark at the original position in the buffer; and it must include code to move the cursor to the beginning of the buffer.

Here is the complete text of the shortened version of the function:

```
(defun simplified-beginning-of-buffer ()
  "Move point to the beginning of the buffer;
leave mark at previous position."
  (interactive)
  (push-mark)
  (goto-char (point-min)))
```

Like all function definitions, this definition has five parts following the macro `defun`:

1. The name: in this example, `simplified-beginning-of-buffer`.

2. A list of the arguments: in this example, an empty list, `()`,

3. The documentation string.

4. The interactive expression.

5. The body.

In this function definition, the argument list is empty; this means that this function does not require any arguments. (When we look at the definition for the complete function, we will see that it may be passed an optional argument.)

The interactive expression tells Emacs that the function is intended to be used interactively. In this example, `interactive` does not have an argument because `simplified-beginning-of-buffer` does not require one.

The body of the function consists of the two lines:

```
(push-mark)
(goto-char (point-min))
```

The first of these lines is the expression, `(push-mark)`. When this expression is evaluated by the Lisp interpreter, it sets a mark at the current position of the cursor, wherever that may be. The position of this mark is saved in the mark ring.

The next line is `(goto-char (point-min))`. This expression jumps the cursor to the minimum point in the buffer, that is, to the beginning of the buffer (or to the beginning of the accessible portion of the buffer if it is narrowed. See Chapter 6 "Narrowing and Widening", page 67.)

The **push-mark** command sets a mark at the place where the cursor was located before it was moved to the beginning of the buffer by the `(goto-char (point-`

min)) expression. Consequently, you can, if you wish, go back to where you were originally by typing *C-x C-x*.

That is all there is to the function definition!

When you are reading code such as this and come upon an unfamiliar function, such as goto-char, you can find out what it does by using the describe-function command. To use this command, type *C-h f* and then type in the name of the function and press RET. The describe-function command will print the function's documentation string in a *Help* window. For example, the documentation for goto-char is:

```
Set point to POSITION, a number or marker.
Beginning of buffer is position (point-min), end is (point-max).
```

The function's one argument is the desired position.

(The prompt for describe-function will offer you the symbol under or preceding the cursor, so you can save typing by positioning the cursor right over or after the function and then typing *C-h f RET*.)

The end-of-buffer function definition is written in the same way as the beginning-of-buffer definition except that the body of the function contains the expression (goto-char (point-max)) in place of (goto-char (point-min)).

4.3 The Definition of mark-whole-buffer

The mark-whole-buffer function is no harder to understand than the simplified-beginning-of-buffer function. In this case, however, we will look at the complete function, not a shortened version.

The mark-whole-buffer function is not as commonly used as the beginning-of-buffer function, but is useful nonetheless: it marks a whole buffer as a region by putting point at the beginning and a mark at the end of the buffer. It is generally bound to *C-x h*.

In GNU Emacs 22, the code for the complete function looks like this:

```
(defun mark-whole-buffer ()
  "Put point at beginning and mark at end of buffer.
You probably should not use this function in Lisp programs;
it is usually a mistake for a Lisp function to use any subroutine
that uses or sets the mark."
  (interactive)
  (push-mark (point))
  (push-mark (point-max) nil t)
  (goto-char (point-min)))
```

Like all other functions, the mark-whole-buffer function fits into the template for a function definition. The template looks like this:

```
(defun name-of-function (argument-list)
  "documentation..."
  (interactive-expression...)
  body...)
```

Here is how the function works: the name of the function is mark-whole-buffer; it is followed by an empty argument list, '()', which means that the function does not require arguments. The documentation comes next.

The next line is an `(interactive)` expression that tells Emacs that the function will be used interactively. These details are similar to the `simplified-beginning-of-buffer` function described in the previous section.

4.3.1 Body of `mark-whole-buffer`

The body of the `mark-whole-buffer` function consists of three lines of code:

```
(push-mark (point))
(push-mark (point-max) nil t)
(goto-char (point-min))
```

The first of these lines is the expression, `(push-mark (point))`.

This line does exactly the same job as the first line of the body of the `simplified-beginning-of-buffer` function, which is written `(push-mark)`. In both cases, the Lisp interpreter sets a mark at the current position of the cursor.

I don't know why the expression in `mark-whole-buffer` is written `(push-mark (point))` and the expression in `beginning-of-buffer` is written `(push-mark)`. Perhaps whoever wrote the code did not know that the arguments for `push-mark` are optional and that if `push-mark` is not passed an argument, the function automatically sets mark at the location of point by default. Or perhaps the expression was written so as to parallel the structure of the next line. In any case, the line causes Emacs to determine the position of point and set a mark there.

In earlier versions of GNU Emacs, the next line of `mark-whole-buffer` was `(push-mark (point-max))`. This expression sets a mark at the point in the buffer that has the highest number. This will be the end of the buffer (or, if the buffer is narrowed, the end of the accessible portion of the buffer. See Chapter 6 "Narrowing and Widening", page 67, for more about narrowing.) After this mark has been set, the previous mark, the one set at point, is no longer set, but Emacs remembers its position, just as all other recent marks are always remembered. This means that you can, if you wish, go back to that position by typing *C-u C-SPC* twice.

In GNU Emacs 22, the `(point-max)` is slightly more complicated. The line reads

```
(push-mark (point-max) nil t)
```

The expression works nearly the same as before. It sets a mark at the highest numbered place in the buffer that it can. However, in this version, `push-mark` has two additional arguments. The second argument to `push-mark` is `nil`. This tells the function it *should* display a message that says "Mark set" when it pushes the mark. The third argument is `t`. This tells `push-mark` to activate the mark when Transient Mark mode is turned on. Transient Mark mode highlights the currently active region. It is often turned off.

Finally, the last line of the function is `(goto-char (point-min)))`. This is written exactly the same way as it is written in `beginning-of-buffer`. The expression moves the cursor to the minimum point in the buffer, that is, to the beginning of the buffer (or to the beginning of the accessible portion of the buffer). As a result of this, point is placed at the beginning of the buffer and mark is set at the end of the buffer. The whole buffer is, therefore, the region.

4.4 The Definition of `append-to-buffer`

The `append-to-buffer` command is more complex than the `mark-whole-buffer` command. What it does is copy the region (that is, the part of the buffer between point and mark) from the current buffer to a specified buffer.

The `append-to-buffer` command uses the `insert-buffer-substring` function to copy the region. `insert-buffer-substring` is described by its name: it takes a substring from a buffer, and inserts it into another buffer.

Most of `append-to-buffer` is concerned with setting up the conditions for `insert-buffer-substring` to work: the code must specify both the buffer to which the text will go, the window it comes from and goes to, and the region that will be copied.

Here is the complete text of the function:

```
(defun append-to-buffer (buffer start end)
  "Append to specified buffer the text of the region.
It is inserted into that buffer before its point.

When calling from a program, give three arguments:
BUFFER (or buffer name), START and END.
START and END specify the portion of the current buffer to be copied."
  (interactive
   (list (read-buffer "Append to buffer: " (other-buffer
                                            (current-buffer) t))
         (region-beginning) (region-end)))
  (let ((oldbuf (current-buffer)))
    (save-excursion
      (let* ((append-to (get-buffer-create buffer))
             (windows (get-buffer-window-list append-to t t))
             point)
        (set-buffer append-to)
        (setq point (point))
        (barf-if-buffer-read-only)
        (insert-buffer-substring oldbuf start end)
        (dolist (window windows)
          (when (= (window-point window) point)
            (set-window-point window (point)))))))))
```

The function can be understood by looking at it as a series of filled-in templates.

The outermost template is for the function definition. In this function, it looks like this (with several slots filled in):

```
(defun append-to-buffer (buffer start end)
  "documentation..."
  (interactive ...)
  body...)
```

The first line of the function includes its name and three arguments. The arguments are the **buffer** to which the text will be copied, and the **start** and **end** of the region in the current buffer that will be copied.

The next part of the function is the documentation, which is clear and complete. As is conventional, the three arguments are written in upper case so you will notice them easily. Even better, they are described in the same order as in the argument list.

Note that the documentation distinguishes between a buffer and its name. (The function can handle either.)

4.4.1 The `append-to-buffer` Interactive Expression

Since the `append-to-buffer` function will be used interactively, the function must have an `interactive` expression. (For a review of `interactive`, see Section 3.3 "Making a Function Interactive", page 29.) The expression reads as follows:

```
(interactive
 (list (read-buffer
         "Append to buffer: "
         (other-buffer (current-buffer) t))
       (region-beginning)
       (region-end)))
```

This expression is not one with letters standing for parts, as described earlier. Instead, it starts a list with these parts:

The first part of the list is an expression to read the name of a buffer and return it as a string. That is `read-buffer`. The function requires a prompt as its first argument, '`"Append to buffer: "`'. Its second argument tells the command what value to provide if you don't specify anything.

In this case that second argument is an expression containing the function `other-buffer`, an exception, and a 't', standing for true.

The first argument to `other-buffer`, the exception, is yet another function, `current-buffer`. That is not going to be returned. The second argument is the symbol for true, `t`. that tells `other-buffer` that it may show visible buffers (except in this case, it will not show the current buffer, which makes sense).

The expression looks like this:

```
(other-buffer (current-buffer) t)
```

The second and third arguments to the `list` expression are `(region-beginning)` and `(region-end)`. These two functions specify the beginning and end of the text to be appended.

Originally, the command used the letters 'B' and 'r'. The whole `interactive` expression looked like this:

```
(interactive "BAppend to buffer: \nr")
```

But when that was done, the default value of the buffer switched to was invisible. That was not wanted.

(The prompt was separated from the second argument with a newline, '\n'. It was followed by an 'r' that told Emacs to bind the two arguments that follow the symbol `buffer` in the function's argument list (that is, `start` and `end`) to the values of point and mark. That argument worked fine.)

4.4.2 The Body of `append-to-buffer`

The body of the `append-to-buffer` function begins with `let`.

As we have seen before (see Section 3.6 "`let`", page 33), the purpose of a `let` expression is to create and give initial values to one or more variables that will only be used within the body of the `let`. This means that such a variable will not be confused with any variable of the same name outside the `let` expression.

We can see how the `let` expression fits into the function as a whole by showing a template for `append-to-buffer` with the `let` expression in outline:

```
(defun append-to-buffer (buffer start end)
  "documentation..."
  (interactive ...)
  (let ((variable value))
        body...)
```

The `let` expression has three elements:

1. The symbol `let`;

2. A varlist containing, in this case, a single two-element list, (*variable value*);

3. The body of the `let` expression.

In the `append-to-buffer` function, the varlist looks like this:

```
(oldbuf (current-buffer))
```

In this part of the `let` expression, the one variable, `oldbuf`, is bound to the value returned by the (`current-buffer`) expression. The variable, `oldbuf`, is used to keep track of the buffer in which you are working and from which you will copy.

The element or elements of a varlist are surrounded by a set of parentheses so the Lisp interpreter can distinguish the varlist from the body of the `let`. As a consequence, the two-element list within the varlist is surrounded by a circumscribing set of parentheses. The line looks like this:

```
(let ((oldbuf (current-buffer)))
   ... )
```

The two parentheses before `oldbuf` might surprise you if you did not realize that the first parenthesis before `oldbuf` marks the boundary of the varlist and the second parenthesis marks the beginning of the two-element list, (`oldbuf (current-buffer)`).

4.4.3 `save-excursion` in `append-to-buffer`

The body of the `let` expression in `append-to-buffer` consists of a `save-excursion` expression.

The `save-excursion` function saves the location of point, and restores it to that position after the expressions in the body of the `save-excursion` complete execution. In addition, `save-excursion` keeps track of the original buffer, and restores it. This is how `save-excursion` is used in `append-to-buffer`.

Incidentally, it is worth noting here that a Lisp function is normally formatted so that everything that is enclosed in a multi-line spread is indented more to the right than the first symbol. In this function definition, the `let` is indented more than the `defun`, and the `save-excursion` is indented more than the `let`, like this:

```
(defun ...
  ...
  ...
  (let...
    (save-excursion
      ...
```

This formatting convention makes it easy to see that the lines in the body of the `save-excursion` are enclosed by the parentheses associated with `save-excursion`, just as the `save-excursion` itself is enclosed by the parentheses associated with the `let`:

```
(let ((oldbuf (current-buffer)))
  (save-excursion
    ...
    (set-buffer ...)
    (insert-buffer-substring oldbuf start end)
    ...))
```

The use of the `save-excursion` function can be viewed as a process of filling in the slots of a template:

```
(save-excursion
  first-expression-in-body
  second-expression-in-body
  ...
  last-expression-in-body)
```

In this function, the body of the `save-excursion` contains only one expression, the `let*` expression. You know about a `let` function. The `let*` function is different. It has a '*' in its name. It enables Emacs to set each variable in its varlist in sequence, one after another.

Its critical feature is that variables later in the varlist can make use of the values to which Emacs set variables earlier in the varlist. See "The `let*` expression", page 135.

We will skip functions like `let*` and focus on two: the `set-buffer` function and the `insert-buffer-substring` function.

In the old days, the `set-buffer` expression was simply

```
(set-buffer (get-buffer-create buffer))
```

but now it is

```
(set-buffer append-to)
```

`append-to` is bound to `(get-buffer-create buffer)` earlier on in the `let*` expression. That extra binding would not be necessary except for that `append-to` is used later in the varlist as an argument to `get-buffer-window-list`.

The `append-to-buffer` function definition inserts text from the buffer in which you are currently to a named buffer. It happens that `insert-buffer-substring` copies text from another buffer to the current buffer, just the reverse—that is why the `append-to-buffer` definition starts out with a `let` that binds the local symbol `oldbuf` to the value returned by `current-buffer`.

The `insert-buffer-substring` expression looks like this:

```
(insert-buffer-substring oldbuf start end)
```

The `insert-buffer-substring` function copies a string *from* the buffer specified as its first argument and inserts the string into the present buffer. In this case, the argument to `insert-buffer-substring` is the value of the variable created and bound by the `let`, namely the value of `oldbuf`, which was the current buffer when you gave the `append-to-buffer` command.

After `insert-buffer-substring` has done its work, `save-excursion` will restore the action to the original buffer and `append-to-buffer` will have done its job.

Written in skeletal form, the workings of the body look like this:

```
(let (bind-oldbuf-to-value-of-current-buffer)
  (save-excursion                          ; Keep track of buffer.
    change-buffer
    insert-substring-from-oldbuf-into-buffer)

  change-back-to-original-buffer-when-finished
let-the-local-meaning-of-oldbuf-disappear-when-finished
```

In summary, `append-to-buffer` works as follows: it saves the value of the current buffer in the variable called `oldbuf`. It gets the new buffer (creating one if need be) and switches Emacs's attention to it. Using the value of `oldbuf`, it inserts the region of text from the old buffer into the new buffer; and then using `save-excursion`, it brings you back to your original buffer.

In looking at `append-to-buffer`, you have explored a fairly complex function. It shows how to use `let` and `save-excursion`, and how to change to and come back from another buffer. Many function definitions use `let`, `save-excursion`, and `set-buffer` this way.

4.5 Review

Here is a brief summary of the various functions discussed in this chapter.

`describe-function`
`describe-variable`

> Print the documentation for a function or variable. Conventionally bound to *C-h f* and *C-h v*.

`find-tag`   Find the file containing the source for a function or variable and switch buffers to it, positioning point at the beginning of the item. Conventionally bound to *M-.* (that's a period following the META key).

`save-excursion`

> Save the location of point and restore its value after the arguments to `save-excursion` have been evaluated. Also, remember the current buffer and return to it.

push-mark   Set mark at a location and record the value of the previous mark on the mark ring. The mark is a location in the buffer that will keep its relative position even if text is added to or removed from the buffer.

goto-char   Set point to the location specified by the value of the argument, which can be a number, a marker, or an expression that returns the number of a position, such as `(point-min)`.

insert-buffer-substring

Copy a region of text from a buffer that is passed to the function as an argument and insert the region into the current buffer.

mark-whole-buffer

Mark the whole buffer as a region. Normally bound to *C-x h*.

set-buffer

Switch the attention of Emacs to another buffer, but do not change the window being displayed. Used when the program rather than a human is to work on a different buffer.

get-buffer-create
get-buffer

Find a named buffer or create one if a buffer of that name does not exist. The `get-buffer` function returns `nil` if the named buffer does not exist.

4.6 Exercises

- Write your own `simplified-end-of-buffer` function definition; then test it to see whether it works.

- Use `if` and `get-buffer` to write a function that prints a message telling you whether a buffer exists.

- Using `find-tag`, find the source for the `copy-to-buffer` function.

5 A Few More Complex Functions

In this chapter, we build on what we have learned in previous chapters by looking at more complex functions. The `copy-to-buffer` function illustrates use of two `save-excursion` expressions in one definition, while the `insert-buffer` function illustrates use of an asterisk in an `interactive` expression, use of `or`, and the important distinction between a name and the object to which the name refers.

5.1 The Definition of `copy-to-buffer`

After understanding how `append-to-buffer` works, it is easy to understand `copy-to-buffer`. This function copies text into a buffer, but instead of adding to the second buffer, it replaces all the previous text in the second buffer.

The body of `copy-to-buffer` looks like this,

```
...
(interactive "BCopy to buffer: \nr")
(let ((oldbuf (current-buffer)))
  (with-current-buffer (get-buffer-create buffer)
    (barf-if-buffer-read-only)
    (erase-buffer)
    (save-excursion
      (insert-buffer-substring oldbuf start end)))))
```

The `copy-to-buffer` function has a simpler `interactive` expression than `append-to-buffer`.

The definition then says

```
(with-current-buffer (get-buffer-create buffer) ...
```

First, look at the earliest inner expression; that is evaluated first. That expression starts with `get-buffer-create buffer`. The function tells the computer to use the buffer with the name specified as the one to which you are copying, or if such a buffer does not exist, to create it. Then, the `with-current-buffer` function evaluates its body with that buffer temporarily current.

(This demonstrates another way to shift the computer's attention but not the user's. The `append-to-buffer` function showed how to do the same with `save-excursion` and `set-buffer`. `with-current-buffer` is a newer, and arguably easier, mechanism.)

The `barf-if-buffer-read-only` function sends you an error message saying the buffer is read-only if you cannot modify it.

The next line has the `erase-buffer` function as its sole contents. That function erases the buffer.

Finally, the last two lines contain the `save-excursion` expression with `insert-buffer-substring` as its body. The `insert-buffer-substring` expression copies the text from the buffer you are in (and you have not seen the computer shift its attention, so you don't know that that buffer is now called `oldbuf`).

Incidentally, this is what is meant by "replacement". To replace text, Emacs erases the previous text and then inserts new text.

In outline, the body of `copy-to-buffer` looks like this:

```
(let (bind-oldbuf-to-value-of-current-buffer)
    (with-the-buffer-you-are-copying-to
      (but-do-not-erase-or-copy-to-a-read-only-buffer)
      (erase-buffer)
      (save-excursion
        insert-substring-from-oldbuf-into-buffer)))
```

5.2 The Definition of `insert-buffer`

`insert-buffer` is yet another buffer-related function. This command copies another buffer *into* the current buffer. It is the reverse of `append-to-buffer` or `copy-to-buffer`, since they copy a region of text *from* the current buffer to another buffer.

Here is a discussion based on the original code. The code was simplified in 2003 and is harder to understand.

(See Section 5.2.6 "New Body for `insert-buffer`", page 60, to see a discussion of the new body.)

In addition, this code illustrates the use of `interactive` with a buffer that might be *read-only* and the important distinction between the name of an object and the object actually referred to.

Here is the earlier code:

```
(defun insert-buffer (buffer)
  "Insert after point the contents of BUFFER.
Puts mark after the inserted text.
BUFFER may be a buffer or a buffer name."
  (interactive "*bInsert buffer: ")
  (or (bufferp buffer)
      (setq buffer (get-buffer buffer)))
  (let (start end newmark)
    (save-excursion
      (save-excursion
        (set-buffer buffer)
        (setq start (point-min) end (point-max)))
      (insert-buffer-substring buffer start end)
      (setq newmark (point)))
    (push-mark newmark)))
```

As with other function definitions, you can use a template to see an outline of the function:

```
(defun insert-buffer (buffer)
  "documentation..."
  (interactive "*bInsert buffer: ")
  body...)
```

5.2.1 The Interactive Expression in `insert-buffer`

In `insert-buffer`, the argument to the `interactive` declaration has two parts, an asterisk, '`*`', and '`bInsert buffer: `'.

A Read-only Buffer

The asterisk is for the situation when the current buffer is a read-only buffer—a buffer that cannot be modified. If `insert-buffer` is called when the current buffer is read-only, a message to this effect is printed in the echo area and the terminal may beep or blink at you; you will not be permitted to insert anything into current buffer. The asterisk does not need to be followed by a newline to separate it from the next argument.

'b' in an Interactive Expression

The next argument in the interactive expression starts with a lower case 'b'. (This is different from the code for `append-to-buffer`, which uses an upper-case 'B'. See Section 4.4 "The Definition of `append-to-buffer`", page 49.) The lower-case 'b' tells the Lisp interpreter that the argument for `insert-buffer` should be an existing buffer or else its name. (The upper-case 'B' option provides for the possibility that the buffer does not exist.) Emacs will prompt you for the name of the buffer, offering you a default buffer, with name completion enabled. If the buffer does not exist, you receive a message that says "No match"; your terminal may beep at you as well.

The new and simplified code generates a list for `interactive`. It uses the `barf-if-buffer-read-only` and `read-buffer` functions with which we are already familiar and the `progn` special form with which we are not. (It will be described later.)

5.2.2 The Body of the `insert-buffer` Function

The body of the `insert-buffer` function has two major parts: an `or` expression and a `let` expression. The purpose of the `or` expression is to ensure that the argument `buffer` is bound to a buffer and not just the name of a buffer. The body of the `let` expression contains the code which copies the other buffer into the current buffer.

In outline, the two expressions fit into the `insert-buffer` function like this:

```
(defun insert-buffer (buffer)
  "documentation..."
  (interactive "*bInsert buffer: ")
  (or ...
      ...
  (let (varlist)
      body-of-let... )
```

To understand how the `or` expression ensures that the argument `buffer` is bound to a buffer and not to the name of a buffer, it is first necessary to understand the `or` function.

Before doing this, let me rewrite this part of the function using `if` so that you can see what is done in a manner that will be familiar.

5.2.3 `insert-buffer` With an `if` Instead of an `or`

The job to be done is to make sure the value of `buffer` is a buffer itself and not the name of a buffer. If the value is the name, then the buffer itself must be got.

You can imagine yourself at a conference where an usher is wandering around holding a list with your name on it and looking for you: the usher is bound to your name, not to you; but when the usher finds you and takes your arm, the usher becomes bound to you.

In Lisp, you might describe this situation like this:

```
(if (not (holding-on-to-guest))
    (find-and-take-arm-of-guest))
```

We want to do the same thing with a buffer—if we do not have the buffer itself, we want to get it.

Using a predicate called `bufferp` that tells us whether we have a buffer (rather than its name), we can write the code like this:

```
(if (not (bufferp buffer))            ; if-part
    (setq buffer (get-buffer buffer)))  ; then-part
```

Here, the true-or-false-test of the `if` expression is `(not (bufferp buffer))`; and the then-part is the expression `(setq buffer (get-buffer buffer))`.

In the test, the function `bufferp` returns true if its argument is a buffer—but false if its argument is the name of the buffer. (The last character of the function name `bufferp` is the character 'p'; as we saw earlier, such use of 'p' is a convention that indicates that the function is a predicate, which is a term that means that the function will determine whether some property is true or false. See Section 1.8.4 "Using the Wrong Type Object as an Argument", page 13.)

The function `not` precedes the expression `(bufferp buffer)`, so the true-or-false-test looks like this:

```
(not (bufferp buffer))
```

`not` is a function that returns true if its argument is false and false if its argument is true. So if `(bufferp buffer)` returns true, the `not` expression returns false and vice versa.

Using this test, the `if` expression works as follows: when the value of the variable `buffer` is actually a buffer rather than its name, the true-or-false-test returns false and the `if` expression does not evaluate the then-part. This is fine, since we do not need to do anything to the variable `buffer` if it really is a buffer.

On the other hand, when the value of `buffer` is not a buffer itself, but the name of a buffer, the true-or-false-test returns true and the then-part of the expression is evaluated. In this case, the then-part is `(setq buffer (get-buffer buffer))`. This expression uses the `get-buffer` function to return an actual buffer itself, given its name. The `setq` then sets the variable `buffer` to the value of the buffer itself, replacing its previous value (which was the name of the buffer).

5.2.4 The `or` in the Body

The purpose of the `or` expression in the `insert-buffer` function is to ensure that the argument `buffer` is bound to a buffer and not just to the name of a buffer. The previous section shows how the job could have been done using an `if` expression. However, the `insert-buffer` function actually uses `or`. To understand this, it is necessary to understand how `or` works.

An `or` function can have any number of arguments. It evaluates each argument in turn and returns the value of the first of its arguments that is not `nil`. Also, and this is a crucial feature of `or`, it does not evaluate any subsequent arguments after returning the first non-`nil` value.

The `or` expression looks like this:

```
(or (bufferp buffer)
    (setq buffer (get-buffer buffer)))
```

The first argument to `or` is the expression (`bufferp buffer`). This expression returns true (a non-`nil` value) if the buffer is actually a buffer, and not just the name of a buffer. In the `or` expression, if this is the case, the `or` expression returns this true value and does not evaluate the next expression—and this is fine with us, since we do not want to do anything to the value of `buffer` if it really is a buffer.

On the other hand, if the value of (`bufferp buffer`) is `nil`, which it will be if the value of `buffer` is the name of a buffer, the Lisp interpreter evaluates the next element of the `or` expression. This is the expression (`setq buffer (get-buffer buffer)`). This expression returns a non-`nil` value, which is the value to which it sets the variable `buffer`—and this value is a buffer itself, not the name of a buffer.

The result of all this is that the symbol `buffer` is always bound to a buffer itself rather than to the name of a buffer. All this is necessary because the `set-buffer` function in a following line only works with a buffer itself, not with the name to a buffer.

Incidentally, using `or`, the situation with the usher would be written like this:

```
(or (holding-on-to-guest) (find-and-take-arm-of-guest))
```

5.2.5 The `let` Expression in `insert-buffer`

After ensuring that the variable `buffer` refers to a buffer itself and not just to the name of a buffer, the `insert-buffer function` continues with a `let` expression. This specifies three local variables, `start`, `end`, and `newmark` and binds them to the initial value `nil`. These variables are used inside the remainder of the `let` and temporarily hide any other occurrence of variables of the same name in Emacs until the end of the `let`.

The body of the `let` contains two `save-excursion` expressions. First, we will look at the inner `save-excursion` expression in detail. The expression looks like this:

```
(save-excursion
  (set-buffer buffer)
  (setq start (point-min) end (point-max)))
```

The expression (`set-buffer buffer`) changes Emacs's attention from the current buffer to the one from which the text will copied. In that buffer, the variables `start` and `end` are set to the beginning and end of the buffer, using the commands `point-min` and `point-max`. Note that we have here an illustration of how `setq` is able to set two variables in the same expression. The first argument of `setq` is set to the value of its second, and its third argument is set to the value of its fourth.

After the body of the inner `save-excursion` is evaluated, the `save-excursion` restores the original buffer, but `start` and `end` remain set to the values of the beginning and end of the buffer from which the text will be copied.

The outer `save-excursion` expression looks like this:

```
(save-excursion
  (inner-save-excursion-expression
    (go-to-new-buffer-and-set-start-and-end)
  (insert-buffer-substring buffer start end)
  (setq newmark (point)))
```

The `insert-buffer-substring` function copies the text *into* the current buffer *from* the region indicated by `start` and `end` in `buffer`. Since the whole of the second buffer lies between `start` and `end`, the whole of the second buffer is copied into the buffer you are editing. Next, the value of point, which will be at the end of the inserted text, is recorded in the variable `newmark`.

After the body of the outer `save-excursion` is evaluated, point is relocated to its original place.

However, it is convenient to locate a mark at the end of the newly inserted text and locate point at its beginning. The `newmark` variable records the end of the inserted text. In the last line of the `let` expression, the `(push-mark newmark)` expression function sets a mark to this location. (The previous location of the mark is still accessible; it is recorded on the mark ring and you can go back to it with *C-u C-SPC*.) Meanwhile, point is located at the beginning of the inserted text, which is where it was before you called the insert function, the position of which was saved by the first `save-excursion`.

The whole `let` expression looks like this:

```
(let (start end newmark)
  (save-excursion
    (save-excursion
      (set-buffer buffer)
      (setq start (point-min) end (point-max)))
    (insert-buffer-substring buffer start end)
    (setq newmark (point)))
  (push-mark newmark))
```

Like the `append-to-buffer` function, the `insert-buffer` function uses `let`, `save-excursion`, and `set-buffer`. In addition, the function illustrates one way to use `or`. All these functions are building blocks that we will find and use again and again.

5.2.6 New Body for `insert-buffer`

The body in the GNU Emacs 22 version is more confusing than the original.

It consists of two expressions,

```
(push-mark
 (save-excursion
   (insert-buffer-substring (get-buffer buffer))
   (point)))

nil
```

except, and this is what confuses novices, very important work is done inside the `push-mark` expression.

The `get-buffer` function returns a buffer with the name provided. You will note that the function is *not* called `get-buffer-create`; it does not create a buffer if one does not already exist. The buffer returned by `get-buffer`, an existing buffer, is passed to `insert-buffer-substring`, which inserts the whole of the buffer (since you did not specify anything else).

The location into which the buffer is inserted is recorded by `push-mark`. Then the function returns `nil`, the value of its last command. Put another way, the `insert-buffer` function exists only to produce a side effect, inserting another buffer, not to return any value.

5.3 Complete Definition of `beginning-of-buffer`

The basic structure of the `beginning-of-buffer` function has already been discussed. (See Section 4.2 "A Simplified `beginning-of-buffer` Definition", page 45.) This section describes the complex part of the definition.

As previously described, when invoked without an argument, `beginning-of-buffer` moves the cursor to the beginning of the buffer (in truth, the beginning of the accessible portion of the buffer), leaving the mark at the previous position. However, when the command is invoked with a number between one and ten, the function considers that number to be a fraction of the length of the buffer, measured in tenths, and Emacs moves the cursor that fraction of the way from the beginning of the buffer. Thus, you can either call this function with the key command *M-<*, which will move the cursor to the beginning of the buffer, or with a key command such as *C-u 7 M-<* which will move the cursor to a point 70% of the way through the buffer. If a number bigger than ten is used for the argument, it moves to the end of the buffer.

The `beginning-of-buffer` function can be called with or without an argument. The use of the argument is optional.

5.3.1 Optional Arguments

Unless told otherwise, Lisp expects that a function with an argument in its function definition will be called with a value for that argument. If that does not happen, you get an error and a message that says '`Wrong number of arguments`'.

However, optional arguments are a feature of Lisp: a particular *keyword* is used to tell the Lisp interpreter that an argument is optional. The keyword is `&optional`. (The '`&`' in front of '`optional`' is part of the keyword.) In a function definition, if an argument follows the keyword &optional, no value need be passed to that argument when the function is called.

The first line of the function definition of beginning-of-buffer therefore looks like this:

```
(defun beginning-of-buffer (&optional arg)
```

In outline, the whole function looks like this:

```
(defun beginning-of-buffer (&optional arg)
  "documentation..."
  (interactive "P")
  (or (is-the-argument-a-cons-cell arg)
      (and are-both-transient-mark-mode-and-mark-active-true)
      (push-mark))
  (let (determine-size-and-set-it)
  (goto-char
    (if-there-is-an-argument
        figure-out-where-to-go
      else-go-to
      (point-min))))
   do-nicety
```

The function is similar to the simplified-beginning-of-buffer function except that the interactive expression has "P" as an argument and the goto-char function is followed by an if-then-else expression that figures out where to put the cursor if there is an argument that is not a cons cell.

(Since I do not explain a cons cell for many more chapters, please consider ignoring the function consp. See Chapter 9 "How Lists are Implemented", page 99, and Section "Cons Cell and List Types" in *The GNU Emacs Lisp Reference Manual*.)

The "P" in the interactive expression tells Emacs to pass a prefix argument, if there is one, to the function in raw form. A prefix argument is made by typing the META key followed by a number, or by typing *C-u* and then a number. (If you don't type a number, *C-u* defaults to a cons cell with a 4. A lowercase "p" in the interactive expression causes the function to convert a prefix arg to a number.)

The true-or-false-test of the if expression looks complex, but it is not: it checks whether arg has a value that is not nil and whether it is a cons cell. (That is what consp does; it checks whether its argument is a cons cell.) If arg has a value that is not nil (and is not a cons cell), which will be the case if beginning-of-buffer is called with a numeric argument, then this true-or-false-test will return true and the then-part of the if expression will be evaluated. On the other hand, if beginning-of-buffer is not called with an argument, the value of arg will be nil and the else-part of the if expression will be evaluated. The else-part is simply point-min, and when this is the outcome, the whole goto-char expression is (goto-char (point-min)), which is how we saw the beginning-of-buffer function in its simplified form.

5.3.2 beginning-of-buffer with an Argument

When beginning-of-buffer is called with an argument, an expression is evaluated which calculates what value to pass to goto-char. This expression is rather complicated at first sight. It includes an inner `if` expression and much arithmetic. It looks like this:

```
(if (> (buffer-size) 10000)
        ;; Avoid overflow for large buffer sizes!
                        (* (prefix-numeric-value arg)
                           (/ size 10))
   (/
    (+ 10
       (*
         size (prefix-numeric-value arg))) 10)))
```

Like other complex-looking expressions, the conditional expression within `beginning-of-buffer` can be disentangled by looking at it as parts of a template, in this case, the template for an if-then-else expression. In skeletal form, the expression looks like this:

```
(if (buffer-is-large
       divide-buffer-size-by-10-and-multiply-by-arg
     else-use-alternate-calculation
```

The true-or-false-test of this inner `if` expression checks the size of the buffer. The reason for this is that the old version 18 Emacs used numbers that are no bigger than eight million or so and in the computation that followed, the programmer feared that Emacs might try to use over-large numbers if the buffer were large. The term "overflow", mentioned in the comment, means numbers that are over large. More recent versions of Emacs use larger numbers, but this code has not been touched, if only because people now look at buffers that are far, far larger than ever before.

There are two cases: if the buffer is large and if it is not.

What happens in a large buffer

In `beginning-of-buffer`, the inner `if` expression tests whether the size of the buffer is greater than 10,000 characters. To do this, it uses the `>` function and the computation of `size` that comes from the let expression.

In the old days, the function `buffer-size` was used. Not only was that function called several times, it gave the size of the whole buffer, not the accessible part. The computation makes much more sense when it handles just the accessible part. (See Chapter 6 "Narrowing and Widening", page 67, for more information on focusing attention to an accessible part.)

The line looks like this:

```
(if (> size 10000)
```

When the buffer is large, the then-part of the `if` expression is evaluated. It reads like this (after formatting for easy reading):

```
(*
  (prefix-numeric-value arg)
  (/ size 10))
```

This expression is a multiplication, with two arguments to the function `*`.

The first argument is (`prefix-numeric-value arg`). When `"P"` is used as the argument for `interactive`, the value passed to the function as its argument is passed a *raw prefix argument*, and not a number. (It is a number in a list.) To perform the arithmetic, a conversion is necessary, and `prefix-numeric-value` does the job.

The second argument is `(/ size 10)`. This expression divides the numeric value by ten—the numeric value of the size of the accessible portion of the buffer. This produces a number that tells how many characters make up one tenth of the buffer size. (In Lisp, `/` is used for division, just as `*` is used for multiplication.)

In the multiplication expression as a whole, this amount is multiplied by the value of the prefix argument—the multiplication looks like this:

```
(* numeric-value-of-prefix-arg
   number-of-characters-in-one-tenth-of-the-accessible-buffer)
```

If, for example, the prefix argument is '7', the one-tenth value will be multiplied by 7 to give a position 70% of the way through.

The result of all this is that if the accessible portion of the buffer is large, the `goto-char` expression reads like this:

```
(goto-char (* (prefix-numeric-value arg)
              (/ size 10)))
```

This puts the cursor where we want it.

What happens in a small buffer

If the buffer contains fewer than 10,000 characters, a slightly different computation is performed. You might think this is not necessary, since the first computation could do the job. However, in a small buffer, the first method may not put the cursor on exactly the desired line; the second method does a better job.

The code looks like this:

```
(/ (+ 10 (* size (prefix-numeric-value arg))) 10))
```

This is code in which you figure out what happens by discovering how the functions are embedded in parentheses. It is easier to read if you reformat it with each expression indented more deeply than its enclosing expression:

```
(/
 (+ 10
    (*
     size
     (prefix-numeric-value arg)))
 10))
```

Looking at parentheses, we see that the innermost operation is (`prefix-numeric-value arg`), which converts the raw argument to a number. In the following expression, this number is multiplied by the size of the accessible portion of the buffer:

```
(* size (prefix-numeric-value arg))
```

This multiplication creates a number that may be larger than the size of the buffer—seven times larger if the argument is 7, for example. Ten is then added to this number and finally the large number is divided by ten to provide a value that is one character larger than the percentage position in the buffer.

The number that results from all this is passed to `goto-char` and the cursor is moved to that point.

5.3.3 The Complete `beginning-of-buffer`

Here is the complete text of the `beginning-of-buffer` function:

```
(defun beginning-of-buffer (&optional arg)
  "Move point to the beginning of the buffer;
leave mark at previous position.
With \\[universal-argument] prefix,
do not set mark at previous position.
With numeric arg N,
put point N/10 of the way from the beginning.

If the buffer is narrowed,
this command uses the beginning and size
of the accessible part of the buffer.

Don't use this command in Lisp programs!
\(goto-char (point-min)) is faster
and avoids clobbering the mark."
  (interactive "P")
  (or (consp arg)
      (and transient-mark-mode mark-active)
      (push-mark))
  (let ((size (- (point-max) (point-min))))
    (goto-char (if (and arg (not (consp arg)))
                   (+ (point-min)
                      (if (> size 10000)
                          ;; Avoid overflow for large buffer sizes!
                          (* (prefix-numeric-value arg)
                             (/ size 10))
                        (/ (+ 10 (* size (prefix-numeric-value arg)))
                           10)))
                 (point-min))))
  (if (and arg (not (consp arg))) (forward-line 1)))
```

Except for two small points, the previous discussion shows how this function works.
The first point deals with a detail in the documentation string, and the second point
concerns the last line of the function.

In the documentation string, there is reference to an expression:

```
\\[universal-argument]
```

A '\\' is used before the first square bracket of this expression. This '\\' tells the
Lisp interpreter to substitute whatever key is currently bound to the '[...]'. In
the case of `universal-argument`, that is usually `C-u`, but it might be different.
(See Section "Tips for Documentation Strings" in *The GNU Emacs Lisp Reference
Manual*, for more information.)

Finally, the last line of the `beginning-of-buffer` command says to move point to the beginning of the next line if the command is invoked with an argument:

    (if (and arg (not (consp arg))) (forward-line 1))

This puts the cursor at the beginning of the first line after the appropriate tenths position in the buffer. This is a flourish that means that the cursor is always located *at least* the requested tenths of the way through the buffer, which is a nicety that is, perhaps, not necessary, but which, if it did not occur, would be sure to draw complaints. (The `(not (consp arg))` portion is so that if you specify the command with a *C-u*, but without a number, that is to say, if the raw prefix argument is simply a cons cell, the command does not put you at the beginning of the second line.)

5.4 Review

Here is a brief summary of some of the topics covered in this chapter.

or
: Evaluate each argument in sequence, and return the value of the first argument that is not `nil`; if none return a value that is not `nil`, return `nil`. In brief, return the first true value of the arguments; return a true value if one *or* any of the others are true.

and
: Evaluate each argument in sequence, and if any are `nil`, return `nil`; if none are `nil`, return the value of the last argument. In brief, return a true value only if all the arguments are true; return a true value if one *and* each of the others is true.

&optional
: A keyword used to indicate that an argument to a function definition is optional; this means that the function can be evaluated without the argument, if desired.

prefix-numeric-value
: Convert the raw prefix argument produced by `(interactive "P")` to a numeric value.

forward-line
: Move point forward to the beginning of the next line, or if the argument is greater than one, forward that many lines. If it can't move as far forward as it is supposed to, `forward-line` goes forward as far as it can and then returns a count of the number of additional lines it was supposed to move but couldn't.

erase-buffer
: Delete the entire contents of the current buffer.

bufferp
: Return `t` if its argument is a buffer; otherwise return `nil`.

5.5 optional Argument Exercise

Write an interactive function with an optional argument that tests whether its argument, a number, is greater than or equal to, or else, less than the value of `fill-column`, and tells you which, in a message. However, if you do not pass an argument to the function, use 56 as a default value.

6 Narrowing and Widening

Narrowing is a feature of Emacs that makes it possible for you to focus on a specific part of a buffer, and work without accidentally changing other parts. Narrowing is normally disabled since it can confuse novices.

With narrowing, the rest of a buffer is made invisible, as if it weren't there. This is an advantage if, for example, you want to replace a word in one part of a buffer but not in another: you narrow to the part you want and the replacement is carried out only in that section, not in the rest of the buffer. Searches will only work within a narrowed region, not outside of one, so if you are fixing a part of a document, you can keep yourself from accidentally finding parts you do not need to fix by narrowing just to the region you want. (The key binding for `narrow-to-region` is `C-x n n`.)

However, narrowing does make the rest of the buffer invisible, which can scare people who inadvertently invoke narrowing and think they have deleted a part of their file. Moreover, the `undo` command (which is usually bound to `C-x u`) does not turn off narrowing (nor should it), so people can become quite desperate if they do not know that they can return the rest of a buffer to visibility with the `widen` command. (The key binding for `widen` is `C-x n w`.)

Narrowing is just as useful to the Lisp interpreter as to a human. Often, an Emacs Lisp function is designed to work on just part of a buffer; or conversely, an Emacs Lisp function needs to work on all of a buffer that has been narrowed. The `what-line` function, for example, removes the narrowing from a buffer, if it has any narrowing and when it has finished its job, restores the narrowing to what it was. On the other hand, the `count-lines` function uses narrowing to restrict itself to just that portion of the buffer in which it is interested and then restores the previous situation.

6.1 The `save-restriction` Special Form

In Emacs Lisp, you can use the `save-restriction` special form to keep track of whatever narrowing is in effect, if any. When the Lisp interpreter meets with `save-restriction`, it executes the code in the body of the `save-restriction` expression, and then undoes any changes to narrowing that the code caused. If, for example, the buffer is narrowed and the code that follows `save-restriction` gets rid of the narrowing, `save-restriction` returns the buffer to its narrowed region afterwards. In the `what-line` command, any narrowing the buffer may have is undone by the `widen` command that immediately follows the `save-restriction` command. Any original narrowing is restored just before the completion of the function.

The template for a `save-restriction` expression is simple:

```
(save-restriction
  body... )
```

The body of the `save-restriction` is one or more expressions that will be evaluated in sequence by the Lisp interpreter.

Finally, a point to note: when you use both `save-excursion` and `save-restriction`, one right after the other, you should use `save-excursion` outermost. If you write them in reverse order, you may fail to record narrowing in the buffer to which Emacs switches after calling `save-excursion`. Thus, when written together, `save-excursion` and `save-restriction` should be written like this:

```
(save-excursion
  (save-restriction
    body...))
```

In other circumstances, when not written together, the `save-excursion` and `save-restriction` special forms must be written in the order appropriate to the function.

For example,

```
(save-restriction
  (widen)
  (save-excursion
    body...))
```


6.2 `what-line`

The `what-line` command tells you the number of the line in which the cursor is located. The function illustrates the use of the `save-restriction` and `save-excursion` commands. Here is the original text of the function:

```
(defun what-line ()
  "Print the current line number (in the buffer) of point."
  (interactive)
  (save-restriction
    (widen)
    (save-excursion
      (beginning-of-line)
      (message "Line %d"
               (1+ (count-lines 1 (point)))))))
```

(In recent versions of GNU Emacs, the `what-line` function has been expanded to tell you your line number in a narrowed buffer as well as your line number in a widened buffer. The recent version is more complex than the version shown here. If you feel adventurous, you might want to look at it after figuring out how this version works. You will probably need to use *C-h f* (`describe-function`). The newer version uses a conditional to determine whether the buffer has been narrowed.

(Also, it uses `line-number-at-pos`, which among other simple expressions, such as (`goto-char (point-min)`), moves point to the beginning of the current line with (`forward-line 0`) rather than `beginning-of-line`.)

The `what-line` function as shown here has a documentation line and is interactive, as you would expect. The next two lines use the functions `save-restriction` and `widen`.

The `save-restriction` special form notes whatever narrowing is in effect, if any, in the current buffer and restores that narrowing after the code in the body of the `save-restriction` has been evaluated.

The `save-restriction` special form is followed by `widen`. This function undoes any narrowing the current buffer may have had when `what-line` was called. (The narrowing that was there is the narrowing that `save-restriction` remembers.) This widening makes it possible for the line counting commands to count from the beginning of the buffer. Otherwise, they would have been limited to counting within the accessible region. Any original narrowing is restored just before the completion of the function by the `save-restriction` special form.

The call to `widen` is followed by `save-excursion`, which saves the location of the cursor (i.e., of point), and restores it after the code in the body of the `save-excursion` uses the `beginning-of-line` function to move point.

(Note that the `(widen)` expression comes between the `save-restriction` and `save-excursion` special forms. When you write the two `save- ...` expressions in sequence, write `save-excursion` outermost.)

The last two lines of the `what-line` function are functions to count the number of lines in the buffer and then print the number in the echo area.

```
(message "Line %d"
         (1+ (count-lines 1 (point)))))))
```

The `message` function prints a one-line message at the bottom of the Emacs screen. The first argument is inside of quotation marks and is printed as a string of characters. However, it may contain a '%d' expression to print a following argument. '%d' prints the argument as a decimal, so the message will say something such as 'Line 243'.

The number that is printed in place of the '%d' is computed by the last line of the function:

```
(1+ (count-lines 1 (point)))
```

What this does is count the lines from the first position of the buffer, indicated by the 1, up to `(point)`, and then add one to that number. (The `1+` function adds one to its argument.) We add one to it because line 2 has only one line before it, and `count-lines` counts only the lines *before* the current line.

After `count-lines` has done its job, and the message has been printed in the echo area, the `save-excursion` restores point to its original position; and `save-restriction` restores the original narrowing, if any.

6.3 Exercise with Narrowing

Write a function that will display the first 60 characters of the current buffer, even if you have narrowed the buffer to its latter half so that the first line is inaccessible. Restore point, mark, and narrowing. For this exercise, you need to use a whole potpourri of functions, including `save-restriction`, `widen`, `goto-char`, `point-min`, `message`, and `buffer-substring`.

(`buffer-substring` is a previously unmentioned function you will have to investigate yourself; or perhaps you will have to use `buffer-substring-no-properties` or `filter-buffer-substring` ..., yet other functions. Text properties are a feature otherwise not discussed here. See Section "Text Properties" in *The GNU Emacs Lisp Reference Manual*.)

Additionally, do you really need `goto-char` or `point-min`? Or can you write the function without them?

7 `car`, `cdr`, `cons`: Fundamental Functions

In Lisp, `car`, `cdr`, and `cons` are fundamental functions. The `cons` function is used to construct lists, and the `car` and `cdr` functions are used to take them apart.

In the walk through of the `copy-region-as-kill` function, we will see `cons` as well as two variants on `cdr`, namely, `setcdr` and `nthcdr`. (See Section 8.3 "copy-region-as-kill", page 86.)

The name of the `cons` function is not unreasonable: it is an abbreviation of the word "construct". The origins of the names for `car` and `cdr`, on the other hand, are esoteric: `car` is an acronym from the phrase "Contents of the Address part of the Register"; and `cdr` (pronounced "could-er") is an acronym from the phrase "Contents of the Decrement part of the Register". These phrases refer to specific pieces of hardware on the very early computer on which the original Lisp was developed. Besides being obsolete, the phrases have been completely irrelevant for more than 25 years to anyone thinking about Lisp. Nonetheless, although a few brave scholars have begun to use more reasonable names for these functions, the old terms are still in use. In particular, since the terms are used in the Emacs Lisp source code, we will use them in this introduction.

7.1 `car` and `cdr`

The CAR of a list is, quite simply, the first item in the list. Thus the CAR of the list (rose violet daisy buttercup) is rose.

If you are reading this in Info in GNU Emacs, you can see this by evaluating the following:

```
(car '(rose violet daisy buttercup))
```

After evaluating the expression, `rose` will appear in the echo area.

Clearly, a more reasonable name for the `car` function would be `first` and this is often suggested.

`car` does not remove the first item from the list; it only reports what it is. After `car` has been applied to a list, the list is still the same as it was. In the jargon, `car` is "non-destructive". This feature turns out to be important.

The CDR of a list is the rest of the list, that is, the `cdr` function returns the part of the list that follows the first item. Thus, while the CAR of the list `'(rose violet daisy buttercup)` is `rose`, the rest of the list, the value returned by the `cdr` function, is (violet daisy buttercup).

You can see this by evaluating the following in the usual way:

```
(cdr '(rose violet daisy buttercup))
```

When you evaluate this, (violet daisy buttercup) will appear in the echo area.

Like `car`, `cdr` does not remove any elements from the list—it just returns a report of what the second and subsequent elements are.

Incidentally, in the example, the list of flowers is quoted. If it were not, the Lisp interpreter would try to evaluate the list by calling `rose` as a function. In this example, we do not want to do that.

Clearly, a more reasonable name for `cdr` would be `rest`.

(There is a lesson here: when you name new functions, consider very carefully what you are doing, since you may be stuck with the names for far longer than you expect. The reason this document perpetuates these names is that the Emacs Lisp source code uses them, and if I did not use them, you would have a hard time reading the code; but do, please, try to avoid using these terms yourself. The people who come after you will be grateful to you.)

When `car` and `cdr` are applied to a list made up of symbols, such as the list (`pine fir oak maple`), the element of the list returned by the function `car` is the symbol `pine` without any parentheses around it. `pine` is the first element in the list. However, the CDR of the list is a list itself, (`fir oak maple`), as you can see by evaluating the following expressions in the usual way:

```
(car '(pine fir oak maple))
```

```
(cdr '(pine fir oak maple))
```

On the other hand, in a list of lists, the first element is itself a list. `car` returns this first element as a list. For example, the following list contains three sub-lists, a list of carnivores, a list of herbivores and a list of sea mammals:

```
(car '((lion tiger cheetah)
       (gazelle antelope zebra)
       (whale dolphin seal)))
```

In this example, the first element or CAR of the list is the list of carnivores, (`lion tiger cheetah`), and the rest of the list is ((`gazelle antelope zebra`) (`whale dolphin seal`)).

```
(cdr '((lion tiger cheetah)
       (gazelle antelope zebra)
       (whale dolphin seal)))
```

It is worth saying again that `car` and `cdr` are non-destructive—that is, they do not modify or change lists to which they are applied. This is very important for how they are used.

Also, in the first chapter, in the discussion about atoms, I said that in Lisp, certain kinds of atom, such as an array, can be separated into parts; but the mechanism for doing this is different from the mechanism for splitting a list. As far as Lisp is concerned, the atoms of a list are unsplittable. (See Section 1.1.1 "Lisp Atoms", page 1.) The `car` and `cdr` functions are used for splitting lists and are considered fundamental to Lisp. Since they cannot split or gain access to the parts of an array, an array is considered an atom. Conversely, the other fundamental function, `cons`, can put together or construct a list, but not an array. (Arrays are handled by array-specific functions. See Section "Arrays" in *The GNU Emacs Lisp Reference Manual*.)

7.2 `cons`

The `cons` function constructs lists; it is the inverse of `car` and `cdr`. For example, `cons` can be used to make a four element list from the three element list, (`fir oak maple`):

```
(cons 'pine '(fir oak maple))
```

After evaluating this list, you will see

```
(pine fir oak maple)
```

appear in the echo area. `cons` causes the creation of a new list in which the element is followed by the elements of the original list.

We often say that `cons` puts a new element at the beginning of a list, or that it attaches or pushes elements onto the list, but this phrasing can be misleading, since `cons` does not change an existing list, but creates a new one.

Like `car` and `cdr`, `cons` is non-destructive.

`cons` must have a list to attach to.[1] You cannot start from absolutely nothing. If you are building a list, you need to provide at least an empty list at the beginning. Here is a series of `cons` expressions that build up a list of flowers. If you are reading this in Info in GNU Emacs, you can evaluate each of the expressions in the usual way; the value is printed in this text after '⇒', which you may read as "evaluates to".

```
(cons 'buttercup ())
     ⇒ (buttercup)

(cons 'daisy '(buttercup))
     ⇒ (daisy buttercup)

(cons 'violet '(daisy buttercup))
     ⇒ (violet daisy buttercup)

(cons 'rose '(violet daisy buttercup))
     ⇒ (rose violet daisy buttercup)
```

In the first example, the empty list is shown as () and a list made up of `buttercup` followed by the empty list is constructed. As you can see, the empty list is not shown in the list that was constructed. All that you see is (buttercup). The empty list is not counted as an element of a list because there is nothing in an empty list. Generally speaking, an empty list is invisible.

The second example, (cons 'daisy '(buttercup)) constructs a new, two element list by putting `daisy` in front of `buttercup`; and the third example constructs a three element list by putting `violet` in front of `daisy` and `buttercup`.

7.2.1 Find the Length of a List: `length`

You can find out how many elements there are in a list by using the Lisp function `length`, as in the following examples:

```
(length '(buttercup))
     ⇒ 1

(length '(daisy buttercup))
     ⇒ 2
```

---

[1] Actually, you can `cons` an element to an atom to produce a dotted pair. Dotted pairs are not discussed here; see Section "Dotted Pair Notation" in *The GNU Emacs Lisp Reference Manual*.

```
(length (cons 'violet '(daisy buttercup)))
     ⇒ 3
```

In the third example, the `cons` function is used to construct a three element list which is then passed to the `length` function as its argument.

We can also use `length` to count the number of elements in an empty list:

```
(length ())
     ⇒ 0
```

As you would expect, the number of elements in an empty list is zero.

An interesting experiment is to find out what happens if you try to find the length of no list at all; that is, if you try to call `length` without giving it an argument, not even an empty list:

```
(length )
```

What you see, if you evaluate this, is the error message

```
Lisp error: (wrong-number-of-arguments length 0)
```

This means that the function receives the wrong number of arguments, zero, when it expects some other number of arguments. In this case, one argument is expected, the argument being a list whose length the function is measuring. (Note that *one* list is *one* argument, even if the list has many elements inside it.)

The part of the error message that says '`length`' is the name of the function.

7.3 `nthcdr`

The `nthcdr` function is associated with the `cdr` function. What it does is take the CDR of a list repeatedly.

If you take the CDR of the list (`pine fir oak maple`), you will be returned the list (`fir oak maple`). If you repeat this on what was returned, you will be returned the list (`oak maple`). (Of course, repeated CDRing on the original list will just give you the original CDR since the function does not change the list. You need to evaluate the CDR of the CDR and so on.) If you continue this, eventually you will be returned an empty list, which in this case, instead of being shown as () is shown as `nil`.

For review, here is a series of repeated CDRs, the text following the '⇒' shows what is returned.

```
(cdr '(pine fir oak maple))
     ⇒(fir oak maple)

(cdr '(fir oak maple))
     ⇒ (oak maple)

(cdr '(oak maple))
     ⇒(maple)

(cdr '(maple))
     ⇒ nil

(cdr 'nil)
     ⇒ nil
```

```
(cdr ())
    ⇒ nil
```

You can also do several CDRs without printing the values in between, like this:

```
(cdr (cdr '(pine fir oak maple)))
    ⇒ (oak maple)
```

In this example, the Lisp interpreter evaluates the innermost list first. The innermost list is quoted, so it just passes the list as it is to the innermost `cdr`. This `cdr` passes a list made up of the second and subsequent elements of the list to the outermost `cdr`, which produces a list composed of the third and subsequent elements of the original list. In this example, the `cdr` function is repeated and returns a list that consists of the original list without its first two elements.

The `nthcdr` function does the same as repeating the call to `cdr`. In the following example, the argument 2 is passed to the function `nthcdr`, along with the list, and the value returned is the list without its first two items, which is exactly the same as repeating `cdr` twice on the list:

```
(nthcdr 2 '(pine fir oak maple))
    ⇒ (oak maple)
```

Using the original four element list, we can see what happens when various numeric arguments are passed to `nthcdr`, including 0, 1, and 5:

```
;; Leave the list as it was.
(nthcdr 0 '(pine fir oak maple))
    ⇒ (pine fir oak maple)

;; Return a copy without the first element.
(nthcdr 1 '(pine fir oak maple))
    ⇒ (fir oak maple)

;; Return a copy of the list without three elements.
(nthcdr 3 '(pine fir oak maple))
    ⇒ (maple)

;; Return a copy lacking all four elements.
(nthcdr 4 '(pine fir oak maple))
    ⇒ nil

;; Return a copy lacking all elements.
(nthcdr 5 '(pine fir oak maple))
    ⇒ nil
```

7.4 `nth`

The `nthcdr` function takes the CDR of a list repeatedly. The `nth` function takes the CAR of the result returned by `nthcdr`. It returns the Nth element of the list.

Thus, if it were not defined in C for speed, the definition of `nth` would be:

```
(defun nth (n list)
  "Returns the Nth element of LIST.
N counts from zero.  If LIST is not that long, nil is returned."
  (car (nthcdr n list)))
```

(Originally, `nth` was defined in Emacs Lisp in `subr.el`, but its definition was redone in C in the 1980s.)

The `nth` function returns a single element of a list. This can be very convenient.

Note that the elements are numbered from zero, not one. That is to say, the first element of a list, its CAR is the zeroth element. This zero-based counting often bothers people who are accustomed to the first element in a list being number one, which is one-based.

For example:

```
(nth 0 '("one" "two" "three"))
    ⇒ "one"

(nth 1 '("one" "two" "three"))
    ⇒ "two"
```

It is worth mentioning that `nth`, like `nthcdr` and `cdr`, does not change the original list—the function is non-destructive. This is in sharp contrast to the `setcar` and `setcdr` functions.

7.5 `setcar`

As you might guess from their names, the `setcar` and `setcdr` functions set the CAR or the CDR of a list to a new value. They actually change the original list, unlike `car` and `cdr` which leave the original list as it was. One way to find out how this works is to experiment. We will start with the `setcar` function.

First, we can make a list and then set the value of a variable to the list, using the `setq` function. Here is a list of animals:

```
(setq animals '(antelope giraffe lion tiger))
```

If you are reading this in Info inside of GNU Emacs, you can evaluate this expression in the usual fashion, by positioning the cursor after the expression and typing `C-x C-e`. (I'm doing this right here as I write this. This is one of the advantages of having the interpreter built into the computing environment. Incidentally, when there is nothing on the line after the final parentheses, such as a comment, point can be on the next line. Thus, if your cursor is in the first column of the next line, you do not need to move it. Indeed, Emacs permits any amount of white space after the final parenthesis.)

When we evaluate the variable `animals`, we see that it is bound to the list `(antelope giraffe lion tiger)`:

```
animals
        ⇒ (antelope giraffe lion tiger)
```

Put another way, the variable `animals` points to the list `(antelope giraffe lion tiger)`.

Next, evaluate the function `setcar` while passing it two arguments, the variable `animals` and the quoted symbol `hippopotamus`; this is done by writing the three element list (`setcar animals 'hippopotamus`) and then evaluating it in the usual fashion:

        (setcar animals 'hippopotamus)

After evaluating this expression, evaluate the variable `animals` again. You will see that the list of animals has changed:

        animals
             ⇒ (hippopotamus giraffe lion tiger)

The first element on the list, `antelope` is replaced by `hippopotamus`.

So we can see that `setcar` did not add a new element to the list as `cons` would have; it replaced `antelope` with `hippopotamus`; it *changed* the list.

7.6 setcdr

The `setcdr` function is similar to the `setcar` function, except that the function replaces the second and subsequent elements of a list rather than the first element.

(To see how to change the last element of a list, look ahead to "The `kill-new` function", page 89, which uses the `nthcdr` and `setcdr` functions.)

To see how this works, set the value of the variable to a list of domesticated animals by evaluating the following expression:

        (setq domesticated-animals '(horse cow sheep goat))

If you now evaluate the list, you will be returned the list (`horse cow sheep goat`):

        domesticated-animals
             ⇒ (horse cow sheep goat)

Next, evaluate `setcdr` with two arguments, the name of the variable which has a list as its value, and the list to which the CDR of the first list will be set;

        (setcdr domesticated-animals '(cat dog))

If you evaluate this expression, the list (`cat dog`) will appear in the echo area. This is the value returned by the function. The result we are interested in is the side effect, which we can see by evaluating the variable `domesticated-animals`:

        domesticated-animals
             ⇒ (horse cat dog)

Indeed, the list is changed from (`horse cow sheep goat`) to (`horse cat dog`). The CDR of the list is changed from (`cow sheep goat`) to (`cat dog`).

7.7 Exercise

Construct a list of four birds by evaluating several expressions with `cons`. Find out what happens when you `cons` a list onto itself. Replace the first element of the list of four birds with a fish. Replace the rest of that list with a list of other fish.

8 Cutting and Storing Text

Whenever you cut or clip text out of a buffer with a *kill* command in GNU Emacs, it is stored in a list and you can bring it back with a *yank* command.

(The use of the word "kill" in Emacs for processes which specifically *do not* destroy the values of the entities is an unfortunate historical accident. A much more appropriate word would be "clip" since that is what the kill commands do; they clip text out of a buffer and put it into storage from which it can be brought back. I have often been tempted to replace globally all occurrences of "kill" in the Emacs sources with "clip" and all occurrences of "killed" with "clipped".)

When text is cut out of a buffer, it is stored on a list. Successive pieces of text are stored on the list successively, so the list might look like this:

```
("a piece of text" "previous piece")
```

The function **cons** can be used to create a new list from a piece of text (an "atom", to use the jargon) and an existing list, like this:

```
(cons "another piece"
      '("a piece of text" "previous piece"))
```

If you evaluate this expression, a list of three elements will appear in the echo area:

```
("another piece" "a piece of text" "previous piece")
```

With the **car** and **nthcdr** functions, you can retrieve whichever piece of text you want. For example, in the following code, **nthcdr 1 ...** returns the list with the first item removed; and the **car** returns the first element of that remainder—the second element of the original list:

```
(car (nthcdr 1 '("another piece"
                 "a piece of text"
                 "previous piece")))
     ⇒ "a piece of text"
```

The actual functions in Emacs are more complex than this, of course. The code for cutting and retrieving text has to be written so that Emacs can figure out which element in the list you want—the first, second, third, or whatever. In addition, when you get to the end of the list, Emacs should give you the first element of the list, rather than nothing at all.

The list that holds the pieces of text is called the *kill ring*. This chapter leads up to a description of the kill ring and how it is used by first tracing how the **zap-to-char** function works. This function calls a function that invokes a function that manipulates the kill ring. Thus, before reaching the mountains, we climb the foothills.

A subsequent chapter describes how text that is cut from the buffer is retrieved. See Chapter 10 "Yanking Text Back", page 103.

8.1 zap-to-char

Let us look at the interactive **zap-to-char** function.

The **zap-to-char** function removes the text in the region between the location of the cursor (i.e., of point) up to and including the next occurrence of a specified character. The text that **zap-to-char** removes is put in the kill ring; and it can be retrieved from the kill ring by typing `C-y` (yank). If the command is given an argument, it removes text through that number of occurrences. Thus, if the cursor were at the beginning of this sentence and the character were 's', 'Thus' would be removed. If the argument were two, 'Thus, if the curs' would be removed, up to and including the 's' in 'cursor'.

If the specified character is not found, `zap-to-char` will say "Search failed", tell you the character you typed, and not remove any text.

In order to determine how much text to remove, `zap-to-char` uses a search function. Searches are used extensively in code that manipulates text, and we will focus attention on them as well as on the deletion command.

Here is the complete text of the version 22 implementation of the function:

```
(defun zap-to-char (arg char)
  "Kill up to and including ARG'th occurrence of CHAR.
Case is ignored if `case-fold-search' is non-nil in the current buffer.
Goes backward if ARG is negative; error if CHAR not found."
  (interactive "p\ncZap to char: ")
  (if (char-table-p translation-table-for-input)
      (setq char (or (aref translation-table-for-input char) char)))
  (kill-region (point) (progn
                         (search-forward (char-to-string char)
                                         nil nil arg)
                         (point)))))
```

The documentation is thorough. You do need to know the jargon meaning of the word "kill".

The version 22 documentation string for `zap-to-char` uses ASCII grave accent and apostrophe to quote a symbol, so it appears as `` `case-fold-search' ``. This quoting style was inspired by 1970s-era displays in which grave accent and apostrophe were often mirror images suitable for use as quotes. On most modern displays this is no longer true, and when these two ASCII characters appear in documentation strings or diagnostic message formats, Emacs typically transliterates them to *curved quotes* (left and right single quotation marks), so that the abovequoted symbol appears as `'case-fold-search'`. Source-code strings can also simply use curved quotes directly.

8.1.1 The `interactive` Expression

The interactive expression in the `zap-to-char` command looks like this:

```
(interactive "p\ncZap to char: ")
```

The part within quotation marks, `"p\ncZap to char: "`, specifies two different things. First, and most simply, is the 'p'. This part is separated from the next part by a newline, '\n'. The 'p' means that the first argument to the function will be passed the value of a *processed prefix*. The prefix argument is passed by typing `C-u` and a number, or `M-` and a number. If the function is called interactively without a prefix, 1 is passed to this argument.

The second part of `"p\ncZap to char: "` is 'cZap to char: '. In this part, the lower case 'c' indicates that `interactive` expects a prompt and that the argument will be a character. The prompt follows the 'c' and is the string 'Zap to char: ' (with a space after the colon to make it look good).

What all this does is prepare the arguments to zap-to-char so they are of the right type, and give the user a prompt.

In a read-only buffer, the zap-to-char function copies the text to the kill ring, but does not remove it. The echo area displays a message saying that the buffer is read-only. Also, the terminal may beep or blink at you.

8.1.2 The Body of zap-to-char

The body of the zap-to-char function contains the code that kills (that is, removes) the text in the region from the current position of the cursor up to and including the specified character.

The first part of the code looks like this:

```
(if (char-table-p translation-table-for-input)
    (setq char (or (aref translation-table-for-input char) char)))
(kill-region (point) (progn
                      (search-forward (char-to-string char) nil nil arg)
                      (point)))
```

char-table-p is an hitherto unseen function. It determines whether its argument is a character table. When it is, it sets the character passed to zap-to-char to one of them, if that character exists, or to the character itself. (This becomes important for certain characters in non-European languages. The aref function extracts an element from an array. It is an array-specific function that is not described in this document. See Section "Arrays" in *The GNU Emacs Lisp Reference Manual*.) (point) is the current position of the cursor.

The next part of the code is an expression using progn. The body of the progn consists of calls to search-forward and point.

It is easier to understand how progn works after learning about search-forward, so we will look at search-forward and then at progn.

8.1.3 The search-forward Function

The search-forward function is used to locate the zapped-for-character in zap-to-char. If the search is successful, search-forward leaves point immediately after the last character in the target string. (In zap-to-char, the target string is just one character long. zap-to-char uses the function char-to-string to ensure that the computer treats that character as a string.) If the search is backwards, search-forward leaves point just before the first character in the target. Also, search-forward returns t for true. (Moving point is therefore a side effect.)

In zap-to-char, the search-forward function looks like this:

```
(search-forward (char-to-string char) nil nil arg)
```

The search-forward function takes four arguments:

1. The first argument is the target, what is searched for. This must be a string, such as '"z"'.

   As it happens, the argument passed to zap-to-char is a single character. Because of the way computers are built, the Lisp interpreter may treat a single character as being different from a string of characters. Inside the computer, a single character has a different electronic format than a string of one character. (A single character can often be recorded in the computer using exactly one byte; but a string may be longer, and the computer needs to be ready for this.) Since the `search-forward` function searches for a string, the character that the `zap-to-char` function receives as its argument must be converted inside the computer from one format to the other; otherwise the `search-forward` function will fail. The `char-to-string` function is used to make this conversion.

2. The second argument bounds the search; it is specified as a position in the buffer. In this case, the search can go to the end of the buffer, so no bound is set and the second argument is `nil`.

3. The third argument tells the function what it should do if the search fails—it can signal an error (and print a message) or it can return `nil`. A `nil` as the third argument causes the function to signal an error when the search fails.

4. The fourth argument to `search-forward` is the repeat count—how many occurrences of the string to look for. This argument is optional and if the function is called without a repeat count, this argument is passed the value 1. If this argument is negative, the search goes backwards.

In template form, a `search-forward` expression looks like this:

```
(search-forward "target-string"
                limit-of-search
                what-to-do-if-search-fails
                repeat-count)
```

We will look at `progn` next.

8.1.4 The `progn` Special Form

`progn` is a special form that causes each of its arguments to be evaluated in sequence and then returns the value of the last one. The preceding expressions are evaluated only for the side effects they perform. The values produced by them are discarded.

The template for a `progn` expression is very simple:

```
(progn
  body...)
```

In `zap-to-char`, the `progn` expression has to do two things: put point in exactly the right position; and return the location of point so that `kill-region` will know how far to kill to.

The first argument to the `progn` is `search-forward`. When `search-forward` finds the string, the function leaves point immediately after the last character in the target string. (In this case the target string is just one character long.) If the search is backwards, `search-forward` leaves point just before the first character in the target. The movement of point is a side effect.

The second and last argument to `progn` is the expression (`point`). This expression returns the value of point, which in this case will be the location to which it has been moved by `search-forward`. (In the source, a line that tells the function to go to the previous character, if it is going forward, was commented out in 1999; I don't remember whether that feature or mis-feature was ever a part of the distributed source.) The value of `point` is returned by the `progn` expression and is passed to `kill-region` as `kill-region`'s second argument.

8.1.5 Summing up `zap-to-char`

Now that we have seen how `search-forward` and `progn` work, we can see how the `zap-to-char` function works as a whole.

The first argument to `kill-region` is the position of the cursor when the `zap-to-char` command is given—the value of point at that time. Within the `progn`, the search function then moves point to just after the zapped-to-character and `point` returns the value of this location. The `kill-region` function puts together these two values of point, the first one as the beginning of the region and the second one as the end of the region, and removes the region.

The `progn` special form is necessary because the `kill-region` command takes two arguments; and it would fail if `search-forward` and `point` expressions were written in sequence as two additional arguments. The `progn` expression is a single argument to `kill-region` and returns the one value that `kill-region` needs for its second argument.

8.2 `kill-region`

The `zap-to-char` function uses the `kill-region` function. This function clips text from a region and copies that text to the kill ring, from which it may be retrieved.

The Emacs 22 version of that function uses `condition-case` and `copy-region-as-kill`, both of which we will explain. `condition-case` is an important special form.

In essence, the `kill-region` function calls `condition-case`, which takes three arguments. In this function, the first argument does nothing. The second argument contains the code that does the work when all goes well. The third argument contains the code that is called in the event of an error.

We will go through the `condition-case` code in a moment. First, let us look at the definition of `kill-region`, with comments added:

```
(defun kill-region (beg end)
  "Kill (\"cut\") text between point and mark.
This deletes the text from the buffer and saves it in the kill ring.
The command \\[yank] can retrieve it from there. ... "

  ;; • Since order matters, pass point first.
  (interactive (list (point) (mark)))
  ;; • And tell us if we cannot cut the text.
  ;; 'unless' is an 'if' without a then-part.
  (unless (and beg end)
    (error "The mark is not set now, so there is no region"))
```

```
;; • 'condition-case' takes three arguments.
;;    If the first argument is nil, as it is here,
;;    information about the error signal is not
;;    stored for use by another function.
(condition-case nil

    ;; • The second argument to 'condition-case' tells the
    ;;     Lisp interpreter what to do when all goes well.

    ;;     It starts with a 'let' function that extracts the string
    ;;     and tests whether it exists.  If so (that is what the
    ;;     'when' checks), it calls an 'if' function that determines
    ;;     whether the previous command was another call to
    ;;     'kill-region'; if it was, then the new text is appended to
    ;;     the previous text; if not, then a different function,
    ;;     'kill-new', is called.

    ;;     The 'kill-append' function concatenates the new string and
    ;;     the old.  The 'kill-new' function inserts text into a new
    ;;     item in the kill ring.

    ;;     'when' is an 'if' without an else-part.  The second 'when'
    ;;     again checks whether the current string exists; in
    ;;     addition, it checks whether the previous command was
    ;;     another call to 'kill-region'.  If one or the other
    ;;     condition is true, then it sets the current command to
    ;;     be 'kill-region'.
    (let ((string (filter-buffer-substring beg end t)))
      (when string                           ;STRING is nil if BEG = END
        ;; Add that string to the kill ring, one way or another.
        (if (eq last-command 'kill-region)
            ;;   - 'yank-handler' is an optional argument to
            ;;     'kill-region' that tells the 'kill-append' and
            ;;     'kill-new' functions how deal with properties
            ;;     added to the text, such as 'bold' or 'italics'.
            (kill-append string (< end beg) yank-handler)
          (kill-new string nil yank-handler)))
      (when (or string (eq last-command 'kill-region))
        (setq this-command 'kill-region))
      nil)

  ;; • The third argument to 'condition-case' tells the interpreter
  ;;    what to do with an error.
  ;;    The third argument has a conditions part and a body part.
  ;;    If the conditions are met (in this case,
  ;;             if text or buffer are read-only)
  ;;    then the body is executed.
  ;;    The first part of the third argument is the following:
  ((buffer-read-only text-read-only) ;; the if-part
   ;; ... the then-part
   (copy-region-as-kill beg end)
```

```
;;    Next, also as part of the then-part, set this-command, so
;;    it will be set in an error
(setq this-command 'kill-region)
;;    Finally, in the then-part, send a message if you may copy
;;    the text to the kill ring without signaling an error, but
;;    don't if you may not.
(if kill-read-only-ok
    (progn (message "Read only text copied to kill ring") nil)
  (barf-if-buffer-read-only)
  ;; If the buffer isn't read-only, the text is.
  (signal 'text-read-only (list (current-buffer)))))))
```

8.2.1 `condition-case`

As we have seen earlier (see Section 1.3 "Generate an Error Message", page 4), when the Emacs Lisp interpreter has trouble evaluating an expression, it provides you with help; in the jargon, this is called "signaling an error". Usually, the computer stops the program and shows you a message.

However, some programs undertake complicated actions. They should not simply stop on an error. In the `kill-region` function, the most likely error is that you will try to kill text that is read-only and cannot be removed. So the `kill-region` function contains code to handle this circumstance. This code, which makes up the body of the `kill-region` function, is inside of a `condition-case` special form.

The template for `condition-case` looks like this:

```
(condition-case
  var
  bodyform
  error-handler...)
```

The second argument, *bodyform*, is straightforward. The `condition-case` special form causes the Lisp interpreter to evaluate the code in *bodyform*. If no error occurs, the special form returns the code's value and produces the side-effects, if any.

In short, the *bodyform* part of a `condition-case` expression determines what should happen when everything works correctly.

However, if an error occurs, among its other actions, the function generating the error signal will define one or more error condition names.

An error handler is the third argument to `condition-case`. An error handler has two parts, a *condition-name* and a *body*. If the *condition-name* part of an error handler matches a condition name generated by an error, then the *body* part of the error handler is run.

As you will expect, the *condition-name* part of an error handler may be either a single condition name or a list of condition names.

Also, a complete `condition-case` expression may contain more than one error handler. When an error occurs, the first applicable handler is run.

Lastly, the first argument to the `condition-case` expression, the *var* argument, is sometimes bound to a variable that contains information about the error. However, if that argument is nil, as is the case in `kill-region`, that information is discarded.

In brief, in the `kill-region` function, the code `condition-case` works like this:

```
If no errors, run only this code
    but, if errors, run this other code.
```

8.2.2 Lisp macro

The part of the `condition-case` expression that is evaluated in the expectation that all goes well has a `when`. The code uses `when` to determine whether the `string` variable points to text that exists.

A `when` expression is simply a programmers' convenience. It is an `if` without the possibility of an else clause. In your mind, you can replace `when` with `if` and understand what goes on. That is what the Lisp interpreter does.

Technically speaking, `when` is a Lisp macro. A Lisp macro enables you to define new control constructs and other language features. It tells the interpreter how to compute another Lisp expression which will in turn compute the value. In this case, the other expression is an `if` expression.

The `kill-region` function definition also has an `unless` macro; it is the converse of `when`. The `unless` macro is an `if` without a then clause

For more about Lisp macros, see Section "Macros" in *The GNU Emacs Lisp Reference Manual*. The C programming language also provides macros. These are different, but also useful.

Regarding the `when` macro, in the `condition-case` expression, when the string has content, then another conditional expression is executed. This is an `if` with both a then-part and an else-part.

```
(if (eq last-command 'kill-region)
    (kill-append string (< end beg) yank-handler)
  (kill-new string nil yank-handler))
```

The then-part is evaluated if the previous command was another call to `kill-region`; if not, the else-part is evaluated.

`yank-handler` is an optional argument to `kill-region` that tells the `kill-append` and `kill-new` functions how deal with properties added to the text, such as bold or italics.

`last-command` is a variable that comes with Emacs that we have not seen before. Normally, whenever a function is executed, Emacs sets the value of `last-command` to the previous command.

In this segment of the definition, the `if` expression checks whether the previous command was `kill-region`. If it was,

```
(kill-append string (< end beg) yank-handler)
```

concatenates a copy of the newly clipped text to the just previously clipped text in the kill ring.

8.3 `copy-region-as-kill`

The `copy-region-as-kill` function copies a region of text from a buffer and (via either `kill-append` or `kill-new`) saves it in the `kill-ring`.

If you call `copy-region-as-kill` immediately after a `kill-region` command, Emacs appends the newly copied text to the previously copied text. This means that if you yank back the text, you get it all, from both this and the previous operation. On the other hand, if some other command precedes the `copy-region-as-kill`, the function copies the text into a separate entry in the kill ring.

Here is the complete text of the version 22 `copy-region-as-kill` function:

```
(defun copy-region-as-kill (beg end)
  "Save the region as if killed, but don't kill it.
In Transient Mark mode, deactivate the mark.
If `interprogram-cut-function' is non-nil, also save the text for a window
system cut and paste."
  (interactive "r")
  (if (eq last-command 'kill-region)
      (kill-append (filter-buffer-substring beg end) (< end beg))
    (kill-new (filter-buffer-substring beg end)))
  (if transient-mark-mode
      (setq deactivate-mark t))
  nil)
```

As usual, this function can be divided into its component parts:

```
(defun copy-region-as-kill (argument-list)
  "documentation..."
  (interactive "r")
  body...)
```

The arguments are `beg` and `end` and the function is interactive with `"r"`, so the two arguments must refer to the beginning and end of the region. If you have been reading through this document from the beginning, understanding these parts of a function is almost becoming routine.

The documentation is somewhat confusing unless you remember that the word "kill" has a meaning different from usual. The Transient Mark and `interprogram-cut-function` comments explain certain side-effects.

After you once set a mark, a buffer always contains a region. If you wish, you can use Transient Mark mode to highlight the region temporarily. (No one wants to highlight the region all the time, so Transient Mark mode highlights it only at appropriate times. Many people turn off Transient Mark mode, so the region is never highlighted.)

Also, a windowing system allows you to copy, cut, and paste among different programs. In the X windowing system, for example, the `interprogram-cut-function`

function is `x-select-text`, which works with the windowing system's equivalent of the Emacs kill ring.

The body of the `copy-region-as-kill` function starts with an `if` clause. What this clause does is distinguish between two different situations: whether or not this command is executed immediately after a previous `kill-region` command. In the first case, the new region is appended to the previously copied text. Otherwise, it is inserted into the beginning of the kill ring as a separate piece of text from the previous piece.

The last two lines of the function prevent the region from lighting up if Transient Mark mode is turned on.

The body of `copy-region-as-kill` merits discussion in detail.

8.3.1 The Body of `copy-region-as-kill`

The `copy-region-as-kill` function works in much the same way as the `kill-region` function. Both are written so that two or more kills in a row combine their text into a single entry. If you yank back the text from the kill ring, you get it all in one piece. Moreover, kills that kill forward from the current position of the cursor are added to the end of the previously copied text and commands that copy text backwards add it to the beginning of the previously copied text. This way, the words in the text stay in the proper order.

Like `kill-region`, the `copy-region-as-kill` function makes use of the `last-command` variable that keeps track of the previous Emacs command.

Normally, whenever a function is executed, Emacs sets the value of `this-command` to the function being executed (which in this case would be `copy-region-as-kill`). At the same time, Emacs sets the value of `last-command` to the previous value of `this-command`.

In the first part of the body of the `copy-region-as-kill` function, an `if` expression determines whether the value of `last-command` is `kill-region`. If so, the then-part of the `if` expression is evaluated; it uses the `kill-append` function to concatenate the text copied at this call to the function with the text already in the first element (the CAR) of the kill ring. On the other hand, if the value of `last-command` is not `kill-region`, then the `copy-region-as-kill` function attaches a new element to the kill ring using the `kill-new` function.

The `if` expression reads as follows; it uses eq:

```
(if (eq last-command 'kill-region)
    ;; then-part
    (kill-append  (filter-buffer-substring beg end) (< end beg))
  ;; else-part
  (kill-new  (filter-buffer-substring beg end)))
```

(The `filter-buffer-substring` function returns a filtered substring of the buffer, if any. Optionally—the arguments are not here, so neither is done—the function may delete the initial text or return the text without its properties; this function is a replacement for the older `buffer-substring` function, which came before text properties were implemented.)

The `eq` function tests whether its first argument is the same Lisp object as its second argument. The `eq` function is similar to the `equal` function in that it is used to test for equality, but differs in that it determines whether two representations are actually the same object inside the computer, but with different names. `equal` determines whether the structure and contents of two expressions are the same.

If the previous command was `kill-region`, then the Emacs Lisp interpreter calls the `kill-append` function

The `kill-append` function

The `kill-append` function looks like this:

```
(defun kill-append (string before-p &optional yank-handler)
  "Append STRING to the end of the latest kill in the kill ring.
If BEFORE-P is non-nil, prepend STRING to the kill.
... "
  (let* ((cur (car kill-ring)))
    (kill-new (if before-p (concat string cur) (concat cur string))
              (or (= (length cur) 0)
                  (equal yank-handler
                         (get-text-property 0 'yank-handler cur)))
              yank-handler)))
```

The `kill-append` function is fairly straightforward. It uses the `kill-new` function, which we will discuss in more detail in a moment.

(Also, the function provides an optional argument called `yank-handler`; when invoked, this argument tells the function how to deal with properties added to the text, such as bold or italics.)

It has a `let*` function to set the value of the first element of the kill ring to `cur`. (I do not know why the function does not use `let` instead; only one value is set in the expression. Perhaps this is a bug that produces no problems?)

Consider the conditional that is one of the two arguments to `kill-new`. It uses `concat` to concatenate the new text to the CAR of the kill ring. Whether it prepends or appends the text depends on the results of an `if` expression:

```
(if before-p                        ; if-part
    (concat string cur)             ; then-part
    (concat cur string))            ; else-part
```

If the region being killed is before the region that was killed in the last command, then it should be prepended before the material that was saved in the previous kill; and conversely, if the killed text follows what was just killed, it should be appended after the previous text. The `if` expression depends on the predicate `before-p` to decide whether the newly saved text should be put before or after the previously saved text.

The symbol `before-p` is the name of one of the arguments to `kill-append`. When the `kill-append` function is evaluated, it is bound to the value returned by evaluating the actual argument. In this case, this is the expression `(< end beg)`. This expression does not directly determine whether the killed text in this command is located before or after the kill text of the last command; what it does is determine whether the value of the variable `end` is less than the value of the variable `beg`. If it is, it means that the user is most likely heading towards the beginning of the buffer. Also, the result of evaluating the predicate expression, (< end beg), will be true and the text will be prepended before the previous text. On the other hand, if the value of the variable `end` is greater than the value of the variable `beg`, the text will be appended after the previous text.

When the newly saved text will be prepended, then the string with the new text will be concatenated before the old text:

```
(concat string cur)
```

But if the text will be appended, it will be concatenated after the old text:

```
(concat cur string))
```

To understand how this works, we first need to review the `concat` function. The `concat` function links together or unites two strings of text. The result is a string. For example:

```
(concat "abc" "def")
     ⇒ "abcdef"

(concat "new "
        (car '("first element" "second element")))
     ⇒ "new first element"

(concat (car
        '("first element" "second element")) " modified")
     ⇒ "first element modified"
```

We can now make sense of `kill-append`: it modifies the contents of the kill ring. The kill ring is a list, each element of which is saved text. The `kill-append` function uses the `kill-new` function which in turn uses the `setcar` function.

The `kill-new` function

In version 22 the `kill-new` function looks like this:

```
(defun kill-new (string &optional replace yank-handler)
  "Make STRING the latest kill in the kill ring.
Set `kill-ring-yank-pointer' to point to it.

If `interprogram-cut-function' is non-nil, apply it to STRING.
Optional second argument REPLACE non-nil means that STRING will replace
the front of the kill ring, rather than being added to the list.
..."
  (if (> (length string) 0)
      (if yank-handler
          (put-text-property 0 (length string)
                             'yank-handler yank-handler string))
    (if yank-handler
        (signal 'args-out-of-range
                (list string "yank-handler specified for empty string"))))
  (if (fboundp 'menu-bar-update-yank-menu)
      (menu-bar-update-yank-menu string (and replace (car kill-ring))))
```

```
(if (and replace kill-ring)
    (setcar kill-ring string)
  (push string kill-ring)
  (if (> (length kill-ring) kill-ring-max)
      (setcdr (nthcdr (1- kill-ring-max) kill-ring) nil)))
(setq kill-ring-yank-pointer kill-ring)
(if interprogram-cut-function
    (funcall interprogram-cut-function string (not replace))))
```

(Notice that the function is not interactive.)

As usual, we can look at this function in parts.

The function definition has an optional `yank-handler` argument, which when invoked tells the function how to deal with properties added to the text, such as bold or italics. We will skip that.

The first line of the documentation makes sense:

```
Make STRING the latest kill in the kill ring.
```

Let's skip over the rest of the documentation for the moment.

Also, let's skip over the initial `if` expression and those lines of code involving `menu-bar-update-yank-menu`. We will explain them below.

The critical lines are these:

```
(if (and replace kill-ring)
    ;; then
    (setcar kill-ring string)
  ;; else
  (push string kill-ring)
  (if (> (length kill-ring) kill-ring-max)
      ;; avoid overly long kill ring
      (setcdr (nthcdr (1- kill-ring-max) kill-ring) nil)))
(setq kill-ring-yank-pointer kill-ring)
(if interprogram-cut-function
    (funcall interprogram-cut-function string (not replace))))
```

The conditional test is (`and replace kill-ring`). This will be true when two conditions are met: the kill ring has something in it, and the `replace` variable is true.

When the `kill-append` function sets `replace` to be true and when the kill ring has at least one item in it, the `setcar` expression is executed:

```
(setcar kill-ring string)
```

The `setcar` function actually changes the first element of the `kill-ring` list to the value of `string`. It replaces the first element.

On the other hand, if the kill ring is empty, or replace is false, the else-part of the condition is executed:

```
(push string kill-ring)
```

`push` puts its first argument onto the second. It is similar to the older

```
(setq kill-ring (cons string kill-ring))
```

or the newer

```
(add-to-list kill-ring string)
```

When it is false, the expression first constructs a new version of the kill ring by prepending `string` to the existing kill ring as a new element (that is what the `push` does). Then it executes a second `if` clause. This second `if` clause keeps the kill ring from growing too long.

Let's look at these two expressions in order.

The `push` line of the else-part sets the new value of the kill ring to what results from adding the string being killed to the old kill ring.

We can see how this works with an example.

First,

```
(setq example-list '("here is a clause" "another clause"))
```

After evaluating this expression with *C-x C-e*, you can evaluate `example-list` and see what it returns:

```
example-list
     ⇒ ("here is a clause" "another clause")
```

Now, we can add a new element on to this list by evaluating the following expression:

```
(push "a third clause" example-list)
```

When we evaluate `example-list`, we find its value is:

```
example-list
     ⇒ ("a third clause" "here is a clause" "another clause")
```

Thus, the third clause is added to the list by `push`.

Now for the second part of the `if` clause. This expression keeps the kill ring from growing too long. It looks like this:

```
(if (> (length kill-ring) kill-ring-max)
    (setcdr (nthcdr (1- kill-ring-max) kill-ring) nil))
```

The code checks whether the length of the kill ring is greater than the maximum permitted length. This is the value of `kill-ring-max` (which is 60, by default). If the length of the kill ring is too long, then this code sets the last element of the kill ring to `nil`. It does this by using two functions, `nthcdr` and `setcdr`.

We looked at `setcdr` earlier (see Section 7.6 "setcdr", page 77). It sets the CDR of a list, just as `setcar` sets the CAR of a list. In this case, however, `setcdr` will not be setting the CDR of the whole kill ring; the `nthcdr` function is used to cause it to set the CDR of the next to last element of the kill ring—this means that since the CDR of the next to last element is the last element of the kill ring, it will set the last element of the kill ring.

The `nthcdr` function works by repeatedly taking the CDR of a list—it takes the CDR of the CDR of the CDR ... It does this N times and returns the results. (See Section 7.3 "nthcdr", page 74.)

Thus, if we had a four element list that was supposed to be three elements long, we could set the CDR of the next to last element to `nil`, and thereby shorten the list. (If you set the last element to some other value than `nil`, which you could do, then you would not have shortened the list. See Section 7.6 "setcdr", page 77.)

You can see shortening by evaluating the following three expressions in turn. First set the value of `trees` to (maple oak pine birch), then set the CDR of its second CDR to `nil` and then find the value of `trees`:

```
(setq trees '(maple oak pine birch))
     ⇒ (maple oak pine birch)

(setcdr (nthcdr 2 trees) nil)
     ⇒ nil

 trees
     ⇒ (maple oak pine)
```

(The value returned by the `setcdr` expression is `nil` since that is what the CDR is set to.)

To repeat, in `kill-new`, the `nthcdr` function takes the CDR a number of times that is one less than the maximum permitted size of the kill ring and `setcdr` sets the CDR of that element (which will be the rest of the elements in the kill ring) to `nil`. This prevents the kill ring from growing too long.

The next to last expression in the `kill-new` function is

```
(setq kill-ring-yank-pointer kill-ring)
```

The `kill-ring-yank-pointer` is a global variable that is set to be the `kill-ring`.

Even though the `kill-ring-yank-pointer` is called a 'pointer', it is a variable just like the kill ring. However, the name has been chosen to help humans understand how the variable is used.

Now, to return to an early expression in the body of the function:

```
(if (fboundp 'menu-bar-update-yank-menu)
        (menu-bar-update-yank-menu string (and replace (car kill-ring))))
```

It starts with an `if` expression

In this case, the expression tests first to see whether `menu-bar-update-yank-menu` exists as a function, and if so, calls it. The `fboundp` function returns true if the symbol it is testing has a function definition that is not void. If the symbol's function definition were void, we would receive an error message, as we did when we created errors intentionally (see Section 1.3 "Generate an Error Message", page 4). The then-part contains an expression whose first element is the function `and`.

The `and` special form evaluates each of its arguments until one of the arguments returns a value of `nil`, in which case the `and` expression returns `nil`; however, if none of the arguments returns a value of `nil`, the value resulting from evaluating the last argument is returned. (Since such a value is not `nil`, it is considered true in Emacs Lisp.) In other words, an `and` expression returns a true value only if all its arguments are true. (See Section 5.4 "Second Buffer Related Review", page 66.)

The expression determines whether the second argument to `menu-bar-update-yank-menu` is true or not.

menu-bar-update-yank-menu is one of the functions that make it possible to use the "Select and Paste" menu in the Edit item of a menu bar; using a mouse, you can look at the various pieces of text you have saved and select one piece to paste.

The last expression in the kill-new function adds the newly copied string to whatever facility exists for copying and pasting among different programs running in a windowing system. In the X Windowing system, for example, the x-select-text function takes the string and stores it in memory operated by X. You can paste the string in another program, such as an Xterm.

The expression looks like this:

```
(if interprogram-cut-function
    (funcall interprogram-cut-function string (not replace))))
```

If an interprogram-cut-function exists, then Emacs executes funcall, which in turn calls its first argument as a function and passes the remaining arguments to it. (Incidentally, as far as I can see, this if expression could be replaced by an **and** expression similar to the one in the first part of the function.)

We are not going to discuss windowing systems and other programs further, but merely note that this is a mechanism that enables GNU Emacs to work easily and well with other programs.

This code for placing text in the kill ring, either concatenated with an existing element or as a new element, leads us to the code for bringing back text that has been cut out of the buffer—the yank commands. However, before discussing the yank commands, it is better to learn how lists are implemented in a computer. This will make clear such mysteries as the use of the term "pointer". But before that, we will digress into C.

8.4 Digression into C

The copy-region-as-kill function (see Section 8.3 "copy-region-as-kill", page 86) uses the filter-buffer-substring function, which in turn uses the delete-and-extract-region function. It removes the contents of a region and you cannot get them back.

Unlike the other code discussed here, the delete-and-extract-region function is not written in Emacs Lisp; it is written in C and is one of the primitives of the GNU Emacs system. Since it is very simple, I will digress briefly from Lisp and describe it here.

Like many of the other Emacs primitives, `delete-and-extract-region` is written as an instance of a C macro, a macro being a template for code. The complete macro looks like this:

```
DEFUN ("delete-and-extract-region", Fdelete_and_extract_region,
       Sdelete_and_extract_region, 2, 2, 0,
       doc: /* Delete the text between START and END and return it.  */)
       (Lisp_Object start, Lisp_Object end)
{
  validate_region (&start, &end);
  if (XINT (start) == XINT (end))
    return empty_unibyte_string;
  return del_range_1 (XINT (start), XINT (end), 1, 1);
}
```

Without going into the details of the macro writing process, let me point out that this macro starts with the word `DEFUN`. The word `DEFUN` was chosen since the code serves the same purpose as **defun** does in Lisp. (The `DEFUN` C macro is defined in `emacs/src/lisp.h`.)

The word `DEFUN` is followed by seven parts inside of parentheses:

- The first part is the name given to the function in Lisp, `delete-and-extract-region`.

- The second part is the name of the function in C, `Fdelete_and_extract_region`. By convention, it starts with 'F'. Since C does not use hyphens in names, underscores are used instead.

- The third part is the name for the C constant structure that records information on this function for internal use. It is the name of the function in C but begins with an 'S' instead of an 'F'.

- The fourth and fifth parts specify the minimum and maximum number of arguments the function can have. This function demands exactly 2 arguments.

- The sixth part is nearly like the argument that follows the **interactive** declaration in a function written in Lisp: a letter followed, perhaps, by a prompt. The only difference from Lisp is when the macro is called with no arguments. Then you write a `0` (which is a null string), as in this macro.

  If you were to specify arguments, you would place them between quotation marks. The C macro for `goto-char` includes `"NGoto char: "` in this position to indicate that the function expects a raw prefix, in this case, a numerical location in a buffer, and provides a prompt.

- The seventh part is a documentation string, just like the one for a function written in Emacs Lisp. This is written as a C comment. (When you build Emacs, the program `lib-src/make-docfile` extracts these comments and uses them to make the documentation.)

In a C macro, the formal parameters come next, with a statement of what kind of object they are, followed by the body of the macro. For **delete-and-extract-region** the body consists of the following four lines:

```
validate_region (&start, &end);
if (XINT (start) == XINT (end))
  return empty_unibyte_string;
return del_range_1 (XINT (start), XINT (end), 1, 1);
```

The `validate_region` function checks whether the values passed as the beginning and end of the region are the proper type and are within range. If the beginning and end positions are the same, then return an empty string.

The `del_range_1` function actually deletes the text. It is a complex function we will not look into. It updates the buffer and does other things. However, it is worth looking at the two arguments passed to `del_range_1`. These are `XINT (start)` and `XINT (end)`.

As far as the C language is concerned, `start` and `end` are two integers that mark the beginning and end of the region to be deleted[1].

Integer widths depend on the machine, and are typically 32 or 64 bits. A few of the bits are used to specify the type of information; the remaining bits are used as content.

'XINT' is a C macro that extracts the relevant number from the longer collection of bits; the type bits are discarded.

The command in **delete-and-extract-region** looks like this:

```
del_range_1 (XINT (start), XINT (end), 1, 1);
```

It deletes the region between the beginning position, `start`, and the ending position, `end`.

From the point of view of the person writing Lisp, Emacs is all very simple; but hidden underneath is a great deal of complexity to make it all work.

8.5 Initializing a Variable with `defvar`

The `copy-region-as-kill` function is written in Emacs Lisp. Two functions within it, `kill-append` and `kill-new`, copy a region in a buffer and save it in a variable called the `kill-ring`. This section describes how the `kill-ring` variable is created and initialized using the `defvar` special form.

(Again we note that the term `kill-ring` is a misnomer. The text that is clipped out of the buffer can be brought back; it is not a ring of corpses, but a ring of resurrectable text.)

In Emacs Lisp, a variable such as the `kill-ring` is created and given an initial value by using the `defvar` special form. The name comes from "define variable".

The `defvar` special form is similar to `setq` in that it sets the value of a variable. It is unlike `setq` in two ways: first, it only sets the value of the variable if the variable does not already have a value. If the variable already has a value, `defvar` does not override the existing value. Second, `defvar` has a documentation string.

---

[1] More precisely, and requiring more expert knowledge to understand, the two integers are of type `Lisp_Object`, which can also be a C union instead of an integer type.

(There is a related macro, `defcustom`, designed for variables that people customize. It has more features than `defvar`. (See Section 16.2 "Setting Variables with `defcustom`", page 183.)

You can see the current value of a variable, any variable, by using the `describe-variable` function, which is usually invoked by typing *C-h v*. If you type *C-h v* and then `kill-ring` (followed by RET) when prompted, you will see what is in your current kill ring—this may be quite a lot! Conversely, if you have been doing nothing this Emacs session except read this document, you may have nothing in it. Also, you will see the documentation for `kill-ring`:

```
Documentation:
List of killed text sequences.
Since the kill ring is supposed to interact nicely with cut-and-paste
facilities offered by window systems, use of this variable should
interact nicely with `interprogram-cut-function' and
`interprogram-paste-function'.  The functions `kill-new',
`kill-append', and `current-kill' are supposed to implement this
interaction; you may want to use them instead of manipulating the kill
ring directly.
```

The kill ring is defined by a `defvar` in the following way:

```
(defvar kill-ring nil
  "List of killed text sequences.
  ...")
```

In this variable definition, the variable is given an initial value of `nil`, which makes sense, since if you have saved nothing, you want nothing back if you give a `yank` command. The documentation string is written just like the documentation string of a `defun`. As with the documentation string of the `defun`, the first line of the documentation should be a complete sentence, since some commands, like `apropos`, print only the first line of documentation. Succeeding lines should not be indented; otherwise they look odd when you use *C-h v* (`describe-variable`).

8.5.1 `defvar` and an asterisk

In the past, Emacs used the `defvar` special form both for internal variables that you would not expect a user to change and for variables that you do expect a user to change. Although you can still use `defvar` for user customizable variables, please use `defcustom` instead, since it provides a path into the Customization commands. (See Section 16.2 "Specifying Variables using `defcustom`", page 183.)

When you specified a variable using the `defvar` special form, you could distinguish a variable that a user might want to change from others by typing an asterisk, '*', in the first column of its documentation string. For example:

```
(defvar shell-command-default-error-buffer nil
  "*Buffer name for `shell-command' ... error output.
  ... ")
```

You could (and still can) use the `set-variable` command to change the value of `shell-command-default-error-buffer` temporarily. However, options set using `set-variable` are set only for the duration of your editing session. The new values are not saved between sessions. Each time Emacs starts, it reads the original value, unless you change the value within your `.emacs` file, either by setting it manually or by using `customize`. See Chapter 16 "Your `.emacs` File", page 182.

For me, the major use of the `set-variable` command is to suggest variables that I might want to set in my `.emacs` file. There are now more than 700 such variables, far too many to remember readily. Fortunately, you can press `TAB` after calling the `M-x set-variable` command to see the list of variables. (See Section "Examining and Setting Variables" in *The GNU Emacs Manual*.)

8.6 Review

Here is a brief summary of some recently introduced functions.

`car`
`cdr`

`car` returns the first element of a list; `cdr` returns the second and subsequent elements of a list.

For example:

```
(car '(1 2 3 4 5 6 7))
     ⇒ 1
(cdr '(1 2 3 4 5 6 7))
     ⇒ (2 3 4 5 6 7)
```

`cons`

`cons` constructs a list by prepending its first argument to its second argument.

For example:

```
(cons 1 '(2 3 4))
     ⇒ (1 2 3 4)
```

`funcall`

`funcall` evaluates its first argument as a function. It passes its remaining arguments to its first argument.

`nthcdr`

Return the result of taking CDR n times on a list. The nth `cdr`. The "rest of the rest", as it were.

For example:

```
(nthcdr 3 '(1 2 3 4 5 6 7))
     ⇒ (4 5 6 7)
```

`setcar`
`setcdr`

`setcar` changes the first element of a list; `setcdr` changes the second and subsequent elements of a list.

For example:

```
(setq triple '(1 2 3))

(setcar triple '37)

triple
     ⇒ (37 2 3)

(setcdr triple '("foo" "bar"))

triple
     ⇒ (37 "foo" "bar")
```

progn   Evaluate each argument in sequence and then return the value of the
               last.

               For example:

                   (progn 1 2 3 4)
                          ⇒ 4

save-restriction
               Record whatever narrowing is in effect in the current buffer, if any,
               and restore that narrowing after evaluating the arguments.

search-forward
               Search for a string, and if the string is found, move point. With a reg-
               ular expression, use the similar **re-search-forward**. (See Chapter 12
               "Regular Expression Searches", page 129, for an explanation of regular
               expression patterns and searches.)

               search-forward and **re-search-forward** take four arguments:

               1. The string or regular expression to search for.

               2. Optionally, the limit of the search.

               3. Optionally, what to do if the search fails, return **nil** or an error
                   message.

               4. Optionally, how many times to repeat the search; if negative, the
                   search goes backwards.

kill-region
delete-and-extract-region
copy-region-as-kill
               kill-region cuts the text between point and mark from the buffer
               and stores that text in the kill ring, so you can get it back by yanking.

               copy-region-as-kill copies the text between point and mark into
               the kill ring, from which you can get it by yanking. The function does
               not cut or remove the text from the buffer.

          delete-and-extract-region removes the text between point and mark from
the buffer and throws it away. You cannot get it back. (This is not an interactive
command.)

8.7 Searching Exercises

- Write an interactive function that searches for a string. If the search finds the
  string, leave point after it and display a message that says "Found!". (Do not
  use **search-forward** for the name of this function; if you do, you will overwrite
  the existing version of **search-forward** that comes with Emacs. Use a name
  such as **test-search** instead.)

- Write a function that prints the third element of the kill ring in the echo area,
  if any; if the kill ring does not contain a third element, print an appropriate
  message.

9 How Lists are Implemented

In Lisp, atoms are recorded in a straightforward fashion; if the implementation is not straightforward in practice, it is, nonetheless, straightforward in theory. The atom 'rose', for example, is recorded as the four contiguous letters 'r', 'o', 's', 'e'. A list, on the other hand, is kept differently. The mechanism is equally simple, but it takes a moment to get used to the idea. A list is kept using a series of pairs of pointers. In the series, the first pointer in each pair points to an atom or to another list, and the second pointer in each pair points to the next pair, or to the symbol nil, which marks the end of the list.

A pointer itself is quite simply the electronic address of what is pointed to. Hence, a list is kept as a series of electronic addresses.

For example, the list (rose violet buttercup) has three elements, 'rose', 'violet', and 'buttercup'. In the computer, the electronic address of 'rose' is recorded in a segment of computer memory along with the address that gives the electronic address of where the atom 'violet' is located; and that address (the one that tells where 'violet' is located) is kept along with an address that tells where the address for the atom 'buttercup' is located.

This sounds more complicated than it is and is easier seen in a diagram:

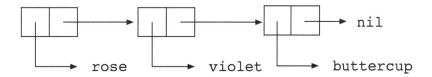

In the diagram, each box represents a word of computer memory that holds a Lisp object, usually in the form of a memory address. The boxes, i.e., the addresses, are in pairs. Each arrow points to what the address is the address of, either an atom or another pair of addresses. The first box is the electronic address of 'rose' and the arrow points to 'rose'; the second box is the address of the next pair of boxes, the first part of which is the address of 'violet' and the second part of which is the address of the next pair. The very last box points to the symbol nil, which marks the end of the list.

When a variable is set to a list with a function such as setq, it stores the address of the first box in the variable. Thus, evaluation of the expression

    (setq bouquet '(rose violet buttercup))

creates a situation like this:

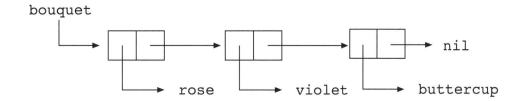

In this example, the symbol `bouquet` holds the address of the first pair of boxes.

This same list can be illustrated in a different sort of box notation like this:

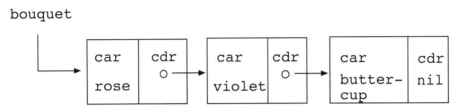

(Symbols consist of more than pairs of addresses, but the structure of a symbol is made up of addresses. Indeed, the symbol `bouquet` consists of a group of address-boxes, one of which is the address of the printed word 'bouquet', a second of which is the address of a function definition attached to the symbol, if any, a third of which is the address of the first pair of address-boxes for the list (`rose violet buttercup`), and so on. Here we are showing that the symbol's third address-box points to the first pair of address-boxes for the list.)

If a symbol is set to the CDR of a list, the list itself is not changed; the symbol simply has an address further down the list. (In the jargon, CAR and CDR are "non-destructive".) Thus, evaluation of the following expression

```
(setq flowers (cdr bouquet))
```

produces this:

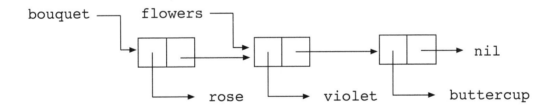

The value of `flowers` is (`violet buttercup`), which is to say, the symbol `flowers` holds the address of the pair of address-boxes, the first of which holds the address of `violet`, and the second of which holds the address of `buttercup`.

A pair of address-boxes is called a *cons cell* or *dotted pair.* See Section "Cons Cell and List Types" in *The GNU Emacs Lisp Reference Manual*, and Section "Dotted Pair Notation" in *The GNU Emacs Lisp Reference Manual*, for more information about cons cells and dotted pairs.

The function `cons` adds a new pair of addresses to the front of a series of addresses like that shown above. For example, evaluating the expression

```
(setq bouquet (cons 'lily bouquet))
```
produces:

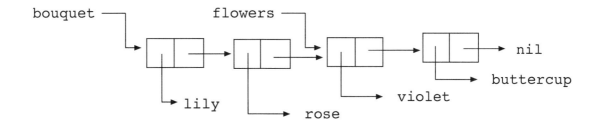

However, this does not change the value of the symbol `flowers`, as you can see by evaluating the following,

```
(eq (cdr (cdr bouquet)) flowers)
```
which returns `t` for true.

Until it is reset, `flowers` still has the value `(violet buttercup)`; that is, it has the address of the cons cell whose first address is of `violet`. Also, this does not alter any of the pre-existing cons cells; they are all still there.

Thus, in Lisp, to get the CDR of a list, you just get the address of the next cons cell in the series; to get the CAR of a list, you get the address of the first element of the list; to `cons` a new element on a list, you add a new cons cell to the front of the list. That is all there is to it! The underlying structure of Lisp is brilliantly simple!

And what does the last address in a series of cons cells refer to? It is the address of the empty list, of `nil`.

In summary, when a Lisp variable is set to a value, it is provided with the address of the list to which the variable refers.

9.1 Symbols as a Chest of Drawers

In an earlier section, I suggested that you might imagine a symbol as being a chest of drawers. The function definition is put in one drawer, the value in another, and so on. What is put in the drawer holding the value can be changed without affecting the contents of the drawer holding the function definition, and vice versa.

Actually, what is put in each drawer is the address of the value or function definition. It is as if you found an old chest in the attic, and in one of its drawers you found a map giving you directions to where the buried treasure lies.

(In addition to its name, symbol definition, and variable value, a symbol has a drawer for a *property list* which can be used to record other information. Property lists are not discussed here; see Section "Property Lists" in *The GNU Emacs Lisp Reference Manual*.)

Here is a fanciful representation:

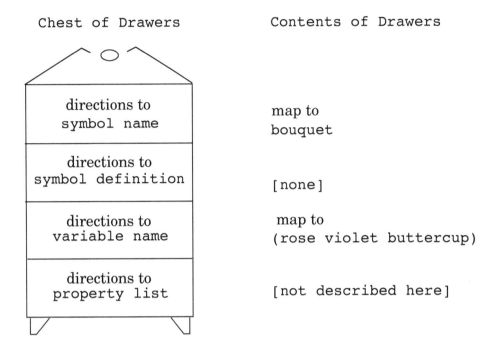

Chest of Drawers	Contents of Drawers
directions to symbol name	map to bouquet
directions to symbol definition	[none]
directions to variable name	map to (rose violet buttercup)
directions to property list	[not described here]

9.2 Exercise

Set `flowers` to `violet` and `buttercup`. Cons two more flowers on to this list and set this new list to `more-flowers`. Set the CAR of `flowers` to a fish. What does the `more-flowers` list now contain?

10 Yanking Text Back

Whenever you cut text out of a buffer with a kill command in GNU Emacs, you can bring it back with a yank command. The text that is cut out of the buffer is put in the kill ring and the yank commands insert the appropriate contents of the kill ring back into a buffer (not necessarily the original buffer).

A simple `C-y` (`yank`) command inserts the first item from the kill ring into the current buffer. If the `C-y` command is followed immediately by `M-y`, the first element is replaced by the second element. Successive `M-y` commands replace the second element with the third, fourth, or fifth element, and so on. When the last element in the kill ring is reached, it is replaced by the first element and the cycle is repeated. (Thus the kill ring is called a "ring" rather than just a "list". However, the actual data structure that holds the text is a list. See Appendix B "Handling the Kill Ring", page 210, for the details of how the list is handled as a ring.)

10.1 Kill Ring Overview

The kill ring is a list of textual strings. This is what it looks like:

```
("some text" "a different piece of text" "yet more text")
```

If this were the contents of my kill ring and I pressed `C-y`, the string of characters saying 'some text' would be inserted in this buffer where my cursor is located.

The `yank` command is also used for duplicating text by copying it. The copied text is not cut from the buffer, but a copy of it is put on the kill ring and is inserted by yanking it back.

Three functions are used for bringing text back from the kill ring: `yank`, which is usually bound to `C-y`; `yank-pop`, which is usually bound to `M-y`; and `rotate-yank-pointer`, which is used by the two other functions.

These functions refer to the kill ring through a variable called the `kill-ring-yank-pointer`. Indeed, the insertion code for both the `yank` and `yank-pop` functions is:

```
(insert (car kill-ring-yank-pointer))
```

(Well, no more. In GNU Emacs 22, the function has been replaced by `insert-for-yank` which calls `insert-for-yank-1` repetitively for each `yank-handler` segment. In turn, `insert-for-yank-1` strips text properties from the inserted text according to `yank-excluded-properties`. Otherwise, it is just like `insert`. We will stick with plain `insert` since it is easier to understand.)

To begin to understand how `yank` and `yank-pop` work, it is first necessary to look at the `kill-ring-yank-pointer` variable.

10.2 The `kill-ring-yank-pointer` Variable

`kill-ring-yank-pointer` is a variable, just as `kill-ring` is a variable. It points to something by being bound to the value of what it points to, like any other Lisp variable.

Thus, if the value of the kill ring is:

    ("some text" "a different piece of text" "yet more text")

and the `kill-ring-yank-pointer` points to the second clause, the value of
`kill-ring-yank-pointer` is:

    ("a different piece of text" "yet more text")

As explained in the previous chapter (see Chapter 9 "List Implementation",
page 99), the computer does not keep two different copies of the text being pointed to
by both the `kill-ring` and the `kill-ring-yank-pointer`. The words "a different
piece of text" and "yet more text" are not duplicated. Instead, the two Lisp variables
point to the same pieces of text. Here is a diagram:

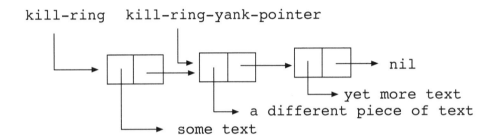

Both the variable `kill-ring` and the variable `kill-ring-yank-pointer` are
pointers. But the kill ring itself is usually described as if it were actually what
it is composed of. The `kill-ring` is spoken of as if it were the list rather than
that it points to the list. Conversely, the `kill-ring-yank-pointer` is spoken of as
pointing to a list.

These two ways of talking about the same thing sound confusing at first but
make sense on reflection. The kill ring is generally thought of as the complete
structure of data that holds the information of what has recently been cut out of
the Emacs buffers. The `kill-ring-yank-pointer` on the other hand, serves to
indicate—that is, to point to—that part of the kill ring of which the first element
(the CAR) will be inserted.

10.3 Exercises with `yank` and `nthcdr`

- Using *C-h v* (`describe-variable`), look at the value of your kill ring. Add
  several items to your kill ring; look at its value again. Using *M-y* (`yank-pop`),
  move all the way around the kill ring. How many items were in your kill ring?
  Find the value of `kill-ring-max`. Was your kill ring full, or could you have
  kept more blocks of text within it?

- Using `nthcdr` and `car`, construct a series of expressions to return the first,
  second, third, and fourth elements of a list.

11 Loops and Recursion

Emacs Lisp has two primary ways to cause an expression, or a series of expressions, to be evaluated repeatedly: one uses a `while` loop, and the other uses *recursion*.

Repetition can be very valuable. For example, to move forward four sentences, you need only write a program that will move forward one sentence and then repeat the process four times. Since a computer does not get bored or tired, such repetitive action does not have the deleterious effects that excessive or the wrong kinds of repetition can have on humans.

People mostly write Emacs Lisp functions using `while` loops and their kin; but you can use recursion, which provides a very powerful way to think about and then to solve problems[1].

11.1 `while`

The `while` special form tests whether the value returned by evaluating its first argument is true or false. This is similar to what the Lisp interpreter does with an `if`; what the interpreter does next, however, is different.

In a `while` expression, if the value returned by evaluating the first argument is false, the Lisp interpreter skips the rest of the expression (the *body* of the expression) and does not evaluate it. However, if the value is true, the Lisp interpreter evaluates the body of the expression and then again tests whether the first argument to `while` is true or false. If the value returned by evaluating the first argument is again true, the Lisp interpreter again evaluates the body of the expression.

The template for a `while` expression looks like this:

```
(while true-or-false-test
    body...)
```

So long as the true-or-false-test of the `while` expression returns a true value when it is evaluated, the body is repeatedly evaluated. This process is called a loop since the Lisp interpreter repeats the same thing again and again, like an airplane doing a loop. When the result of evaluating the true-or-false-test is false, the Lisp interpreter does not evaluate the rest of the `while` expression and exits the loop.

Clearly, if the value returned by evaluating the first argument to `while` is always true, the body following will be evaluated again and again ... and again ... forever. Conversely, if the value returned is never true, the expressions in the body will never be evaluated. The craft of writing a `while` loop consists of choosing a mechanism such that the true-or-false-test returns true just the number of times that you want the subsequent expressions to be evaluated, and then have the test return false.

The value returned by evaluating a `while` is the value of the true-or-false-test. An interesting consequence of this is that a `while` loop that evaluates without error

---

[1] You can write recursive functions to be frugal or wasteful of mental or computer resources; as it happens, methods that people find easy—that are frugal of mental resources—sometimes use considerable computer resources. Emacs was designed to run on machines that we now consider limited and its default settings are conservative. You may want to increase the values of `max-specpdl-size` and `max-lisp-eval-depth`. In my `.emacs` file, I set them to 15 and 30 times their default value.

will return `nil` or false regardless of whether it has looped 1 or 100 times or none at all. A `while` expression that evaluates successfully never returns a true value! What this means is that `while` is always evaluated for its side effects, which is to say, the consequences of evaluating the expressions within the body of the `while` loop. This makes sense. It is not the mere act of looping that is desired, but the consequences of what happens when the expressions in the loop are repeatedly evaluated.

11.1.1 A `while` Loop and a List

A common way to control a `while` loop is to test whether a list has any elements. If it does, the loop is repeated; but if it does not, the repetition is ended. Since this is an important technique, we will create a short example to illustrate it.

A simple way to test whether a list has elements is to evaluate the list: if it has no elements, it is an empty list and will return the empty list, (), which is a synonym for `nil` or false. On the other hand, a list with elements will return those elements when it is evaluated. Since Emacs Lisp considers as true any value that is not `nil`, a list that returns elements will test true in a `while` loop.

For example, you can set the variable `empty-list` to `nil` by evaluating the following `setq` expression:

```
(setq empty-list ())
```

After evaluating the `setq` expression, you can evaluate the variable `empty-list` in the usual way, by placing the cursor after the symbol and typing *C-x C-e*; `nil` will appear in your echo area:

```
empty-list
```

On the other hand, if you set a variable to be a list with elements, the list will appear when you evaluate the variable, as you can see by evaluating the following two expressions:

```
(setq animals '(gazelle giraffe lion tiger))


animals
```

Thus, to create a `while` loop that tests whether there are any items in the list `animals`, the first part of the loop will be written like this:

```
(while animals
     ...
```

When the `while` tests its first argument, the variable `animals` is evaluated. It returns a list. So long as the list has elements, the `while` considers the results of the test to be true; but when the list is empty, it considers the results of the test to be false.

To prevent the `while` loop from running forever, some mechanism needs to be provided to empty the list eventually. An oft-used technique is to have one of the subsequent forms in the `while` expression set the value of the list to be the CDR of the list. Each time the `cdr` function is evaluated, the list will be made shorter, until eventually only the empty list will be left. At this point, the test of the `while` loop will return false, and the arguments to the `while` will no longer be evaluated.

For example, the list of animals bound to the variable `animals` can be set to be the CDR of the original list with the following expression:

```
(setq animals (cdr animals))
```

If you have evaluated the previous expressions and then evaluate this expression, you will see (giraffe lion tiger) appear in the echo area. If you evaluate the expression again, (lion tiger) will appear in the echo area. If you evaluate it again and yet again, (tiger) appears and then the empty list, shown by `nil`.

A template for a `while` loop that uses the `cdr` function repeatedly to cause the true-or-false-test eventually to test false looks like this:

```
(while test-whether-list-is-empty
  body...
  set-list-to-cdr-of-list)
```

This test and use of `cdr` can be put together in a function that goes through a list and prints each element of the list on a line of its own.

11.1.2 An Example: `print-elements-of-list`

The `print-elements-of-list` function illustrates a `while` loop with a list.

The function requires several lines for its output. If you are reading this in a recent instance of GNU Emacs, you can evaluate the following expression inside of Info, as usual.

If you are using an earlier version of Emacs, you need to copy the necessary expressions to your *scratch* buffer and evaluate them there. This is because the echo area had only one line in the earlier versions.

You can copy the expressions by marking the beginning of the region with *C-SPC* (`set-mark-command`), moving the cursor to the end of the region and then copying the region using *M-w* (`kill-ring-save`, which calls `copy-region-as-kill` and then provides visual feedback). In the *scratch* buffer, you can yank the expressions back by typing *C-y* (`yank`).

After you have copied the expressions to the *scratch* buffer, evaluate each expression in turn. Be sure to evaluate the last expression, (print-elements-of-list animals), by typing *C-u C-x C-e*, that is, by giving an argument to `eval-last-sexp`. This will cause the result of the evaluation to be printed in the *scratch* buffer instead of being printed in the echo area. (Otherwise you will see something like this in your echo area: ^Jgazelle^J^Jgiraffe^J^Jlion^J^Jtiger^Jnil, in which each '^J' stands for a newline.)

In a recent instance of GNU Emacs, you can evaluate these expressions directly in the Info buffer, and the echo area will grow to show the results.

```
(setq animals '(gazelle giraffe lion tiger))

(defun print-elements-of-list (list)
  "Print each element of LIST on a line of its own."
  (while list
    (print (car list))
    (setq list (cdr list))))

(print-elements-of-list animals)
```

When you evaluate the three expressions in sequence, you will see this:

```
gazelle

giraffe

lion

tiger
nil
```

Each element of the list is printed on a line of its own (that is what the function `print` does) and then the value returned by the function is printed. Since the last expression in the function is the `while` loop, and since `while` loops always return `nil`, a `nil` is printed after the last element of the list.

11.1.3 A Loop with an Incrementing Counter

A loop is not useful unless it stops when it ought. Besides controlling a loop with a list, a common way of stopping a loop is to write the first argument as a test that returns false when the correct number of repetitions are complete. This means that the loop must have a counter—an expression that counts how many times the loop repeats itself.

The test for a loop with an incrementing counter can be an expression such as `(< count desired-number)` which returns `t` for true if the value of `count` is less than the `desired-number` of repetitions and `nil` for false if the value of `count` is equal to or is greater than the `desired-number`. The expression that increments the count can be a simple `setq` such as `(setq count (1+ count))`, where `1+` is a built-in function in Emacs Lisp that adds 1 to its argument. (The expression `(1+ count)` has the same result as `(+ count 1)`, but is easier for a human to read.)

The template for a `while` loop controlled by an incrementing counter looks like this:

```
set-count-to-initial-value
(while (< count desired-number)          ; true-or-false-test
    body...
    (setq count (1+ count)))             ; incrementer
```

Note that you need to set the initial value of `count`; usually it is set to 1.

Example with incrementing counter

Suppose you are playing on the beach and decide to make a triangle of pebbles, putting one pebble in the first row, two in the second row, three in the third row and so on, like this:

(About 2500 years ago, Pythagoras and others developed the beginnings of number theory by considering questions such as this.)

Suppose you want to know how many pebbles you will need to make a triangle with 7 rows?

Clearly, what you need to do is add up the numbers from 1 to 7. There are two ways to do this; start with the smallest number, one, and add up the list in sequence, 1, 2, 3, 4 and so on; or start with the largest number and add the list going down: 7, 6, 5, 4 and so on. Because both mechanisms illustrate common ways of writing `while` loops, we will create two examples, one counting up and the other counting down. In this first example, we will start with 1 and add 2, 3, 4 and so on.

If you are just adding up a short list of numbers, the easiest way to do it is to add up all the numbers at once. However, if you do not know ahead of time how many numbers your list will have, or if you want to be prepared for a very long list, then you need to design your addition so that what you do is repeat a simple process many times instead of doing a more complex process once.

For example, instead of adding up all the pebbles all at once, what you can do is add the number of pebbles in the first row, 1, to the number in the second row, 2, and then add the total of those two rows to the third row, 3. Then you can add the number in the fourth row, 4, to the total of the first three rows; and so on.

The critical characteristic of the process is that each repetitive action is simple. In this case, at each step we add only two numbers, the number of pebbles in the row and the total already found. This process of adding two numbers is repeated again and again until the last row has been added to the total of all the preceding rows. In a more complex loop the repetitive action might not be so simple, but it will be simpler than doing everything all at once.

The parts of the function definition

The preceding analysis gives us the bones of our function definition: first, we will need a variable that we can call `total` that will be the total number of pebbles. This will be the value returned by the function.

Second, we know that the function will require an argument: this argument will be the total number of rows in the triangle. It can be called `number-of-rows`.

Finally, we need a variable to use as a counter. We could call this variable `counter`, but a better name is `row-number`. That is because what the counter does in this function is count rows, and a program should be written to be as understandable as possible.

When the Lisp interpreter first starts evaluating the expressions in the function, the value of `total` should be set to zero, since we have not added anything to it. Then the function should add the number of pebbles in the first row to the total, and then add the number of pebbles in the second to the total, and then add the number of pebbles in the third row to the total, and so on, until there are no more rows left to add.

Both `total` and `row-number` are used only inside the function, so they can be declared as local variables with `let` and given initial values. Clearly, the initial value for `total` should be 0. The initial value of `row-number` should be 1, since we start with the first row. This means that the `let` statement will look like this:

```
(let ((total 0)
      (row-number 1))
  body...)
```

After the internal variables are declared and bound to their initial values, we can begin the `while` loop. The expression that serves as the test should return a value of `t` for true so long as the `row-number` is less than or equal to the `number-of-rows`. (If the expression tests true only so long as the row number is less than the number of rows in the triangle, the last row will never be added to the total; hence the row number has to be either less than or equal to the number of rows.)

Lisp provides the `<=` function that returns true if the value of its first argument is less than or equal to the value of its second argument and false otherwise. So the expression that the `while` will evaluate as its test should look like this:

```
(<= row-number number-of-rows)
```

The total number of pebbles can be found by repeatedly adding the number of pebbles in a row to the total already found. Since the number of pebbles in the row is equal to the row number, the total can be found by adding the row number to the total. (Clearly, in a more complex situation, the number of pebbles in the row might be related to the row number in a more complicated way; if this were the case, the row number would be replaced by the appropriate expression.)

```
(setq total (+ total row-number))
```

What this does is set the new value of `total` to be equal to the sum of adding the number of pebbles in the row to the previous total.

After setting the value of `total`, the conditions need to be established for the next repetition of the loop, if there is one. This is done by incrementing the value of the `row-number` variable, which serves as a counter. After the `row-number` variable has been incremented, the true-or-false-test at the beginning of the `while` loop tests whether its value is still less than or equal to the value of the `number-of-rows` and if it is, adds the new value of the `row-number` variable to the `total` of the previous repetition of the loop.

The built-in Emacs Lisp function `1+` adds 1 to a number, so the `row-number` variable can be incremented with this expression:

```
(setq row-number (1+ row-number))
```

Putting the function definition together

We have created the parts for the function definition; now we need to put them together.

First, the contents of the `while` expression:

```
(while (<= row-number number-of-rows)    ; true-or-false-test
  (setq total (+ total row-number))
  (setq row-number (1+ row-number)))      ; incrementer
```

Along with the `let` expression varlist, this very nearly completes the body of the function definition. However, it requires one final element, the need for which is somewhat subtle.

The final touch is to place the variable `total` on a line by itself after the `while` expression. Otherwise, the value returned by the whole function is the value of the last expression that is evaluated in the body of the `let`, and this is the value returned by the `while`, which is always `nil`.

This may not be evident at first sight. It almost looks as if the incrementing expression is the last expression of the whole function. But that expression is part of the body of the `while`; it is the last element of the list that starts with the symbol `while`. Moreover, the whole of the `while` loop is a list within the body of the `let`.

In outline, the function will look like this:

```
(defun name-of-function (argument-list)
  "documentation..."
  (let (varlist)
    (while (true-or-false-test)
      body-of-while... )
    ... ))                            ; Need final expression here.
```

The result of evaluating the `let` is what is going to be returned by the `defun` since the `let` is not embedded within any containing list, except for the `defun` as a whole. However, if the `while` is the last element of the `let` expression, the function will always return `nil`. This is not what we want! Instead, what we want is the value of the variable `total`. This is returned by simply placing the symbol as the last element of the list starting with `let`. It gets evaluated after the preceding elements of the list are evaluated, which means it gets evaluated after it has been assigned the correct value for the total.

It may be easier to see this by printing the list starting with `let` all on one line. This format makes it evident that the *varlist* and `while` expressions are the second and third elements of the list starting with `let`, and the `total` is the last element:

```
(let (varlist) (while (true-or-false-test) body-of-while... ) total)
```

Putting everything together, the `triangle` function definition looks like this:

```
(defun triangle (number-of-rows)    ; Version with
                                    ;   incrementing counter.
  "Add up the number of pebbles in a triangle.
The first row has one pebble, the second row two pebbles,
the third row three pebbles, and so on.
The argument is NUMBER-OF-ROWS."
  (let ((total 0)
        (row-number 1))
    (while (<= row-number number-of-rows)
      (setq total (+ total row-number))
      (setq row-number (1+ row-number)))
    total))
```

After you have installed `triangle` by evaluating the function, you can try it out. Here are two examples:

```
(triangle 4)
```

```
(triangle 7)
```

The sum of the first four numbers is 10 and the sum of the first seven numbers is 28.

11.1.4 Loop with a Decrementing Counter

Another common way to write a `while` loop is to write the test so that it determines whether a counter is greater than zero. So long as the counter is greater than zero, the loop is repeated. But when the counter is equal to or less than zero, the loop is stopped. For this to work, the counter has to start out greater than zero and then be made smaller and smaller by a form that is evaluated repeatedly.

The test will be an expression such as `(> counter 0)` which returns `t` for true if the value of `counter` is greater than zero, and `nil` for false if the value of `counter` is equal to or less than zero. The expression that makes the number smaller and smaller can be a simple `setq` such as `(setq counter (1- counter))`, where `1-` is a built-in function in Emacs Lisp that subtracts 1 from its argument.

The template for a decrementing `while` loop looks like this:

```
(while (> counter 0)                    ; true-or-false-test
  body...
  (setq counter (1- counter)))          ; decrementer
```

Example with decrementing counter

To illustrate a loop with a decrementing counter, we will rewrite the `triangle` function so the counter decreases to zero.

This is the reverse of the earlier version of the function. In this case, to find out how many pebbles are needed to make a triangle with 3 rows, add the number of pebbles in the third row, 3, to the number in the preceding row, 2, and then add the total of those two rows to the row that precedes them, which is 1.

Likewise, to find the number of pebbles in a triangle with 7 rows, add the number of pebbles in the seventh row, 7, to the number in the preceding row, which is 6, and then add the total of those two rows to the row that precedes them, which is 5, and so on. As in the previous example, each addition only involves adding two numbers, the total of the rows already added up and the number of pebbles in the row that is being added to the total. This process of adding two numbers is repeated again and again until there are no more pebbles to add.

We know how many pebbles to start with: the number of pebbles in the last row is equal to the number of rows. If the triangle has seven rows, the number of pebbles in the last row is 7. Likewise, we know how many pebbles are in the preceding row: it is one less than the number in the row.

The parts of the function definition

We start with three variables: the total number of rows in the triangle; the number of pebbles in a row; and the total number of pebbles, which is what we want to calculate. These variables can be named `number-of-rows`, `number-of-pebbles-in-row`, and `total`, respectively.

Both `total` and `number-of-pebbles-in-row` are used only inside the function and are declared with `let`. The initial value of `total` should, of course, be zero. However, the initial value of `number-of-pebbles-in-row` should be equal to the number of rows in the triangle, since the addition will start with the longest row.

This means that the beginning of the `let` expression will look like this:

```
(let ((total 0)
      (number-of-pebbles-in-row number-of-rows))
  body...)
```

The total number of pebbles can be found by repeatedly adding the number of pebbles in a row to the total already found, that is, by repeatedly evaluating the following expression:

```
(setq total (+ total number-of-pebbles-in-row))
```

After the `number-of-pebbles-in-row` is added to the `total`, the `number-of-pebbles-in-row` should be decremented by one, since the next time the loop repeats, the preceding row will be added to the total.

The number of pebbles in a preceding row is one less than the number of pebbles in a row, so the built-in Emacs Lisp function `1-` can be used to compute the number of pebbles in the preceding row. This can be done with the following expression:

```
(setq number-of-pebbles-in-row
      (1- number-of-pebbles-in-row))
```

Finally, we know that the `while` loop should stop making repeated additions when there are no pebbles in a row. So the test for the `while` loop is simply:

```
(while (> number-of-pebbles-in-row 0)
```

Putting the function definition together

We can put these expressions together to create a function definition that works. However, on examination, we find that one of the local variables is unneeded!

The function definition looks like this:

```
;;; First subtractive version.
(defun triangle (number-of-rows)
  "Add up the number of pebbles in a triangle."
  (let ((total 0)
        (number-of-pebbles-in-row number-of-rows))
    (while (> number-of-pebbles-in-row 0)
      (setq total (+ total number-of-pebbles-in-row))
      (setq number-of-pebbles-in-row
            (1- number-of-pebbles-in-row)))
    total))
```

As written, this function works.

However, we do not need `number-of-pebbles-in-row`.

When the `triangle` function is evaluated, the symbol `number-of-rows` will be bound to a number, giving it an initial value. That number can be changed in the body of the function as if it were a local variable, without any fear that such a change will effect the value of the variable outside of the function. This is a very useful characteristic of Lisp; it means that the variable `number-of-rows` can be used anywhere in the function where `number-of-pebbles-in-row` is used.

Here is a second version of the function written a bit more cleanly:

```
(defun triangle (number)                   ; Second version.
  "Return sum of numbers 1 through NUMBER inclusive."
  (let ((total 0))
    (while (> number 0)
      (setq total (+ total number))
      (setq number (1- number)))
    total))
```

In brief, a properly written **while** loop will consist of three parts:

1. A test that will return false after the loop has repeated itself the correct number of times.

2. An expression the evaluation of which will return the value desired after being repeatedly evaluated.

3. An expression to change the value passed to the true-or-false-test so that the test returns false after the loop has repeated itself the right number of times.

11.2 Save your time: `dolist` and `dotimes`

In addition to **while**, both **dolist** and **dotimes** provide for looping. Sometimes these are quicker to write than the equivalent **while** loop. Both are Lisp macros. (See Section "Macros" in *The GNU Emacs Lisp Reference Manual.*)

dolist works like a **while** loop that CDRs down a list: **dolist** automatically shortens the list each time it loops—takes the CDR of the list—and binds the CAR of each shorter version of the list to the first of its arguments.

dotimes loops a specific number of times: you specify the number.

The `dolist` Macro

Suppose, for example, you want to reverse a list, so that "first" "second" "third" becomes "third" "second" "first".

In practice, you would use the **reverse** function, like this:

```
(setq animals '(gazelle giraffe lion tiger))

(reverse animals)
```

Here is how you could reverse the list using a **while** loop:

```
(setq animals '(gazelle giraffe lion tiger))

(defun reverse-list-with-while (list)
  "Using while, reverse the order of LIST."
  (let (value)  ; make sure list starts empty
    (while list
      (setq value (cons (car list) value))
      (setq list (cdr list)))
    value))

(reverse-list-with-while animals)
```

And here is how you could use the `dolist` macro:

```
(setq animals '(gazelle giraffe lion tiger))

(defun reverse-list-with-dolist (list)
  "Using dolist, reverse the order of LIST."
  (let (value)  ; make sure list starts empty
    (dolist (element list value)
      (setq value (cons element value)))))

(reverse-list-with-dolist animals)
```

In Info, you can place your cursor after the closing parenthesis of each expression and type *C-x C-e*; in each case, you should see

```
(tiger lion giraffe gazelle)
```

in the echo area.

For this example, the existing **reverse** function is obviously best. The **while** loop is just like our first example (see Section 11.1.1 "A **while** Loop and a List", page 106). The **while** first checks whether the list has elements; if so, it constructs a new list by adding the first element of the list to the existing list (which in the first iteration of the loop is **nil**). Since the second element is prepended in front of the first element, and the third element is prepended in front of the second element, the list is reversed.

In the expression using a **while** loop, the `(setq list (cdr list))` expression shortens the list, so the **while** loop eventually stops. In addition, it provides the **cons** expression with a new first element by creating a new and shorter list at each repetition of the loop.

The **dolist** expression does very much the same as the **while** expression, except that the **dolist** macro does some of the work you have to do when writing a **while** expression.

Like a **while** loop, a **dolist** loops. What is different is that it automatically shortens the list each time it loops—it CDRs down the list on its own—and it automatically binds the CAR of each shorter version of the list to the first of its arguments.

In the example, the CAR of each shorter version of the list is referred to using the symbol '**element**', the list itself is called '**list**', and the value returned is called '**value**'. The remainder of the **dolist** expression is the body.

The **dolist** expression binds the CAR of each shorter version of the list to **element** and then evaluates the body of the expression; and repeats the loop. The result is returned in **value**.

The `dotimes` Macro

The **dotimes** macro is similar to **dolist**, except that it loops a specific number of times.

The first argument to **dotimes** is assigned the numbers 0, 1, 2 and so forth each time around the loop, and the value of the third argument is returned. You need to provide the value of the second argument, which is how many times the macro loops.

For example, the following binds the numbers from 0 up to, but not including, the number 3 to the first argument, *number*, and then constructs a list of the three numbers. (The first number is 0, the second number is 1, and the third number is 2; this makes a total of three numbers in all, starting with zero as the first number.)

```
(let (value)        ; otherwise a value is a void variable
  (dotimes (number 3 value)
    (setq value (cons number value))))
```

⇒ (2 1 0)

dotimes returns value, so the way to use dotimes is to operate on some expression *number* number of times and then return the result, either as a list or an atom.

Here is an example of a defun that uses dotimes to add up the number of pebbles in a triangle.

```
(defun triangle-using-dotimes (number-of-rows)
  "Using `dotimes', add up the number of pebbles in a triangle."
(let ((total 0))  ; otherwise a total is a void variable
  (dotimes (number number-of-rows total)
    (setq total (+ total (1+ number))))))

(triangle-using-dotimes 4)
```

11.3 Recursion

A recursive function contains code that tells the Lisp interpreter to call a program that runs exactly like itself, but with slightly different arguments. The code runs exactly the same because it has the same name. However, even though the program has the same name, it is not the same entity. It is different. In the jargon, it is a different "instance".

Eventually, if the program is written correctly, the slightly different arguments will become sufficiently different from the first arguments that the final instance will stop.

11.3.1 Building Robots: Extending the Metaphor

It is sometimes helpful to think of a running program as a robot that does a job. In doing its job, a recursive function calls on a second robot to help it. The second robot is identical to the first in every way, except that the second robot helps the first and has been passed different arguments than the first.

In a recursive function, the second robot may call a third; and the third may call a fourth, and so on. Each of these is a different entity; but all are clones.

Since each robot has slightly different instructions—the arguments will differ from one robot to the next—the last robot should know when to stop.

Let's expand on the metaphor in which a computer program is a robot.

A function definition provides the blueprints for a robot. When you install a function definition, that is, when you evaluate a defun macro, you install the necessary equipment to build robots. It is as if you were in a factory, setting up an assembly line. Robots with the same name are built according to the same blueprints. So they have the same model number, but a different serial number.

We often say that a recursive function "calls itself". What we mean is that the instructions in a recursive function cause the Lisp interpreter to run a different function that has the same name and does the same job as the first, but with different arguments.

It is important that the arguments differ from one instance to the next; otherwise, the process will never stop.

11.3.2 The Parts of a Recursive Definition

A recursive function typically contains a conditional expression which has three parts:

1. A true-or-false-test that determines whether the function is called again, here called the *do-again-test*.

2. The name of the function. When this name is called, a new instance of the function—a new robot, as it were—is created and told what to do.

3. An expression that returns a different value each time the function is called, here called the *next-step-expression*. Consequently, the argument (or arguments) passed to the new instance of the function will be different from that passed to the previous instance. This causes the conditional expression, the *do-again-test*, to test false after the correct number of repetitions.

Recursive functions can be much simpler than any other kind of function. Indeed, when people first start to use them, they often look so mysteriously simple as to be incomprehensible. Like riding a bicycle, reading a recursive function definition takes a certain knack which is hard at first but then seems simple.

There are several different common recursive patterns. A very simple pattern looks like this:

```
(defun name-of-recursive-function (argument-list)
  "documentation..."
  (if do-again-test
      body...
      (name-of-recursive-function
          next-step-expression)))
```

Each time a recursive function is evaluated, a new instance of it is created and told what to do. The arguments tell the instance what to do.

An argument is bound to the value of the next-step-expression. Each instance runs with a different value of the next-step-expression.

The value in the next-step-expression is used in the do-again-test.

The value returned by the next-step-expression is passed to the new instance of the function, which evaluates it (or some transmogrification of it) to determine whether to continue or stop. The next-step-expression is designed so that the do-again-test returns false when the function should no longer be repeated.

The do-again-test is sometimes called the *stop condition*, since it stops the repetitions when it tests false.

11.3.3 Recursion with a List

The example of a `while` loop that printed the elements of a list of numbers can be written recursively. Here is the code, including an expression to set the value of the variable `animals` to a list.

If you are reading this in Info in Emacs, you can evaluate this expression directly in Info. Otherwise, you must copy the example to the `*scratch*` buffer and evaluate each expression there. Use *C-u C-x C-e* to evaluate the `(print-elements-recursively animals)` expression so that the results are printed in the buffer; otherwise the Lisp interpreter will try to squeeze the results into the one line of the echo area.

Also, place your cursor immediately after the last closing parenthesis of the `print-elements-recursively` function, before the comment. Otherwise, the Lisp interpreter will try to evaluate the comment.

```
(setq animals '(gazelle giraffe lion tiger))

(defun print-elements-recursively (list)
  "Print each element of LIST on a line of its own.
Uses recursion."
  (when list                                ; do-again-test
        (print (car list))                  ; body
        (print-elements-recursively         ; recursive call
          (cdr list))))                     ; next-step-expression

(print-elements-recursively animals)
```

The `print-elements-recursively` function first tests whether there is any content in the list; if there is, the function prints the first element of the list, the CAR of the list. Then the function invokes itself, but gives itself as its argument, not the whole list, but the second and subsequent elements of the list, the CDR of the list.

Put another way, if the list is not empty, the function invokes another instance of code that is similar to the initial code, but is a different thread of execution, with different arguments than the first instance.

Put in yet another way, if the list is not empty, the first robot assembles a second robot and tells it what to do; the second robot is a different individual from the first, but is the same model.

When the second evaluation occurs, the `when` expression is evaluated and if true, prints the first element of the list it receives as its argument (which is the second element of the original list). Then the function calls itself with the CDR of the list it is invoked with, which (the second time around) is the CDR of the CDR of the original list.

Note that although we say that the function "calls itself", what we mean is that the Lisp interpreter assembles and instructs a new instance of the program. The new instance is a clone of the first, but is a separate individual.

Each time the function invokes itself, it does so on a shorter version of the original list. It creates a new instance that works on a shorter list.

Eventually, the function invokes itself on an empty list. It creates a new instance whose argument is `nil`. The conditional expression tests the value of `list`. Since the value of `list` is `nil`, the `when` expression tests false so the then-part is not evaluated. The function as a whole then returns `nil`.

When you evaluate the expression (`print-elements-recursively animals`) in the *scratch* buffer, you see this result:

```
gazelle

giraffe

lion

tiger
nil
```

11.3.4 Recursion in Place of a Counter

The `triangle` function described in a previous section can also be written recursively. It looks like this:

```
(defun triangle-recursively (number)
  "Return the sum of the numbers 1 through NUMBER inclusive.
Uses recursion."
  (if (= number 1)                      ; do-again-test
      1                                 ; then-part
    (+ number                           ; else-part
       (triangle-recursively            ; recursive call
        (1- number)))))                 ; next-step-expression

(triangle-recursively 7)
```

You can install this function by evaluating it and then try it by evaluating (`triangle-recursively 7`). (Remember to put your cursor immediately after the last parenthesis of the function definition, before the comment.) The function evaluates to 28.

To understand how this function works, let's consider what happens in the various cases when the function is passed 1, 2, 3, or 4 as the value of its argument.

First, what happens if the value of the argument is 1?

The function has an `if` expression after the documentation string. It tests whether the value of `number` is equal to 1; if so, Emacs evaluates the then-part of the `if` expression, which returns the number 1 as the value of the function. (A triangle with one row has one pebble in it.)

Suppose, however, that the value of the argument is 2. In this case, Emacs evaluates the else-part of the `if` expression.

The else-part consists of an addition, the recursive call to `triangle-recursively` and a decrementing action; and it looks like this:

```
(+ number (triangle-recursively (1- number)))
```

When Emacs evaluates this expression, the innermost expression is evaluated first; then the other parts in sequence. Here are the steps in detail:

Step 1 *Evaluate the innermost expression.*

The innermost expression is (1- number) so Emacs decrements the value of **number** from 2 to 1.

Step 2 *Evaluate the* `triangle-recursively` *function.*

The Lisp interpreter creates an individual instance of `triangle-recursively`. It does not matter that this function is contained within itself. Emacs passes the result Step 1 as the argument used by this instance of the `triangle-recursively` function

In this case, Emacs evaluates `triangle-recursively` with an argument of 1. This means that this evaluation of `triangle-recursively` returns 1.

Step 3 *Evaluate the value of* **number**.

The variable **number** is the second element of the list that starts with +; its value is 2.

Step 4 *Evaluate the* + *expression.*

The + expression receives two arguments, the first from the evaluation of **number** (Step 3) and the second from the evaluation of `triangle-recursively` (Step 2).

The result of the addition is the sum of 2 plus 1, and the number 3 is returned, which is correct. A triangle with two rows has three pebbles in it.

An argument of 3 or 4

Suppose that `triangle-recursively` is called with an argument of 3.

Step 1 *Evaluate the do-again-test.*

The `if` expression is evaluated first. This is the do-again test and returns false, so the else-part of the `if` expression is evaluated. (Note that in this example, the do-again-test causes the function to call itself when it tests false, not when it tests true.)

Step 2 *Evaluate the innermost expression of the else-part.*

The innermost expression of the else-part is evaluated, which decrements 3 to 2. This is the next-step-expression.

Step 3 *Evaluate the* `triangle-recursively` *function.*

The number 2 is passed to the `triangle-recursively` function.

We already know what happens when Emacs evaluates `triangle-recursively` with an argument of 2. After going through the sequence of actions described earlier, it returns a value of 3. So that is what will happen here.

Step 4   Evaluate the addition.

3 will be passed as an argument to the addition and will be added to the number with which the function was called, which is 3.

The value returned by the function as a whole will be 6.

Now that we know what will happen when `triangle-recursively` is called with an argument of 3, it is evident what will happen if it is called with an argument of 4:

In the recursive call, the evaluation of

```
(triangle-recursively (1- 4))
```

will return the value of evaluating

```
(triangle-recursively 3)
```

which is 6 and this value will be added to 4 by the addition in the third line.

The value returned by the function as a whole will be 10.

Each time `triangle-recursively` is evaluated, it evaluates a version of itself—a different instance of itself—with a smaller argument, until the argument is small enough so that it does not evaluate itself.

Note that this particular design for a recursive function requires that operations be deferred.

Before (`triangle-recursively 7`) can calculate its answer, it must call (`triangle-recursively 6`); and before (`triangle-recursively 6`) can calculate its answer, it must call (`triangle-recursively 5`); and so on. That is to say, the calculation that (`triangle-recursively 7`) makes must be deferred until (`triangle-recursively 6`) makes its calculation; and (`triangle-recursively 6`) must defer until (`triangle-recursively 5`) completes; and so on.

If each of these instances of `triangle-recursively` are thought of as different robots, the first robot must wait for the second to complete its job, which must wait until the third completes, and so on.

There is a way around this kind of waiting, which we will discuss in Section 11.3.7 "Recursion without Deferments", page 125.

11.3.5 Recursion Example Using `cond`

The version of `triangle-recursively` described earlier is written with the `if` special form. It can also be written using another special form called `cond`. The name of the special form `cond` is an abbreviation of the word 'conditional'.

Although the `cond` special form is not used as often in the Emacs Lisp sources as `if`, it is used often enough to justify explaining it.

The template for a `cond` expression looks like this:

```
(cond
  body...)
```

where the *body* is a series of lists.

Written out more fully, the template looks like this:

```
(cond
  (first-true-or-false-test first-consequent)
  (second-true-or-false-test second-consequent)
  (third-true-or-false-test third-consequent)
   ...)
```

When the Lisp interpreter evaluates the `cond` expression, it evaluates the first element (the CAR or true-or-false-test) of the first expression in a series of expressions within the body of the `cond`.

If the true-or-false-test returns `nil` the rest of that expression, the consequent, is skipped and the true-or-false-test of the next expression is evaluated. When an expression is found whose true-or-false-test returns a value that is not `nil`, the consequent of that expression is evaluated. The consequent can be one or more expressions. If the consequent consists of more than one expression, the expressions are evaluated in sequence and the value of the last one is returned. If the expression does not have a consequent, the value of the true-or-false-test is returned.

If none of the true-or-false-tests test true, the `cond` expression returns `nil`.

Written using `cond`, the `triangle` function looks like this:

```
(defun triangle-using-cond (number)
  (cond ((<= number 0) 0)
        ((= number 1) 1)
        ((> number 1)
         (+ number (triangle-using-cond (1- number)))))))
```

In this example, the `cond` returns 0 if the number is less than or equal to 0, it returns 1 if the number is 1 and it evaluates (+ number (`triangle-using-cond` (1- number))) if the number is greater than 1.

11.3.6 Recursive Patterns

Here are three common recursive patterns. Each involves a list. Recursion does not need to involve lists, but Lisp is designed for lists and this provides a sense of its primal capabilities.

Recursive Pattern: *every*

In the `every` recursive pattern, an action is performed on every element of a list.

The basic pattern is:

- If a list be empty, return `nil`.

- Else, act on the beginning of the list (the CAR of the list)

    - through a recursive call by the function on the rest (the CDR) of the list,

    - and, optionally, combine the acted-on element, using `cons`, with the results of acting on the rest.

Here is an example:

```
(defun square-each (numbers-list)
  "Square each of a NUMBERS LIST, recursively."
  (if (not numbers-list)                    ; do-again-test
      nil
    (cons
     (* (car numbers-list) (car numbers-list))
     (square-each (cdr numbers-list))))) ; next-step-expression

(square-each '(1 2 3))
    ⇒ (1 4 9)
```

If `numbers-list` is empty, do nothing. But if it has content, construct a list combining the square of the first number in the list with the result of the recursive call.

(The example follows the pattern exactly: `nil` is returned if the numbers' list is empty. In practice, you would write the conditional so it carries out the action when the numbers' list is not empty.)

The `print-elements-recursively` function (see Section 11.3.3 "Recursion with a List", page 118) is another example of an **every** pattern, except in this case, rather than bring the results together using `cons`, we print each element of output.

The `print-elements-recursively` function looks like this:

```
(setq animals '(gazelle giraffe lion tiger))

(defun print-elements-recursively (list)
  "Print each element of LIST on a line of its own.
Uses recursion."
  (when list                          ; do-again-test
        (print (car list))            ; body
        (print-elements-recursively   ; recursive call
         (cdr list))))                ; next-step-expression

(print-elements-recursively animals)
```

The pattern for `print-elements-recursively` is:

- When the list is empty, do nothing.

- But when the list has at least one element,

    - act on the beginning of the list (the CAR of the list),

    - and make a recursive call on the rest (the CDR) of the list.

Recursive Pattern: *accumulate*

Another recursive pattern is called the `accumulate` pattern. In the `accumulate` recursive pattern, an action is performed on every element of a list and the result of that action is accumulated with the results of performing the action on the other elements.

This is very like the `every` pattern using `cons`, except that `cons` is not used, but some other combiner.

The pattern is:

- If a list be empty, return zero or some other constant.

- Else, act on the beginning of the list (the CAR of the list),

    - and combine that acted-on element, using `+` or some other combining function, with

    - a recursive call by the function on the rest (the CDR) of the list.

Here is an example:

```
(defun add-elements (numbers-list)
  "Add the elements of NUMBERS-LIST together."
  (if (not numbers-list)
      0
    (+ (car numbers-list) (add-elements (cdr numbers-list)))))

(add-elements '(1 2 3 4))
     ⇒ 10
```

See Section 14.9.2 "Making a List of Files", page 166, for an example of the accumulate pattern.

Recursive Pattern: *keep*

A third recursive pattern is called the `keep` pattern. In the `keep` recursive pattern, each element of a list is tested; the element is acted on and the results are kept only if the element meets a criterion.

Again, this is very like the `every` pattern, except the element is skipped unless it meets a criterion.

The pattern has three parts:

- If a list be empty, return `nil`.

- Else, if the beginning of the list (the CAR of the list) passes a test

    - act on that element and combine it, using `cons` with

    - a recursive call by the function on the rest (the CDR) of the list.

- Otherwise, if the beginning of the list (the CAR of the list) fails the test

    - skip on that element,

    - and, recursively call the function on the rest (the CDR) of the list.

Here is an example that uses `cond`:

```
(defun keep-three-letter-words (word-list)
  "Keep three letter words in WORD-LIST."
  (cond
    ;; First do-again-test: stop-condition
    ((not word-list) nil)

    ;; Second do-again-test: when to act
    ((eq 3 (length (symbol-name (car word-list))))
     ;; combine acted-on element with recursive call on shorter list
     (cons (car word-list) (keep-three-letter-words (cdr word-list))))

    ;; Third do-again-test: when to skip element;
    ;;   recursively call shorter list with next-step expression
    (t (keep-three-letter-words (cdr word-list)))))
```

```
(keep-three-letter-words '(one two three four five six))
    ⇒ (one two six)
```

It goes without saying that you need not use `nil` as the test for when to stop; and you can, of course, combine these patterns.

11.3.7 Recursion without Deferments

Let's consider again what happens with the `triangle-recursively` function. We will find that the intermediate calculations are deferred until all can be done.

Here is the function definition:

```
(defun triangle-recursively (number)
  "Return the sum of the numbers 1 through NUMBER inclusive.
Uses recursion."
  (if (= number 1)                          ; do-again-test
      1                                     ; then-part
    (+ number                               ; else-part
       (triangle-recursively                ; recursive call
        (1- number)))))                     ; next-step-expression
```

What happens when we call this function with a argument of 7?

The first instance of the `triangle-recursively` function adds the number 7 to the value returned by a second instance of `triangle-recursively`, an instance that has been passed an argument of 6. That is to say, the first calculation is:

```
(+ 7 (triangle-recursively 6))
```

The first instance of `triangle-recursively`—you may want to think of it as a little robot—cannot complete its job. It must hand off the calculation for (`triangle-recursively` 6) to a second instance of the program, to a second robot. This second individual is completely different from the first one; it is, in the jargon, a "different instantiation". Or, put another way, it is a different robot. It is the same model as the first; it calculates triangle numbers recursively; but it has a different serial number.

And what does (`triangle-recursively` 6) return? It returns the number 6 added to the value returned by evaluating `triangle-recursively` with an argument of 5. Using the robot metaphor, it asks yet another robot to help it.

Now the total is:

```
(+ 7 6 (triangle-recursively 5))
```

And what happens next?

```
(+ 7 6 5 (triangle-recursively 4))
```

Each time `triangle-recursively` is called, except for the last time, it creates another instance of the program—another robot—and asks it to make a calculation.

Eventually, the full addition is set up and performed:

```
(+ 7 6 5 4 3 2 1)
```

This design for the function defers the calculation of the first step until the second can be done, and defers that until the third can be done, and so on. Each deferment means the computer must remember what is being waited on. This is not a problem when there are only a few steps, as in this example. But it can be a problem when there are more steps.

11.3.8 No Deferment Solution

The solution to the problem of deferred operations is to write in a manner that does not defer operations[2]. This requires writing to a different pattern, often one that involves writing two function definitions, an initialization function and a helper function.

The initialization function sets up the job; the helper function does the work.

Here are the two function definitions for adding up numbers. They are so simple, I find them hard to understand.

```
(defun triangle-initialization (number)
  "Return the sum of the numbers 1 through NUMBER inclusive.
This is the initialization component of a two function
duo that uses recursion."
  (triangle-recursive-helper 0 0 number))
(defun triangle-recursive-helper (sum counter number)
  "Return SUM, using COUNTER, through NUMBER inclusive.
This is the helper component of a two function duo
that uses recursion."
  (if (> counter number)
      sum
    (triangle-recursive-helper (+ sum counter)    ; sum
                               (1+ counter)        ; counter
                               number)))           ; number
```

Install both function definitions by evaluating them, then call `triangle-initialization` with 2 rows:

```
(triangle-initialization 2)
     ⇒ 3
```

The initialization function calls the first instance of the helper function with three arguments: zero, zero, and a number which is the number of rows in the triangle.

---

[2] The phrase *tail recursive* is used to describe such a process, one that uses constant space.

The first two arguments passed to the helper function are initialization values. These values are changed when `triangle-recursive-helper` invokes new instances.[3]

Let's see what happens when we have a triangle that has one row. (This triangle will have one pebble in it!)

`triangle-initialization` will call its helper with the arguments 0 0 1. That function will run the conditional test whether (`> counter number`):

```
(> 0 1)
```

and find that the result is false, so it will invoke the else-part of the `if` clause:

```
(triangle-recursive-helper
  (+ sum counter)    ; sum plus counter ⇒ sum
  (1+ counter)       ; increment counter ⇒ counter
  number)            ; number stays the same
```

which will first compute:

```
(triangle-recursive-helper (+ 0 0)    ; sum
                           (1+ 0)     ; counter
                           1)         ; number
```

which is:

```
(triangle-recursive-helper 0 1 1)
```

Again, (`> counter number`) will be false, so again, the Lisp interpreter will evaluate `triangle-recursive-helper`, creating a new instance with new arguments.

This new instance will be;

```
(triangle-recursive-helper
  (+ sum counter)    ; sum plus counter ⇒ sum
  (1+ counter)       ; increment counter ⇒ counter
  number)            ; number stays the same
```

which is:

```
(triangle-recursive-helper 1 2 1)
```

In this case, the (`> counter number`) test will be true! So the instance will return the value of the sum, which will be 1, as expected.

Now, let's pass `triangle-initialization` an argument of 2, to find out how many pebbles there are in a triangle with two rows.

That function calls (`triangle-recursive-helper 0 0 2`).

---

[3] The jargon is mildly confusing: `triangle-recursive-helper` uses a process that is iterative in a procedure that is recursive. The process is called iterative because the computer need only record the three values, `sum`, `counter`, and `number`; the procedure is recursive because the function calls itself. On the other hand, both the process and the procedure used by `triangle-recursively` are called recursive. The word "recursive" has different meanings in the two contexts.

In stages, the instances called will be:

```
                      sum counter number
(triangle-recursive-helper 0    1      2)

(triangle-recursive-helper 1    2      2)

(triangle-recursive-helper 3    3      2)
```

When the last instance is called, the (> counter number) test will be true, so the instance will return the value of sum, which will be 3.

This kind of pattern helps when you are writing functions that can use many resources in a computer.

11.4 Looping Exercise

- Write a function similar to triangle in which each row has a value which is the square of the row number. Use a while loop.

- Write a function similar to triangle that multiplies instead of adds the values.

- Rewrite these two functions recursively. Rewrite these functions using cond.

- Write a function for Texinfo mode that creates an index entry at the beginning of a paragraph for every '@dfn' within the paragraph. (In a Texinfo file, '@dfn' marks a definition. This book is written in Texinfo.)

  Many of the functions you will need are described in two of the previous chapters, Chapter 8 "Cutting and Storing Text", page 78, and Chapter 10 "Yanking Text Back", page 103. If you use forward-paragraph to put the index entry at the beginning of the paragraph, you will have to use *C-h f* (describe-function) to find out how to make the command go backwards.

  For more information, see "Indicating Definitions, Commands, etc." in *Texinfo, The GNU Documentation Format*.

12 Regular Expression Searches

Regular expression searches are used extensively in GNU Emacs. The two functions, `forward-sentence` and `forward-paragraph`, illustrate these searches well. They use regular expressions to find where to move point. The phrase "regular expression" is often written as "regexp".

Regular expression searches are described in Section "Regular Expression Search" in *The GNU Emacs Manual*, as well as in Section "Regular Expressions" in *The GNU Emacs Lisp Reference Manual*. In writing this chapter, I am presuming that you have at least a mild acquaintance with them. The major point to remember is that regular expressions permit you to search for patterns as well as for literal strings of characters. For example, the code in `forward-sentence` searches for the pattern of possible characters that could mark the end of a sentence, and moves point to that spot.

Before looking at the code for the `forward-sentence` function, it is worth considering what the pattern that marks the end of a sentence must be. The pattern is discussed in the next section; following that is a description of the regular expression search function, `re-search-forward`. The `forward-sentence` function is described in the section following. Finally, the `forward-paragraph` function is described in the last section of this chapter. `forward-paragraph` is a complex function that introduces several new features.

12.1 The Regular Expression for `sentence-end`

The symbol `sentence-end` is bound to the pattern that marks the end of a sentence. What should this regular expression be?

Clearly, a sentence may be ended by a period, a question mark, or an exclamation mark. Indeed, in English, only clauses that end with one of those three characters should be considered the end of a sentence. This means that the pattern should include the character set:

```
[.?!]
```

However, we do not want `forward-sentence` merely to jump to a period, a question mark, or an exclamation mark, because such a character might be used in the middle of a sentence. A period, for example, is used after abbreviations. So other information is needed.

According to convention, you type two spaces after every sentence, but only one space after a period, a question mark, or an exclamation mark in the body of a sentence. So a period, a question mark, or an exclamation mark followed by two spaces is a good indicator of an end of sentence. However, in a file, the two spaces may instead be a tab or the end of a line. This means that the regular expression should include these three items as alternatives.

This group of alternatives will look like this:

```
\\($\\| \\|  \\)
       ^   ^^
      TAB  SPC
```

Here, '$' indicates the end of the line, and I have pointed out where the tab and two spaces are inserted in the expression. Both are inserted by putting the actual characters into the expression.

Two backslashes, '\\', are required before the parentheses and vertical bars: the first backslash quotes the following backslash in Emacs; and the second indicates that the following character, the parenthesis or the vertical bar, is special.

Also, a sentence may be followed by one or more carriage returns, like this:

```
[
]*
```

Like tabs and spaces, a carriage return is inserted into a regular expression by inserting it literally. The asterisk indicates that the RET is repeated zero or more times.

But a sentence end does not consist only of a period, a question mark or an exclamation mark followed by appropriate space: a closing quotation mark or a closing brace of some kind may precede the space. Indeed more than one such mark or brace may precede the space. These require a expression that looks like this:

```
[]\"')}]*
```

In this expression, the first ']' is the first character in the expression; the second character is '"', which is preceded by a '\' to tell Emacs the '"' is *not* special. The last three characters are ''', ')', and '}'.

All this suggests what the regular expression pattern for matching the end of a sentence should be; and, indeed, if we evaluate sentence-end we find that it returns the following value:

```
sentence-end
    ⇒ "[.?!][]\"')}]*\\($\\|     \\|  \\)[
]*"
```

(Well, not in GNU Emacs 22; that is because of an effort to make the process simpler and to handle more glyphs and languages. When the value of sentence-end is nil, then use the value defined by the function sentence-end. (Here is a use of the difference between a value and a function in Emacs Lisp.) The function returns a value constructed from the variables sentence-end-base, sentence-end-double-space, sentence-end-without-period, and sentence-end-without-space. The critical variable is sentence-end-base; its global value is similar to the one described above but it also contains two additional quotation marks. These have differing degrees of curliness. The sentence-end-without-period variable, when true, tells Emacs that a sentence may end without a period, such as text in Thai.)

12.2 The re-search-forward Function

The re-search-forward function is very like the search-forward function. (See Section 8.1.3 "The search-forward Function", page 80.)

re-search-forward searches for a regular expression. If the search is successful, it leaves point immediately after the last character in the target. If the search is backwards, it leaves point just before the first character in the target. You may tell re-search-forward to return t for true. (Moving point is therefore a side effect.)

Like search-forward, the re-search-forward function takes four arguments:

1. The first argument is the regular expression that the function searches for. The regular expression will be a string between quotation marks.

2. The optional second argument limits how far the function will search; it is a bound, which is specified as a position in the buffer.

3. The optional third argument specifies how the function responds to failure: `nil` as the third argument causes the function to signal an error (and print a message) when the search fails; any other value causes it to return `nil` if the search fails and `t` if the search succeeds.

4. The optional fourth argument is the repeat count. A negative repeat count causes `re-search-forward` to search backwards.

The template for `re-search-forward` looks like this:

```
(re-search-forward "regular-expression"
            limit-of-search
            what-to-do-if-search-fails
            repeat-count)
```

The second, third, and fourth arguments are optional. However, if you want to pass a value to either or both of the last two arguments, you must also pass a value to all the preceding arguments. Otherwise, the Lisp interpreter will mistake which argument you are passing the value to.

In the `forward-sentence` function, the regular expression will be the value of the variable `sentence-end`. In simple form, that is:

```
"[.?!][]\"')}]*\\($\\|  \\|  \\)[
]*"
```

The limit of the search will be the end of the paragraph (since a sentence cannot go beyond a paragraph). If the search fails, the function will return `nil`; and the repeat count will be provided by the argument to the `forward-sentence` function.

12.3 `forward-sentence`

The command to move the cursor forward a sentence is a straightforward illustration of how to use regular expression searches in Emacs Lisp. Indeed, the function looks longer and more complicated than it is; this is because the function is designed to go backwards as well as forwards; and, optionally, over more than one sentence. The function is usually bound to the key command `M-e`.

Here is the code for `forward-sentence`:

```
(defun forward-sentence (&optional arg)
  "Move forward to next end of sentence.  With argument, repeat.
With negative argument, move backward repeatedly to start of sentence.

The variable `sentence-end' is a regular expression that matches ends of
sentences.  Also, every paragraph boundary terminates sentences as well."
```

```
(interactive "p")
(or arg (setq arg 1))
(let ((opoint (point))
      (sentence-end (sentence-end)))
  (while (< arg 0)
    (let ((pos (point))
          (par-beg (save-excursion (start-of-paragraph-text) (point))))
      (if (and (re-search-backward sentence-end par-beg t)
               (or (< (match-end 0) pos)
                   (re-search-backward sentence-end par-beg t)))
          (goto-char (match-end 0))
        (goto-char par-beg)))
    (setq arg (1+ arg)))
  (while (> arg 0)
    (let ((par-end (save-excursion (end-of-paragraph-text) (point))))
      (if (re-search-forward sentence-end par-end t)
          (skip-chars-backward " \t\n")
        (goto-char par-end)))
    (setq arg (1- arg)))
  (constrain-to-field nil opoint t)))
```

The function looks long at first sight and it is best to look at its skeleton first, and then its muscle. The way to see the skeleton is to look at the expressions that start in the left-most columns:

```
(defun forward-sentence (&optional arg)
  "documentation..."
  (interactive "p")
  (or arg (setq arg 1))
  (let ((opoint (point)) (sentence-end (sentence-end)))
    (while (< arg 0)
      (let ((pos (point))
            (par-beg (save-excursion (start-of-paragraph-text) (point))))
        rest-of-body-of-while-loop-when-going-backwards
    (while (> arg 0)
      (let ((par-end (save-excursion (end-of-paragraph-text) (point))))
        rest-of-body-of-while-loop-when-going-forwards
    handle-forms-and-equivalent
```

This looks much simpler! The function definition consists of documentation, an `interactive` expression, an `or` expression, a `let` expression, and `while` loops.

Let's look at each of these parts in turn.

We note that the documentation is thorough and understandable.

The function has an `interactive "p"` declaration. This means that the processed prefix argument, if any, is passed to the function as its argument. (This will be a number.) If the function is not passed an argument (it is optional) then the argument `arg` will be bound to 1.

When `forward-sentence` is called non-interactively without an argument, `arg` is bound to `nil`. The `or` expression handles this. What it does is either leave the value of `arg` as it is, but only if `arg` is bound to a value; or it sets the value of `arg` to 1, in the case when `arg` is bound to `nil`.

Next is a `let`. That specifies the values of two local variables, `opoint` and `sentence-end`. The local value of point, from before the search, is used in the `constrain-to-field` function which handles forms and equivalents. The `sentence-end` variable is set by the `sentence-end` function.

The `while` loops

Two `while` loops follow. The first `while` has a true-or-false-test that tests true if the prefix argument for `forward-sentence` is a negative number. This is for going backwards. The body of this loop is similar to the body of the second `while` clause, but it is not exactly the same. We will skip this `while` loop and concentrate on the second `while` loop.

The second `while` loop is for moving point forward. Its skeleton looks like this:

```
(while (> arg 0)                ; true-or-false-test
  (let varlist
    (if (true-or-false-test)
        then-part
      else-part)
  (setq arg (1- arg))))         ; while loop decrementer
```

The `while` loop is of the decrementing kind. (See Section 11.1.4 "A Loop with a Decrementing Counter", page 112.) It has a true-or-false-test that tests true so long as the counter (in this case, the variable `arg`) is greater than zero; and it has a decrementer that subtracts 1 from the value of the counter every time the loop repeats.

If no prefix argument is given to `forward-sentence`, which is the most common way the command is used, this `while` loop will run once, since the value of `arg` will be 1.

The body of the `while` loop consists of a `let` expression, which creates and binds a local variable, and has, as its body, an `if` expression.

The body of the `while` loop looks like this:

```
(let ((par-end
        (save-excursion (end-of-paragraph-text) (point))))
  (if (re-search-forward sentence-end par-end t)
      (skip-chars-backward " \t\n")
    (goto-char par-end)))
```

The `let` expression creates and binds the local variable `par-end`. As we shall see, this local variable is designed to provide a bound or limit to the regular expression search. If the search fails to find a proper sentence ending in the paragraph, it will stop on reaching the end of the paragraph.

But first, let us examine how `par-end` is bound to the value of the end of the paragraph. What happens is that the `let` sets the value of `par-end` to the value returned when the Lisp interpreter evaluates the expression

```
(save-excursion (end-of-paragraph-text) (point))
```

In this expression, `(end-of-paragraph-text)` moves point to the end of the paragraph, `(point)` returns the value of point, and then `save-excursion` restores point to its original position. Thus, the `let` binds `par-end` to the value returned by the `save-excursion` expression, which is the position of the end of the paragraph. (The end-of-paragraph-text function uses forward-paragraph, which we will discuss shortly.)

Emacs next evaluates the body of the let, which is an if expression that looks like this:

```
(if (re-search-forward sentence-end par-end t) ; if-part
    (skip-chars-backward " \t\n")              ; then-part
  (goto-char par-end)))                        ; else-part
```

The if tests whether its first argument is true and if so, evaluates its then-part; otherwise, the Emacs Lisp interpreter evaluates the else-part. The true-or-false-test of the if expression is the regular expression search.

It may seem odd to have what looks like the real work of the forward-sentence function buried here, but this is a common way this kind of operation is carried out in Lisp.

The regular expression search

The re-search-forward function searches for the end of the sentence, that is, for the pattern defined by the sentence-end regular expression. If the pattern is found—if the end of the sentence is found—then the re-search-forward function does two things:

1. The re-search-forward function carries out a side effect, which is to move point to the end of the occurrence found.

2. The re-search-forward function returns a value of true. This is the value received by the if, and means that the search was successful.

The side effect, the movement of point, is completed before the if function is handed the value returned by the successful conclusion of the search.

When the if function receives the value of true from a successful call to re-search-forward, the if evaluates the then-part, which is the expression (skip-chars-backward " \t\n"). This expression moves backwards over any blank spaces, tabs or carriage returns until a printed character is found and then leaves point after the character. Since point has already been moved to the end of the pattern that marks the end of the sentence, this action leaves point right after the closing printed character of the sentence, which is usually a period.

On the other hand, if the re-search-forward function fails to find a pattern marking the end of the sentence, the function returns false. The false then causes the if to evaluate its third argument, which is (goto-char par-end): it moves point to the end of the paragraph.

(And if the text is in a form or equivalent, and point may not move fully, then the constrain-to-field function comes into play.)

Regular expression searches are exceptionally useful and the pattern illustrated by re-search-forward, in which the search is the test of an if expression, is handy. You will see or write code incorporating this pattern often.

12.4 `forward-paragraph`: a Goldmine of Functions

The `forward-paragraph` function moves point forward to the end of the paragraph. It is usually bound to *M-}* and makes use of a number of functions that are important in themselves, including `let*`, `match-beginning`, and `looking-at`.

The function definition for `forward-paragraph` is considerably longer than the function definition for `forward-sentence` because it works with a paragraph, each line of which may begin with a fill prefix.

A fill prefix consists of a string of characters that are repeated at the beginning of each line. For example, in Lisp code, it is a convention to start each line of a paragraph-long comment with ';;; '. In Text mode, four blank spaces make up another common fill prefix, creating an indented paragraph. (See Section "Fill Prefix" in *The GNU Emacs Manual*, for more information about fill prefixes.)

The existence of a fill prefix means that in addition to being able to find the end of a paragraph whose lines begin on the left-most column, the `forward-paragraph` function must be able to find the end of a paragraph when all or many of the lines in the buffer begin with the fill prefix.

Moreover, it is sometimes practical to ignore a fill prefix that exists, especially when blank lines separate paragraphs. This is an added complication.

Rather than print all of the `forward-paragraph` function, we will only print parts of it. Read without preparation, the function can be daunting!

In outline, the function looks like this:

```
(defun forward-paragraph (&optional arg)
  "documentation..."
  (interactive "p")
  (or arg (setq arg 1))
  (let*
      varlist
    (while (and (< arg 0) (not (bobp)))    ; backward-moving-code
      ...
    (while (and (> arg 0) (not (eobp)))    ; forward-moving-code
      ...
```

The first parts of the function are routine: the function's argument list consists of one optional argument. Documentation follows.

The lower case 'p' in the `interactive` declaration means that the processed prefix argument, if any, is passed to the function. This will be a number, and is the repeat count of how many paragraphs point will move. The `or` expression in the next line handles the common case when no argument is passed to the function, which occurs if the function is called from other code rather than interactively. This case was described earlier. (See Section 12.3 "forward-sentence", page 131.) Now we reach the end of the familiar part of this function.

The `let*` expression

The next line of the `forward-paragraph` function begins a `let*` expression. This is a different than `let`. The symbol is `let*` not `let`.

The `let*` special form is like `let` except that Emacs sets each variable in sequence, one after another, and variables in the latter part of the varlist can make use of the values to which Emacs set variables in the earlier part of the varlist.

(Section 4.4.3 "save-excursion in `append-to-buffer`", page 51.)

In the `let*` expression in this function, Emacs binds a total of seven variables: `opoint`, `fill-prefix-regexp`, `parstart`, `parsep`, `sp-parstart`, `start`, and `found-start`.

The variable `parsep` appears twice, first, to remove instances of '^', and second, to handle fill prefixes.

The variable `opoint` is just the value of `point`. As you can guess, it is used in a `constrain-to-field` expression, just as in `forward-sentence`.

The variable `fill-prefix-regexp` is set to the value returned by evaluating the following list:

```
(and fill-prefix
     (not (equal fill-prefix ""))
     (not paragraph-ignore-fill-prefix)
     (regexp-quote fill-prefix))
```

This is an expression whose first element is the **and** special form.

As we learned earlier (see "The `kill-new` function", page 89), the **and** special form evaluates each of its arguments until one of the arguments returns a value of `nil`, in which case the **and** expression returns `nil`; however, if none of the arguments returns a value of `nil`, the value resulting from evaluating the last argument is returned. (Since such a value is not `nil`, it is considered true in Lisp.) In other words, an **and** expression returns a true value only if all its arguments are true.

In this case, the variable `fill-prefix-regexp` is bound to a non-`nil` value only if the following four expressions produce a true (i.e., a non-`nil`) value when they are evaluated; otherwise, `fill-prefix-regexp` is bound to `nil`.

`fill-prefix`

>   When this variable is evaluated, the value of the fill prefix, if any, is returned. If there is no fill prefix, this variable returns `nil`.

`(not (equal fill-prefix "")`

>   This expression checks whether an existing fill prefix is an empty string, that is, a string with no characters in it. An empty string is not a useful fill prefix.

`(not paragraph-ignore-fill-prefix)`

>   This expression returns `nil` if the variable `paragraph-ignore-fill-prefix` has been turned on by being set to a true value such as `t`.

`(regexp-quote fill-prefix)`

>   This is the last argument to the **and** special form. If all the arguments to the **and** are true, the value resulting from evaluating this expression will be returned by the **and** expression and bound to the variable `fill-prefix-regexp`,

The result of evaluating this **and** expression successfully is that `fill-prefix-regexp` will be bound to the value of `fill-prefix` as modified by the `regexp-quote` function. What `regexp-quote` does is read a string and return a regular expression that will exactly match the string and match nothing else. This means that `fill-prefix-regexp` will be set to a value that will exactly match the fill prefix if the fill prefix exists. Otherwise, the variable will be set to `nil`.

The next two local variables in the `let*` expression are designed to remove instances of '`^`' from `parstart` and `parsep`, the local variables which indicate the paragraph start and the paragraph separator. The next expression sets `parsep` again. That is to handle fill prefixes.

This is the setting that requires the definition call `let*` rather than `let`. The true-or-false-test for the `if` depends on whether the variable `fill-prefix-regexp` evaluates to `nil` or some other value.

If `fill-prefix-regexp` does not have a value, Emacs evaluates the else-part of the `if` expression and binds `parsep` to its local value. (`parsep` is a regular expression that matches what separates paragraphs.)

But if `fill-prefix-regexp` does have a value, Emacs evaluates the then-part of the `if` expression and binds `parsep` to a regular expression that includes the `fill-prefix-regexp` as part of the pattern.

Specifically, `parsep` is set to the original value of the paragraph separate regular expression concatenated with an alternative expression that consists of the `fill-prefix-regexp` followed by optional whitespace to the end of the line. The whitespace is defined by `"[ \t]*$"`.) The '`\\|`' defines this portion of the regexp as an alternative to `parsep`.

According to a comment in the code, the next local variable, `sp-parstart`, is used for searching, and then the final two, `start` and `found-start`, are set to `nil`.

Now we get into the body of the `let*`. The first part of the body of the `let*` deals with the case when the function is given a negative argument and is therefore moving backwards. We will skip this section.

The forward motion `while` loop

The second part of the body of the `let*` deals with forward motion. It is a `while` loop that repeats itself so long as the value of `arg` is greater than zero. In the most common use of the function, the value of the argument is 1, so the body of the `while` loop is evaluated exactly once, and the cursor moves forward one paragraph.

This part handles three situations: when point is between paragraphs, when there is a fill prefix and when there is no fill prefix.

The `while` loop looks like this:

```
;; going forwards and not at the end of the buffer
(while (and (> arg 0) (not (eobp)))

    ;; between paragraphs
    ;; Move forward over separator lines...
    (while (and (not (eobp))
                (progn (move-to-left-margin) (not (eobp)))
                (looking-at parsep))
      (forward-line 1))
    ;;  This decrements the loop
    (unless (eobp) (setq arg (1- arg)))
    ;; ... and one more line.
    (forward-line 1)

    (if fill-prefix-regexp
        ;; There is a fill prefix; it overrides parstart;
        ;; we go forward line by line
        (while (and (not (eobp))
                    (progn (move-to-left-margin) (not (eobp)))
                    (not (looking-at parsep))
                    (looking-at fill-prefix-regexp))
          (forward-line 1))

      ;; There is no fill prefix;
      ;; we go forward character by character
      (while (and (re-search-forward sp-parstart nil 1)
                  (progn (setq start (match-beginning 0))
                         (goto-char start)
                         (not (eobp)))
                  (progn (move-to-left-margin)
                         (not (looking-at parsep)))
                  (or (not (looking-at parstart))
                      (and use-hard-newlines
                           (not (get-text-property (1- start) 'hard)))))
        (forward-char 1))

      ;; and if there is no fill prefix and if we are not at the end,
      ;;     go to whatever was found in the regular expression search
      ;;     for sp-parstart
      (if (< (point) (point-max))
          (goto-char start)))))
```

We can see that this is a decrementing counter `while` loop, using the expression `(setq arg (1- arg))` as the decrementer. That expression is not far from the `while`, but is hidden in another Lisp macro, an `unless` macro. Unless we are at the end of the buffer—that is what the `eobp` function determines; it is an abbreviation of 'End Of Buffer P'—we decrease the value of `arg` by one.

(If we are at the end of the buffer, we cannot go forward any more and the next loop of the `while` expression will test false since the test is an `and` with `(not (eobp))`. The `not` function means exactly as you expect; it is another name for `null`, a function that returns true when its argument is false.)

Interestingly, the loop count is not decremented until we leave the space between paragraphs, unless we come to the end of buffer or stop seeing the local value of the paragraph separator.

That second `while` also has a (`move-to-left-margin`) expression. The function is self-explanatory. It is inside a `progn` expression and not the last element of its body, so it is only invoked for its side effect, which is to move point to the left margin of the current line.

The `looking-at` function is also self-explanatory; it returns true if the text after point matches the regular expression given as its argument.

The rest of the body of the loop looks difficult at first, but makes sense as you come to understand it.

First consider what happens if there is a fill prefix:

```
(if fill-prefix-regexp
    ;; There is a fill prefix; it overrides parstart;
    ;; we go forward line by line
    (while (and (not (eobp))
                (progn (move-to-left-margin) (not (eobp)))
                (not (looking-at parsep))
                (looking-at fill-prefix-regexp))
      (forward-line 1))
```

This expression moves point forward line by line so long as four conditions are true:

1. Point is not at the end of the buffer.

2. We can move to the left margin of the text and are not at the end of the buffer.

3. The text following point does not separate paragraphs.

4. The pattern following point is the fill prefix regular expression.

The last condition may be puzzling, until you remember that point was moved to the beginning of the line early in the `forward-paragraph` function. This means that if the text has a fill prefix, the `looking-at` function will see it.

Consider what happens when there is no fill prefix.

```
(while (and (re-search-forward sp-parstart nil 1)
            (progn (setq start (match-beginning 0))
                   (goto-char start)
                   (not (eobp)))
            (progn (move-to-left-margin)
                   (not (looking-at parsep)))
            (or (not (looking-at parstart))
                (and use-hard-newlines
                     (not (get-text-property (1- start) 'hard)))))
  (forward-char 1))
```

This `while` loop has us searching forward for `sp-parstart`, which is the combination of possible whitespace with the local value of the start of a paragraph or of a paragraph separator. (The latter two are within an expression starting \(?: so that they are not referenced by the `match-beginning` function.)

The two expressions,

```
(setq start (match-beginning 0))
(goto-char start)
```

mean go to the start of the text matched by the regular expression search.

The (match-beginning 0) expression is new. It returns a number specifying the location of the start of the text that was matched by the last search.

The match-beginning function is used here because of a characteristic of a forward search: a successful forward search, regardless of whether it is a plain search or a regular expression search, moves point to the end of the text that is found. In this case, a successful search moves point to the end of the pattern for sp-parstart.

However, we want to put point at the end of the current paragraph, not somewhere else. Indeed, since the search possibly includes the paragraph separator, point may end up at the beginning of the next one unless we use an expression that includes match-beginning.

When given an argument of 0, match-beginning returns the position that is the start of the text matched by the most recent search. In this case, the most recent search looks for sp-parstart. The (match-beginning 0) expression returns the beginning position of that pattern, rather than the end position of that pattern.

(Incidentally, when passed a positive number as an argument, the match-beginning function returns the location of point at that parenthesized expression in the last search unless that parenthesized expression begins with \(?:. I don't know why \(?: appears here since the argument is 0.)

The last expression when there is no fill prefix is

```
(if (< (point) (point-max))
    (goto-char start))))
```

This says that if there is no fill prefix and if we are not at the end, point should move to the beginning of whatever was found by the regular expression search for sp-parstart.

The full definition for the forward-paragraph function not only includes code for going forwards, but also code for going backwards.

If you are reading this inside of GNU Emacs and you want to see the whole function, you can type *C-h f* (describe-function) and the name of the function. This gives you the function documentation and the name of the library containing the function's source. Place point over the name of the library and press the RET key; you will be taken directly to the source. (Be sure to install your sources! Without them, you are like a person who tries to drive a car with his eyes shut!)

12.5 Review

Here is a brief summary of some recently introduced functions.

while   Repeatedly evaluate the body of the expression so long as the first element of the body tests true. Then return nil. (The expression is evaluated only for its side effects.)

For example:

```
(let ((foo 2))
  (while (> foo 0)
    (insert (format "foo is %d.\n" foo))
    (setq foo (1- foo))))
```

$$\Rightarrow \quad \texttt{foo is 2.}$$
```
           foo is 1.
           nil
```

(The `insert` function inserts its arguments at point; the `format` function returns a string formatted from its arguments the way `message` formats its arguments; `\n` produces a new line.)

`re-search-forward`

Search for a pattern, and if the pattern is found, move point to rest just after it.

Takes four arguments, like `search-forward`:

1. A regular expression that specifies the pattern to search for. (Remember to put quotation marks around this argument!)

2. Optionally, the limit of the search.

3. Optionally, what to do if the search fails, return `nil` or an error message.

4. Optionally, how many times to repeat the search; if negative, the search goes backwards.

`let*`

Bind some variables locally to particular values, and then evaluate the remaining arguments, returning the value of the last one. While binding the local variables, use the local values of variables bound earlier, if any.

For example:

```
(let* ((foo 7)
       (bar (* 3 foo)))
  (message "`bar' is %d." bar))
```
$$\Rightarrow \text{`bar' is 21.}$$

`match-beginning`

Return the position of the start of the text found by the last regular expression search.

`looking-at`

Return `t` for true if the text after point matches the argument, which should be a regular expression.

`eobp`

Return `t` for true if point is at the end of the accessible part of a buffer. The end of the accessible part is the end of the buffer if the buffer is not narrowed; it is the end of the narrowed part if the buffer is narrowed.

12.6 Exercises with `re-search-forward`

- Write a function to search for a regular expression that matches two or more blank lines in sequence.

- Write a function to search for duplicated words, such as "the the". See Section "Syntax of Regular Expressions" in *The GNU Emacs Manual*, for information on how to write a regexp (a regular expression) to match a string that is composed of two identical halves. You can devise several regexps; some are better than others. The function I use is described in an appendix, along with several regexps. See Appendix A   "`the-the` Duplicated Words Function", page 208.

13 Counting via Repetition and Regexps

Repetition and regular expression searches are powerful tools that you often use when you write code in Emacs Lisp. This chapter illustrates the use of regular expression searches through the construction of word count commands using `while` loops and recursion.

The standard Emacs distribution contains functions for counting the number of lines and words within a region.

Certain types of writing ask you to count words. Thus, if you write an essay, you may be limited to 800 words; if you write a novel, you may discipline yourself to write 1000 words a day. It seems odd, but for a long time, Emacs lacked a word count command. Perhaps people used Emacs mostly for code or types of documentation that did not require word counts; or perhaps they restricted themselves to the operating system word count command, `wc`. Alternatively, people may have followed the publishers' convention and computed a word count by dividing the number of characters in a document by five.

There are many ways to implement a command to count words. Here are some examples, which you may wish to compare with the standard Emacs command, `count-words-region`.

13.1 The `count-words-example` Function

A word count command could count words in a line, paragraph, region, or buffer. What should the command cover? You could design the command to count the number of words in a complete buffer. However, the Emacs tradition encourages flexibility—you may want to count words in just a section, rather than all of a buffer. So it makes more sense to design the command to count the number of words in a region. Once you have a command to count words in a region, you can, if you wish, count words in a whole buffer by marking it with `C-x h` (`mark-whole-buffer`).

Clearly, counting words is a repetitive act: starting from the beginning of the region, you count the first word, then the second word, then the third word, and so on, until you reach the end of the region. This means that word counting is ideally suited to recursion or to a `while` loop.

First, we will implement the word count command with a `while` loop, then with recursion. The command will, of course, be interactive.

The template for an interactive function definition is, as always:

```
(defun name-of-function (argument-list)
  "documentation..."
  (interactive-expression...)
  body...)
```

What we need to do is fill in the slots.

The name of the function should be self-explanatory and similar to the existing `count-lines-region` name. This makes the name easier to remember. `count-words-region` is the obvious choice. Since that name is now used for the standard Emacs command to count words, we will name our implementation `count-words-example`.

The function counts words within a region. This means that the argument list must contain symbols that are bound to the two positions, the beginning and end of the region. These two positions can be called 'beginning' and 'end' respectively. The first line of the documentation should be a single sentence, since that is all that is printed as documentation by a command such as apropos. The interactive expression will be of the form '(interactive "r")', since that will cause Emacs to pass the beginning and end of the region to the function's argument list. All this is routine.

The body of the function needs to be written to do three tasks: first, to set up conditions under which the while loop can count words, second, to run the while loop, and third, to send a message to the user.

When a user calls count-words-example, point may be at the beginning or the end of the region. However, the counting process must start at the beginning of the region. This means we will want to put point there if it is not already there. Executing (goto-char beginning) ensures this. Of course, we will want to return point to its expected position when the function finishes its work. For this reason, the body must be enclosed in a save-excursion expression.

The central part of the body of the function consists of a while loop in which one expression jumps point forward word by word, and another expression counts those jumps. The true-or-false-test of the while loop should test true so long as point should jump forward, and false when point is at the end of the region.

We could use (forward-word 1) as the expression for moving point forward word by word, but it is easier to see what Emacs identifies as a "word" if we use a regular expression search.

A regular expression search that finds the pattern for which it is searching leaves point after the last character matched. This means that a succession of successful word searches will move point forward word by word.

As a practical matter, we want the regular expression search to jump over whitespace and punctuation between words as well as over the words themselves. A regexp that refuses to jump over interword whitespace would never jump more than one word! This means that the regexp should include the whitespace and punctuation that follows a word, if any, as well as the word itself. (A word may end a buffer and not have any following whitespace or punctuation, so that part of the regexp must be optional.)

Thus, what we want for the regexp is a pattern defining one or more word constituent characters followed, optionally, by one or more characters that are not word constituents. The regular expression for this is:

```
\w+\W*
```

The buffer's syntax table determines which characters are and are not word constituents. For more information about syntax, see Section "Syntax Tables" in *The GNU Emacs Lisp Reference Manual*.

The search expression looks like this:

```
(re-search-forward "\\w+\\W*")
```

(Note that paired backslashes precede the 'w' and 'W'. A single backslash has special meaning to the Emacs Lisp interpreter. It indicates that the following character is interpreted differently than usual. For example, the two characters, '\n', stand for 'newline', rather than for a backslash followed by 'n'. Two backslashes in a row stand for an ordinary, unspecial backslash, so Emacs Lisp interpreter ends of seeing a single backslash followed by a letter. So it discovers the letter is special.)

We need a counter to count how many words there are; this variable must first be set to 0 and then incremented each time Emacs goes around the `while` loop. The incrementing expression is simply:

```
(setq count (1+ count))
```

Finally, we want to tell the user how many words there are in the region. The `message` function is intended for presenting this kind of information to the user. The message has to be phrased so that it reads properly regardless of how many words there are in the region: we don't want to say that "there are 1 words in the region". The conflict between singular and plural is ungrammatical. We can solve this problem by using a conditional expression that evaluates different messages depending on the number of words in the region. There are three possibilities: no words in the region, one word in the region, and more than one word. This means that the `cond` special form is appropriate.

All this leads to the following function definition:

```
;;; First version; has bugs!
(defun count-words-example (beginning end)
  "Print number of words in the region.
Words are defined as at least one word-constituent
character followed by at least one character that
is not a word-constituent.  The buffer's syntax
table determines which characters these are."
  (interactive "r")
  (message "Counting words in region ... ")

;;; 1. Set up appropriate conditions.
  (save-excursion
    (goto-char beginning)
    (let ((count 0))

;;; 2. Run the while loop.
      (while (< (point) end)
        (re-search-forward "\\w+\\W*")
        (setq count (1+ count)))
```

```
;;; 3. Send a message to the user.
    (cond ((zerop count)
           (message
            "The region does NOT have any words."))
          ((= 1 count)
           (message
            "The region has 1 word."))
          (t
           (message
            "The region has %d words." count)))))))
```
As written, the function works, but not in all circumstances.

13.1.1 The Whitespace Bug in `count-words-example`

The `count-words-example` command described in the preceding section has two
bugs, or rather, one bug with two manifestations. First, if you mark a region
containing only whitespace in the middle of some text, the `count-words-example`
command tells you that the region contains one word! Second, if you mark a region
containing only whitespace at the end of the buffer or the accessible portion of a
narrowed buffer, the command displays an error message that looks like this:

```
Search failed: "\\w+\\W*"
```

If you are reading this in Info in GNU Emacs, you can test for these bugs
yourself.

First, evaluate the function in the usual manner to install it.

If you wish, you can also install this keybinding by evaluating it:

```
(global-set-key "\C-c=" 'count-words-example)
```

To conduct the first test, set mark and point to the beginning and end of the
following line and then type *C-c =* (or *M-x count-words-example* if you have not
bound *C-c =*):

```
        one    two    three
```
Emacs will tell you, correctly, that the region has three words.

Repeat the test, but place mark at the beginning of the line and place point
just *before* the word 'one'. Again type the command *C-c =* (or *M-x count-words-
example*). Emacs should tell you that the region has no words, since it is composed
only of the whitespace at the beginning of the line. But instead Emacs tells you
that the region has one word!

For the third test, copy the sample line to the end of the *scratch* buffer
and then type several spaces at the end of the line. Place mark right after the
word 'three' and point at the end of line. (The end of the line will be the end of
the buffer.) Type *C-c =* (or *M-x count-words-example*) as you did before. Again,
Emacs should tell you that the region has no words, since it is composed only of the
whitespace at the end of the line. Instead, Emacs displays an error message saying
'Search failed'.

The two bugs stem from the same problem.

Consider the first manifestation of the bug, in which the command tells you
that the whitespace at the beginning of the line contains one word. What happens
is this: The M-x `count-words-example` command moves point to the beginning of

the region. The `while` tests whether the value of point is smaller than the value of `end`, which it is. Consequently, the regular expression search looks for and finds the first word. It leaves point after the word. `count` is set to one. The `while` loop repeats; but this time the value of point is larger than the value of `end`, the loop is exited; and the function displays a message saying the number of words in the region is one. In brief, the regular expression search looks for and finds the word even though it is outside the marked region.

In the second manifestation of the bug, the region is whitespace at the end of the buffer. Emacs says '`Search failed`'. What happens is that the true-or-false-test in the `while` loop tests true, so the search expression is executed. But since there are no more words in the buffer, the search fails.

In both manifestations of the bug, the search extends or attempts to extend outside of the region.

The solution is to limit the search to the region—this is a fairly simple action, but as you may have come to expect, it is not quite as simple as you might think.

As we have seen, the `re-search-forward` function takes a search pattern as its first argument. But in addition to this first, mandatory argument, it accepts three optional arguments. The optional second argument bounds the search. The optional third argument, if `t`, causes the function to return `nil` rather than signal an error if the search fails. The optional fourth argument is a repeat count. (In Emacs, you can see a function's documentation by typing *C-h f*, the name of the function, and then RET.)

In the `count-words-example` definition, the value of the end of the region is held by the variable `end` which is passed as an argument to the function. Thus, we can add `end` as an argument to the regular expression search expression:

```
(re-search-forward "\\w+\\W*" end)
```

However, if you make only this change to the `count-words-example` definition and then test the new version of the definition on a stretch of whitespace, you will receive an error message saying '`Search failed`'.

What happens is this: the search is limited to the region, and fails as you expect because there are no word-constituent characters in the region. Since it fails, we receive an error message. But we do not want to receive an error message in this case; we want to receive the message "The region does NOT have any words."

The solution to this problem is to provide `re-search-forward` with a third argument of `t`, which causes the function to return `nil` rather than signal an error if the search fails.

However, if you make this change and try it, you will see the message "Counting words in region ... " and ... you will keep on seeing that message ..., until you type *C-g* (`keyboard-quit`).

Here is what happens: the search is limited to the region, as before, and it fails because there are no word-constituent characters in the region, as expected. Consequently, the `re-search-forward` expression returns `nil`. It does nothing else. In particular, it does not move point, which it does as a side effect if it finds the search target. After the `re-search-forward` expression returns `nil`, the next expression in the `while` loop is evaluated. This expression increments the count.

Then the loop repeats. The true-or-false-test tests true because the value of point is still less than the value of end, since the `re-search-forward` expression did not move point. ... and the cycle repeats ...

The `count-words-example` definition requires yet another modification, to cause the true-or-false-test of the `while` loop to test false if the search fails. Put another way, there are two conditions that must be satisfied in the true-or-false-test before the word count variable is incremented: point must still be within the region and the search expression must have found a word to count.

Since both the first condition and the second condition must be true together, the two expressions, the region test and the search expression, can be joined with an `and` special form and embedded in the `while` loop as the true-or-false-test, like this:

```
(and (< (point) end) (re-search-forward "\\w+\\W*" end t))
```

(For information about `and`, see "The `kill-new` function", page 89.)

The `re-search-forward` expression returns `t` if the search succeeds and as a side effect moves point. Consequently, as words are found, point is moved through the region. When the search expression fails to find another word, or when point reaches the end of the region, the true-or-false-test tests false, the `while` loop exits, and the `count-words-example` function displays one or other of its messages.

After incorporating these final changes, the `count-words-example` works without bugs (or at least, without bugs that I have found!). Here is what it looks like:

```
;;; Final version: while
(defun count-words-example (beginning end)
  "Print number of words in the region."
  (interactive "r")
  (message "Counting words in region ... ")

;;; 1. Set up appropriate conditions.
  (save-excursion
    (let ((count 0))
      (goto-char beginning)

;;; 2. Run the while loop.
      (while (and (< (point) end)
                  (re-search-forward "\\w+\\W*" end t))
        (setq count (1+ count)))

;;; 3. Send a message to the user.
      (cond ((zerop count)
             (message
              "The region does NOT have any words."))
            ((= 1 count)
             (message
              "The region has 1 word."))
            (t
             (message
              "The region has %d words." count)))))))
```

13.2 Count Words Recursively

You can write the function for counting words recursively as well as with a `while` loop. Let's see how this is done.

First, we need to recognize that the `count-words-example` function has three jobs: it sets up the appropriate conditions for counting to occur; it counts the words in the region; and it sends a message to the user telling how many words there are.

If we write a single recursive function to do everything, we will receive a message for every recursive call. If the region contains 13 words, we will receive thirteen messages, one right after the other. We don't want this! Instead, we must write two functions to do the job, one of which (the recursive function) will be used inside of the other. One function will set up the conditions and display the message; the other will return the word count.

Let us start with the function that causes the message to be displayed. We can continue to call this `count-words-example`.

This is the function that the user will call. It will be interactive. Indeed, it will be similar to our previous versions of this function, except that it will call `recursive-count-words` to determine how many words are in the region.

We can readily construct a template for this function, based on our previous versions:

```
;; Recursive version; uses regular expression search
(defun count-words-example (beginning end)
  "documentation..."
  (interactive-expression...)

;;; 1. Set up appropriate conditions.
  (explanatory message)
  (set-up functions...

;;; 2. Count the words.
    recursive call

;;; 3. Send a message to the user.
    message providing word count))
```

The definition looks straightforward, except that somehow the count returned by the recursive call must be passed to the message displaying the word count. A little thought suggests that this can be done by making use of a `let` expression: we can bind a variable in the varlist of a `let` expression to the number of words in the region, as returned by the recursive call; and then the `cond` expression, using binding, can display the value to the user.

Often, one thinks of the binding within a `let` expression as somehow secondary to the primary work of a function. But in this case, what you might consider the primary job of the function, counting words, is done within the `let` expression.

Using `let`, the function definition looks like this:

```
(defun count-words-example (beginning end)
  "Print number of words in the region."
  (interactive "r")

;;; 1. Set up appropriate conditions.
  (message "Counting words in region ... ")
  (save-excursion
    (goto-char beginning)

;;; 2. Count the words.
    (let ((count (recursive-count-words end)))

;;; 3. Send a message to the user.
      (cond ((zerop count)
             (message
              "The region does NOT have any words."))
            ((= 1 count)
             (message
              "The region has 1 word."))
            (t
             (message
              "The region has %d words." count)))))))
```

Next, we need to write the recursive counting function.

A recursive function has at least three parts: the do-again-test, the next-step-expression, and the recursive call.

The do-again-test determines whether the function will or will not be called again. Since we are counting words in a region and can use a function that moves point forward for every word, the do-again-test can check whether point is still within the region. The do-again-test should find the value of point and determine whether point is before, at, or after the value of the end of the region. We can use the `point` function to locate point. Clearly, we must pass the value of the end of the region to the recursive counting function as an argument.

In addition, the do-again-test should also test whether the search finds a word. If it does not, the function should not call itself again.

The next-step-expression changes a value so that when the recursive function is supposed to stop calling itself, it stops. More precisely, the next-step-expression changes a value so that at the right time, the do-again-test stops the recursive function from calling itself again. In this case, the next-step-expression can be the expression that moves point forward, word by word.

The third part of a recursive function is the recursive call.

Somewhere, we also need a part that does the work of the function, a part that does the counting. A vital part!

But already, we have an outline of the recursive counting function:

```
(defun recursive-count-words (region-end)
  "documentation..."
   do-again-test
   next-step-expression
   recursive call)
```

Now we need to fill in the slots. Let's start with the simplest cases first: if point is at or beyond the end of the region, there cannot be any words in the region, so the function should return zero. Likewise, if the search fails, there are no words to count, so the function should return zero.

On the other hand, if point is within the region and the search succeeds, the function should call itself again.

Thus, the do-again-test should look like this:

```
(and (< (point) region-end)
     (re-search-forward "\\w+\\W*" region-end t))
```

Note that the search expression is part of the do-again-test—the function returns t if its search succeeds and nil if it fails. (See Section 13.1.1 "The Whitespace Bug in count-words-example", page 146, for an explanation of how re-search-forward works.)

The do-again-test is the true-or-false test of an if clause. Clearly, if the do-again-test succeeds, the then-part of the if clause should call the function again; but if it fails, the else-part should return zero since either point is outside the region or the search failed because there were no words to find.

But before considering the recursive call, we need to consider the next-step-expression. What is it? Interestingly, it is the search part of the do-again-test.

In addition to returning t or nil for the do-again-test, re-search-forward moves point forward as a side effect of a successful search. This is the action that changes the value of point so that the recursive function stops calling itself when point completes its movement through the region. Consequently, the re-search-forward expression is the next-step-expression.

In outline, then, the body of the recursive-count-words function looks like this:

```
(if do-again-test-and-next-step-combined
    ;; then
    recursive-call-returning-count
  ;; else
  return-zero)
```

How to incorporate the mechanism that counts?

If you are not used to writing recursive functions, a question like this can be troublesome. But it can and should be approached systematically.

We know that the counting mechanism should be associated in some way with the recursive call. Indeed, since the next-step-expression moves point forward by one word, and since a recursive call is made for each word, the counting mechanism must be an expression that adds one to the value returned by a call to recursive-count-words.

Consider several cases:

- If there are two words in the region, the function should return a value resulting from adding one to the value returned when it counts the first word, plus the number returned when it counts the remaining words in the region, which in this case is one.

- If there is one word in the region, the function should return a value resulting from adding one to the value returned when it counts that word, plus the number returned when it counts the remaining words in the region, which in this case is zero.

- If there are no words in the region, the function should return zero.

From the sketch we can see that the else-part of the `if` returns zero for the case of no words. This means that the then-part of the `if` must return a value resulting from adding one to the value returned from a count of the remaining words.

The expression will look like this, where `1+` is a function that adds one to its argument.

```
(1+ (recursive-count-words region-end))
```

The whole `recursive-count-words` function will then look like this:

```
(defun recursive-count-words (region-end)
  "documentation..."

;;; 1. do-again-test
  (if (and (< (point) region-end)
           (re-search-forward "\\w+\\W*" region-end t))

;;; 2. then-part: the recursive call
      (1+ (recursive-count-words region-end))

;;; 3. else-part
    0))
```

Let's examine how this works:

If there are no words in the region, the else part of the `if` expression is evaluated and consequently the function returns zero.

If there is one word in the region, the value of point is less than the value of `region-end` and the search succeeds. In this case, the true-or-false-test of the `if` expression tests true, and the then-part of the `if` expression is evaluated. The counting expression is evaluated. This expression returns a value (which will be the value returned by the whole function) that is the sum of one added to the value returned by a recursive call.

Meanwhile, the next-step-expression has caused point to jump over the first (and in this case only) word in the region. This means that when (`recursive-count-words region-end`) is evaluated a second time, as a result of the recursive call, the value of point will be equal to or greater than the value of region end. So this time, `recursive-count-words` will return zero. The zero will be added to one, and the original evaluation of `recursive-count-words` will return one plus zero, which is one, which is the correct amount.

Clearly, if there are two words in the region, the first call to `recursive-count-words` returns one added to the value returned by calling `recursive-count-words` on a region containing the remaining word—that is, it adds one to one, producing two, which is the correct amount.

Similarly, if there are three words in the region, the first call to `recursive-count-words` returns one added to the value returned by calling `recursive-count-words` on a region containing the remaining two words—and so on and so on.

With full documentation the two functions look like this:

The recursive function:

```
(defun recursive-count-words (region-end)
  "Number of words between point and REGION-END."

;;; 1. do-again-test
  (if (and (< (point) region-end)
           (re-search-forward "\\w+\\W*" region-end t))

;;; 2. then-part: the recursive call
      (1+ (recursive-count-words region-end))

;;; 3. else-part
    0))
```

The wrapper:

```
;;; Recursive version
(defun count-words-example (beginning end)
  "Print number of words in the region.

Words are defined as at least one word-constituent
character followed by at least one character that is
not a word-constituent.  The buffer's syntax table
determines which characters these are."
  (interactive "r")
  (message "Counting words in region ... ")
  (save-excursion
    (goto-char beginning)
    (let ((count (recursive-count-words end)))
      (cond ((zerop count)
             (message
              "The region does NOT have any words."))
            ((= 1 count)
             (message "The region has 1 word."))
            (t
             (message
              "The region has %d words." count)))))))
```

13.3 Exercise: Counting Punctuation

Using a `while` loop, write a function to count the number of punctuation marks in a region—period, comma, semicolon, colon, exclamation mark, and question mark. Do the same using recursion.

14 Counting Words in a `defun`

Our next project is to count the number of words in a function definition. Clearly, this can be done using some variant of `count-words-example`. See Chapter 13 "Counting via Repetition and Regexps", page 143. If we are just going to count the words in one definition, it is easy enough to mark the definition with the *C-M-h* (`mark-defun`) command, and then call `count-words-example`.

However, I am more ambitious: I want to count the words and symbols in every definition in the Emacs sources and then print a graph that shows how many functions there are of each length: how many contain 40 to 49 words or symbols, how many contain 50 to 59 words or symbols, and so on. I have often been curious how long a typical function is, and this will tell.

Described in one phrase, the histogram project is daunting; but divided into numerous small steps, each of which we can take one at a time, the project becomes less fearsome. Let us consider what the steps must be:

- First, write a function to count the words in one definition. This includes the problem of handling symbols as well as words.

- Second, write a function to list the number of words in each function in a file. This function can use the `count-words-in-defun` function.

- Third, write a function to list the number of words in each function in each of several files. This entails automatically finding the various files, switching to them, and counting the words in the definitions within them.

- Fourth, write a function to convert the list of numbers that we created in step three to a form that will be suitable for printing as a graph.

- Fifth, write a function to print the results as a graph.

This is quite a project! But if we take each step slowly, it will not be difficult.

14.1 What to Count?

When we first start thinking about how to count the words in a function definition, the first question is (or ought to be) what are we going to count? When we speak of "words" with respect to a Lisp function definition, we are actually speaking, in large part, of symbols. For example, the following `multiply-by-seven` function contains the five symbols `defun`, `multiply-by-seven`, `number`, `*`, and 7. In addition, in the documentation string, it contains the four words 'Multiply', 'NUMBER', 'by', and 'seven'. The symbol 'number' is repeated, so the definition contains a total of ten words and symbols.

```
(defun multiply-by-seven (number)
  "Multiply NUMBER by seven."
  (* 7 number))
```

However, if we mark the `multiply-by-seven` definition with *C-M-h* (`mark-defun`), and then call `count-words-example` on it, we will find that `count-words-example` claims the definition has eleven words, not ten! Something is wrong!

The problem is twofold: `count-words-example` does not count the '*' as a word, and it counts the single symbol, `multiply-by-seven`, as containing three words.

The hyphens are treated as if they were interword spaces rather than intraword connectors: 'multiply-by-seven' is counted as if it were written 'multiply by seven'.

The cause of this confusion is the regular expression search within the count-words-example definition that moves point forward word by word. In the canonical version of count-words-example, the regexp is:

```
"\\w+\\W*"
```

This regular expression is a pattern defining one or more word constituent characters possibly followed by one or more characters that are not word constituents. What is meant by "word constituent characters" brings us to the issue of syntax, which is worth a section of its own.

14.2 What Constitutes a Word or Symbol?

Emacs treats different characters as belonging to different *syntax categories*. For example, the regular expression, '\\w+', is a pattern specifying one or more *word constituent* characters. Word constituent characters are members of one syntax category. Other syntax categories include the class of punctuation characters, such as the period and the comma, and the class of whitespace characters, such as the blank space and the tab character. (For more information, see Section "Syntax Tables" in *The GNU Emacs Lisp Reference Manual*.)

Syntax tables specify which characters belong to which categories. Usually, a hyphen is not specified as a word constituent character. Instead, it is specified as being in the class of characters that are part of symbol names but not words. This means that the count-words-example function treats it in the same way it treats an interword white space, which is why count-words-example counts 'multiply-by-seven' as three words.

There are two ways to cause Emacs to count 'multiply-by-seven' as one symbol: modify the syntax table or modify the regular expression.

We could redefine a hyphen as a word constituent character by modifying the syntax table that Emacs keeps for each mode. This action would serve our purpose, except that a hyphen is merely the most common character within symbols that is not typically a word constituent character; there are others, too.

Alternatively, we can redefine the regexp used in the count-words-example definition so as to include symbols. This procedure has the merit of clarity, but the task is a little tricky.

The first part is simple enough: the pattern must match at least one character that is a word or symbol constituent. Thus:

```
"\\(\\w\\|\\s_\\)+"
```

The '\\(' is the first part of the grouping construct that includes the '\\w' and the '\\s_' as alternatives, separated by the '\\|'. The '\\w' matches any word-constituent character and the '\\s_' matches any character that is part of a symbol name but not a word-constituent character. The '+' following the group indicates that the word or symbol constituent characters must be matched at least once.

However, the second part of the regexp is more difficult to design. What we want is to follow the first part with optionally one or more characters that are not constituents of a word or symbol. At first, I thought I could define this with the following:

```
"\\(\\W\\|\\S_\\)*"
```

The upper case 'W' and 'S' match characters that are *not* word or symbol constituents. Unfortunately, this expression matches any character that is either not a word constituent or not a symbol constituent. This matches any character!

I then noticed that every word or symbol in my test region was followed by white space (blank space, tab, or newline). So I tried placing a pattern to match one or more blank spaces after the pattern for one or more word or symbol constituents. This failed, too. Words and symbols are often separated by whitespace, but in actual code parentheses may follow symbols and punctuation may follow words. So finally, I designed a pattern in which the word or symbol constituents are followed optionally by characters that are not white space and then followed optionally by white space.

Here is the full regular expression:

```
"\\(\\w\\|\\s_\\)+[^ \t\n]*[ \t\n]*"
```

14.3 The `count-words-in-defun` Function

We have seen that there are several ways to write a `count-words-region` function. To write a `count-words-in-defun`, we need merely adapt one of these versions.

The version that uses a `while` loop is easy to understand, so I am going to adapt that. Because `count-words-in-defun` will be part of a more complex program, it need not be interactive and it need not display a message but just return the count. These considerations simplify the definition a little.

On the other hand, `count-words-in-defun` will be used within a buffer that contains function definitions. Consequently, it is reasonable to ask that the function determine whether it is called when point is within a function definition, and if it is, to return the count for that definition. This adds complexity to the definition, but saves us from needing to pass arguments to the function.

These considerations lead us to prepare the following template:

```
(defun count-words-in-defun ()
  "documentation..."
  (set up...
    (while loop...)
   return count)
```

As usual, our job is to fill in the slots.

First, the set up.

We are presuming that this function will be called within a buffer containing function definitions. Point will either be within a function definition or not. For `count-words-in-defun` to work, point must move to the beginning of the definition, a counter must start at zero, and the counting loop must stop when point reaches the end of the definition.

The `beginning-of-defun` function searches backwards for an opening delimiter such as a '(' at the beginning of a line, and moves point to that position, or else to the limit of the search. In practice, this means that `beginning-of-defun` moves point to the beginning of an enclosing or preceding function definition, or else to the beginning of the buffer. We can use `beginning-of-defun` to place point where we wish to start.

The `while` loop requires a counter to keep track of the words or symbols being counted. A `let` expression can be used to create a local variable for this purpose, and bind it to an initial value of zero.

The `end-of-defun` function works like `beginning-of-defun` except that it moves point to the end of the definition. `end-of-defun` can be used as part of an expression that determines the position of the end of the definition.

The set up for `count-words-in-defun` takes shape rapidly: first we move point to the beginning of the definition, then we create a local variable to hold the count, and finally, we record the position of the end of the definition so the `while` loop will know when to stop looping.

The code looks like this:

```
(beginning-of-defun)
(let ((count 0)
      (end (save-excursion (end-of-defun) (point))))
```

The code is simple. The only slight complication is likely to concern `end`: it is bound to the position of the end of the definition by a `save-excursion` expression that returns the value of point after `end-of-defun` temporarily moves it to the end of the definition.

The second part of the `count-words-in-defun`, after the set up, is the `while` loop.

The loop must contain an expression that jumps point forward word by word and symbol by symbol, and another expression that counts the jumps. The true-or-false-test for the `while` loop should test true so long as point should jump forward, and false when point is at the end of the definition. We have already redefined the regular expression for this, so the loop is straightforward:

```
(while (and (< (point) end)
            (re-search-forward
             "\\(\\w\\|\\s_\\)+[^ \t\n]*[ \t\n]*" end t))
  (setq count (1+ count)))
```

The third part of the function definition returns the count of words and symbols. This part is the last expression within the body of the `let` expression, and can be, very simply, the local variable `count`, which when evaluated returns the count.

Put together, the `count-words-in-defun` definition looks like this:

```
(defun count-words-in-defun ()
  "Return the number of words and symbols in a defun."
  (beginning-of-defun)
  (let ((count 0)
        (end (save-excursion (end-of-defun) (point))))
    (while
        (and (< (point) end)
             (re-search-forward
              "\\(\\w\\|\\s_\\)+[^ \t\n]*[ \t\n]*"
              end t))
      (setq count (1+ count)))
    count))
```

How to test this? The function is not interactive, but it is easy to put a wrapper around the function to make it interactive; we can use almost the same code as for the recursive version of `count-words-example`:

```
;;; Interactive version.
(defun count-words-defun ()
  "Number of words and symbols in a function definition."
  (interactive)
  (message
   "Counting words and symbols in function definition ... ")
  (let ((count (count-words-in-defun)))
    (cond
     ((zerop count)
      (message
       "The definition does NOT have any words or symbols."))
     ((= 1 count)
      (message
       "The definition has 1 word or symbol."))
     (t
      (message
       "The definition has %d words or symbols." count)))))
```

Let's re-use *C-c =* as a convenient keybinding:

```
(global-set-key "\C-c=" 'count-words-defun)
```

Now we can try out `count-words-defun`: install both `count-words-in-defun` and `count-words-defun`, and set the keybinding, and then place the cursor within the following definition:

```
(defun multiply-by-seven (number)
  "Multiply NUMBER by seven."
  (* 7 number))
     ⇒ 10
```

Success! The definition has 10 words and symbols.

The next problem is to count the numbers of words and symbols in several definitions within a single file.

14.4 Count Several `defuns` Within a File

A file such as `simple.el` may have a hundred or more function definitions within it. Our long term goal is to collect statistics on many files, but as a first step, our immediate goal is to collect statistics on one file.

The information will be a series of numbers, each number being the length of a function definition. We can store the numbers in a list.

We know that we will want to incorporate the information regarding one file with information about many other files; this means that the function for counting definition lengths within one file need only return the list of lengths. It need not and should not display any messages.

The word count commands contain one expression to jump point forward word by word and another expression to count the jumps. The function to return the lengths of definitions can be designed to work the same way, with one expression to jump point forward definition by definition and another expression to construct the lengths' list.

This statement of the problem makes it elementary to write the function definition. Clearly, we will start the count at the beginning of the file, so the first command will be `(goto-char (point-min))`. Next, we start the `while` loop; and the true-or-false test of the loop can be a regular expression search for the next function definition—so long as the search succeeds, point is moved forward and then the body of the loop is evaluated. The body needs an expression that constructs the lengths' list. `cons`, the list construction command, can be used to create the list. That is almost all there is to it.

Here is what this fragment of code looks like:

```
(goto-char (point-min))
(while (re-search-forward "^(defun" nil t)
  (setq lengths-list
        (cons (count-words-in-defun) lengths-list)))
```

What we have left out is the mechanism for finding the file that contains the function definitions.

In previous examples, we either used this, the Info file, or we switched back and forth to some other buffer, such as the `*scratch*` buffer.

Finding a file is a new process that we have not yet discussed.

14.5 Find a File

To find a file in Emacs, you use the *C-x C-f* (`find-file`) command. This command is almost, but not quite right for the lengths problem.

Let's look at the source for `find-file`:

```
(defun find-file (filename)
  "Edit file FILENAME.
Switch to a buffer visiting file FILENAME,
creating one if none already exists."
  (interactive "FFind file: ")
  (switch-to-buffer (find-file-noselect filename)))
```

(The most recent version of the `find-file` function definition permits you to specify optional wildcards to visit multiple files; that makes the definition more complex and we will not discuss it here, since it is not relevant. You can see its source using either *M-.* (`find-tag`) or *C-h f* (`describe-function`).)

The definition I am showing possesses short but complete documentation and an interactive specification that prompts you for a file name when you use the command interactively. The body of the definition contains two functions, `find-file-noselect` and `switch-to-buffer`.

According to its documentation as shown by *C-h f* (the `describe-function` command), the `find-file-noselect` function reads the named file into a buffer and returns the buffer. (Its most recent version includes an optional *wildcards* argument, too, as well as another to read a file literally and an other you suppress warning messages. These optional arguments are irrelevant.)

However, the `find-file-noselect` function does not select the buffer in which it puts the file. Emacs does not switch its attention (or yours if you are using `find-file-noselect`) to the selected buffer. That is what `switch-to-buffer` does: it switches the buffer to which Emacs attention is directed; and it switches the buffer displayed in the window to the new buffer. We have discussed buffer switching elsewhere. (See Section 2.3 "Switching Buffers", page 23.)

In this histogram project, we do not need to display each file on the screen as the program determines the length of each definition within it. Instead of employing `switch-to-buffer`, we can work with `set-buffer`, which redirects the attention of the computer program to a different buffer but does not redisplay it on the screen. So instead of calling on `find-file` to do the job, we must write our own expression.

The task is easy: use `find-file-noselect` and `set-buffer`.

14.6 `lengths-list-file` in Detail

The core of the `lengths-list-file` function is a `while` loop containing a function to move point forward defun by defun, and a function to count the number of words and symbols in each defun. This core must be surrounded by functions that do various other tasks, including finding the file, and ensuring that point starts out at the beginning of the file. The function definition looks like this:

```
(defun lengths-list-file (filename)
  "Return list of definitions' lengths within FILE.
The returned list is a list of numbers.
Each number is the number of words or
symbols in one function definition."
```

```
(message "Working on `%s' ... " filename)
(save-excursion
  (let ((buffer (find-file-noselect filename))
        (lengths-list))
    (set-buffer buffer)
    (setq buffer-read-only t)
    (widen)
    (goto-char (point-min))
    (while (re-search-forward "^(defun" nil t)
      (setq lengths-list
            (cons (count-words-in-defun) lengths-list)))
    (kill-buffer buffer)
    lengths-list)))
```

The function is passed one argument, the name of the file on which it will work.
It has four lines of documentation, but no interactive specification. Since people
worry that a computer is broken if they don't see anything going on, the first line
of the body is a message.

The next line contains a `save-excursion` that returns Emacs's attention to the
current buffer when the function completes. This is useful in case you embed this
function in another function that presumes point is restored to the original buffer.

In the varlist of the `let` expression, Emacs finds the file and binds the local
variable `buffer` to the buffer containing the file. At the same time, Emacs creates
`lengths-list` as a local variable.

Next, Emacs switches its attention to the buffer.

In the following line, Emacs makes the buffer read-only. Ideally, this line is
not necessary. None of the functions for counting words and symbols in a function
definition should change the buffer. Besides, the buffer is not going to be saved,
even if it were changed. This line is entirely the consequence of great, perhaps
excessive, caution. The reason for the caution is that this function and those it
calls work on the sources for Emacs and it is inconvenient if they are inadvertently
modified. It goes without saying that I did not realize a need for this line until an
experiment went awry and started to modify my Emacs source files . . .

Next comes a call to widen the buffer if it is narrowed. This function is usually
not needed—Emacs creates a fresh buffer if none already exists; but if a buffer
visiting the file already exists Emacs returns that one. In this case, the buffer may
be narrowed and must be widened. If we wanted to be fully user-friendly, we would
arrange to save the restriction and the location of point, but we won't.

The `(goto-char (point-min))` expression moves point to the beginning of the
buffer.

Then comes a `while` loop in which the work of the function is carried out. In
the loop, Emacs determines the length of each definition and constructs a lengths'
list containing the information.

Emacs kills the buffer after working through it. This is to save space inside of
Emacs. My version of GNU Emacs 19 contained over 300 source files of interest;
GNU Emacs 22 contains over a thousand source files. Another function will apply
`lengths-list-file` to each of the files.

Finally, the last expression within the `let` expression is the `lengths-list` variable; its value is returned as the value of the whole function.

You can try this function by installing it in the usual fashion. Then place your cursor after the following expression and type *C-x C-e* (`eval-last-sexp`).

```
(lengths-list-file
  "/usr/local/share/emacs/22.1/lisp/emacs-lisp/debug.el")
```

You may need to change the pathname of the file; the one here is for GNU Emacs version 22.1. To change the expression, copy it to the `*scratch*` buffer and edit it. Also, to see the full length of the list, rather than a truncated version, you may have to evaluate the following:

```
(custom-set-variables '(eval-expression-print-length nil))
```

(See Section 16.2 "Specifying Variables using `defcustom`", page 183. Then evaluate the `lengths-list-file` expression.)

The lengths' list for `debug.el` takes less than a second to produce and looks like this in GNU Emacs 22:

```
(83 113 105 144 289 22 30 97 48 89 25 52 52 88 28 29 77 49 43 290 232 587)
```

(Using my old machine, the version 19 lengths' list for `debug.el` took seven seconds to produce and looked like this:

```
(75 41 80 62 20 45 44 68 45 12 34 235)
```

The newer version of `debug.el` contains more defuns than the earlier one; and my new machine is much faster than the old one.)

Note that the length of the last definition in the file is first in the list.

14.7 Count Words in `defuns` in Different Files

In the previous section, we created a function that returns a list of the lengths of each definition in a file. Now, we want to define a function to return a master list of the lengths of the definitions in a list of files.

Working on each of a list of files is a repetitious act, so we can use either a `while` loop or recursion.

The design using a `while` loop is routine. The argument passed to the function is a list of files. As we saw earlier (see Section 11.1.1 "Loop Example", page 106), you can write a `while` loop so that the body of the loop is evaluated if such a list contains elements, but to exit the loop if the list is empty. For this design to work, the body of the loop must contain an expression that shortens the list each time the body is evaluated, so that eventually the list is empty. The usual technique is to set the value of the list to the value of the CDR of the list each time the body is evaluated.

The template looks like this:

```
(while test-whether-list-is-empty
    body...
    set-list-to-cdr-of-list)
```

Also, we remember that a `while` loop returns `nil` (the result of evaluating the true-or-false-test), not the result of any evaluation within its body. (The evaluations within the body of the loop are done for their side effects.) However, the expression that sets the lengths' list is part of the body—and that is the value that we want returned by the function as a whole. To do this, we enclose the `while` loop within a `let` expression, and arrange that the last element of the `let` expression contains the value of the lengths' list. (See "Loop Example with an Incrementing Counter", page 108.)

These considerations lead us directly to the function itself:

```
;;; Use while loop.
(defun lengths-list-many-files (list-of-files)
  "Return list of lengths of defuns in LIST-OF-FILES."
  (let (lengths-list)

;;; true-or-false-test
    (while list-of-files
      (setq lengths-list
            (append
              lengths-list

;;; Generate a lengthsfl list.
              (lengths-list-file
                (expand-file-name (car list-of-files)))))

;;; Make filesfl list shorter.
      (setq list-of-files (cdr list-of-files)))

;;; Return final value of lengthsfl list.
    lengths-list))
```

`expand-file-name` is a built-in function that converts a file name to the absolute, long, path name form. The function employs the name of the directory in which the function is called.

Thus, if `expand-file-name` is called on `debug.el` when Emacs is visiting the `/usr/local/share/emacs/22.1.1/lisp/emacs-lisp/` directory,

```
debug.el
```

becomes

```
/usr/local/share/emacs/22.1.1/lisp/emacs-lisp/debug.el
```

The only other new element of this function definition is the as yet unstudied function `append`, which merits a short section for itself.

14.7.1 The `append` Function

The `append` function attaches one list to another. Thus,

```
(append '(1 2 3 4) '(5 6 7 8))
```

produces the list

```
(1 2 3 4 5 6 7 8)
```

This is exactly how we want to attach two lengths' lists produced by `lengths-list-file` to each other. The results contrast with `cons`,

```
(cons '(1 2 3 4) '(5 6 7 8))
```

which constructs a new list in which the first argument to `cons` becomes the first
element of the new list:

```
((1 2 3 4) 5 6 7 8)
```

14.8 Recursively Count Words in Different Files

Besides a `while` loop, you can work on each of a list of files with recursion. A
recursive version of `lengths-list-many-files` is short and simple.

The recursive function has the usual parts: the do-again-test, the next-step-
expression, and the recursive call. The do-again-test determines whether the function should call itself again, which it will do if the `list-of-files` contains any
remaining elements; the next-step-expression resets the `list-of-files` to the CDR
of itself, so eventually the list will be empty; and the recursive call calls itself on
the shorter list. The complete function is shorter than this description!

```
(defun recursive-lengths-list-many-files (list-of-files)
  "Return list of lengths of each defun in LIST-OF-FILES."
  (if list-of-files                    ; do-again-test
      (append
       (lengths-list-file
        (expand-file-name (car list-of-files)))
       (recursive-lengths-list-many-files
        (cdr list-of-files)))))
```

In a sentence, the function returns the lengths' list for the first of the `list-of-files`
appended to the result of calling itself on the rest of the `list-of-files`.

Here is a test of `recursive-lengths-list-many-files`, along with the results
of running `lengths-list-file` on each of the files individually.

Install `recursive-lengths-list-many-files` and `lengths-list-file`, if necessary, and then evaluate the following expressions. You may need to change the
files' pathnames; those here work when this Info file and the Emacs sources are
located in their customary places. To change the expressions, copy them to the
`*scratch*` buffer, edit them, and then evaluate them.

The results are shown after the '⇒'. (These results are for files from Emacs
version 22.1.1; files from other versions of Emacs may produce different results.)

```
(cd "/usr/local/share/emacs/22.1.1/")

(lengths-list-file "./lisp/macros.el")
     ⇒ (283 263 480 90)

(lengths-list-file "./lisp/mail/mailalias.el")
     ⇒ (38 32 29 95 178 180 321 218 324)

(lengths-list-file "./lisp/makesum.el")
     ⇒ (85 181)

  (recursive-lengths-list-many-files
   '("./lisp/macros.el"
     "./lisp/mail/mailalias.el"
     "./lisp/makesum.el"))
     ⇒ (283 263 480 90 38 32 29 95 178 180 321 218 324 85 181)
```

The `recursive-lengths-list-many-files` function produces the output we want.

The next step is to prepare the data in the list for display in a graph.

14.9 Prepare the Data for Display in a Graph

The `recursive-lengths-list-many-files` function returns a list of numbers. Each number records the length of a function definition. What we need to do now is transform this data into a list of numbers suitable for generating a graph. The new list will tell how many functions definitions contain less than 10 words and symbols, how many contain between 10 and 19 words and symbols, how many contain between 20 and 29 words and symbols, and so on.

In brief, we need to go through the lengths' list produced by the `recursive-lengths-list-many-files` function and count the number of defuns within each range of lengths, and produce a list of those numbers.

Based on what we have done before, we can readily foresee that it should not be too hard to write a function that CDRs down the lengths' list, looks at each element, determines which length range it is in, and increments a counter for that range.

However, before beginning to write such a function, we should consider the advantages of sorting the lengths' list first, so the numbers are ordered from smallest to largest. First, sorting will make it easier to count the numbers in each range, since two adjacent numbers will either be in the same length range or in adjacent ranges. Second, by inspecting a sorted list, we can discover the highest and lowest number, and thereby determine the largest and smallest length range that we will need.

14.9.1 Sorting Lists

Emacs contains a function to sort lists, called (as you might guess) `sort`. The `sort` function takes two arguments, the list to be sorted, and a predicate that determines whether the first of two list elements is less than the second.

As we saw earlier (see Section 1.8.4 "Using the Wrong Type Object as an Argument", page 13), a predicate is a function that determines whether some property is true or false. The `sort` function will reorder a list according to whatever property the predicate uses; this means that `sort` can be used to sort non-numeric lists by non-numeric criteria—it can, for example, alphabetize a list.

The `<` function is used when sorting a numeric list. For example,

```
(sort '(4 8 21 17 33 7 21 7) '<)
```

produces this:

```
(4 7 7 8 17 21 21 33)
```

(Note that in this example, both the arguments are quoted so that the symbols are not evaluated before being passed to `sort` as arguments.)

Sorting the list returned by the `recursive-lengths-list-many-files` function is straightforward; it uses the `<` function:

```
(sort
 (recursive-lengths-list-many-files
  '("./lisp/macros.el"
    "./lisp/mailalias.el"
    "./lisp/makesum.el"))
 '<)
```

which produces:

```
(29 32 38 85 90 95 178 180 181 218 263 283 321 324 480)
```

(Note that in this example, the first argument to `sort` is not quoted, since the expression must be evaluated so as to produce the list that is passed to `sort`.)

14.9.2 Making a List of Files

The `recursive-lengths-list-many-files` function requires a list of files as its argument. For our test examples, we constructed such a list by hand; but the Emacs Lisp source directory is too large for us to do for that. Instead, we will write a function to do the job for us. In this function, we will use both a `while` loop and a recursive call.

We did not have to write a function like this for older versions of GNU Emacs, since they placed all the '`.el`' files in one directory. Instead, we were able to use the `directory-files` function, which lists the names of files that match a specified pattern within a single directory.

However, recent versions of Emacs place Emacs Lisp files in sub-directories of the top level `lisp` directory. This re-arrangement eases navigation. For example, all the mail related files are in a `lisp` sub-directory called `mail`. But at the same time, this arrangement forces us to create a file listing function that descends into the sub-directories.

We can create this function, called `files-in-below-directory`, using familiar functions such as `car`, `nthcdr`, and `substring` in conjunction with an existing function called `directory-files-and-attributes`. This latter function not only lists all the filenames in a directory, including the names of sub-directories, but also their attributes.

To restate our goal: to create a function that will enable us to feed filenames to `recursive-lengths-list-many-files` as a list that looks like this (but with more elements):

```
("./lisp/macros.el"
 "./lisp/mail/rmail.el"
 "./lisp/makesum.el")
```

The `directory-files-and-attributes` function returns a list of lists. Each of the lists within the main list consists of 13 elements. The first element is a string that contains the name of the file—which, in GNU/Linux, may be a *directory file*, that is to say, a file with the special attributes of a directory. The second element of the list is `t` for a directory, a string for symbolic link (the string is the name linked to), or `nil`.

For example, the first '`.el`' file in the `lisp/` directory is `abbrev.el`. Its name is `/usr/local/share/emacs/22.1.1/lisp/abbrev.el` and it is not a directory or a symbolic link.

This is how `directory-files-and-attributes` lists that file and its attributes:

```
("abbrev.el"
nil
1
1000
100
(20615 27034 579989 697000)
(17905 55681 0 0)
(20615 26327 734791 805000)
13188
"-rw-r--r--"
t
2971624
773)
```

On the other hand, `mail/` is a directory within the `lisp/` directory. The beginning of its listing looks like this:

```
("mail"
t
...
)
```

(To learn about the different attributes, look at the documentation of `file-attributes`. Bear in mind that the `file-attributes` function does not list the filename, so its first element is `directory-files-and-attributes`'s second element.)

We will want our new function, `files-in-below-directory`, to list the '.el' files in the directory it is told to check, and in any directories below that directory.

This gives us a hint on how to construct `files-in-below-directory`: within a directory, the function should add '.el' filenames to a list; and if, within a directory, the function comes upon a sub-directory, it should go into that sub-directory and repeat its actions.

However, we should note that every directory contains a name that refers to itself, called . ("dot"), and a name that refers to its parent directory, called .. ("dot dot"). (In /, the root directory, .. refers to itself, since / has no parent.) Clearly, we do not want our `files-in-below-directory` function to enter those directories, since they always lead us, directly or indirectly, to the current directory.

Consequently, our `files-in-below-directory` function must do several tasks:

- Check to see whether it is looking at a filename that ends in '.el'; and if so, add its name to a list.

- Check to see whether it is looking at a filename that is the name of a directory; and if so,

  - Check to see whether it is looking at . or ..; and if so skip it.

  - Or else, go into that directory and repeat the process.

Let's write a function definition to do these tasks. We will use a `while` loop to move from one filename to another within a directory, checking what needs to be done; and we will use a recursive call to repeat the actions on each sub-directory.

The recursive pattern is Accumulate (see "Accumulate", page 124), using `append` as the combiner.

Here is the function:

```
(defun files-in-below-directory (directory)
  "List the .el files in DIRECTORY and in its sub-directories."
  ;; Although the function will be used non-interactively,
  ;; it will be easier to test if we make it interactive.
  ;; The directory will have a name such as
  ;;  "/usr/local/share/emacs/22.1.1/lisp/"
  (interactive "DDirectory name: ")
  (let (el-files-list
        (current-directory-list
         (directory-files-and-attributes directory t)))
    ;; while we are in the current directory
    (while current-directory-list
      (cond
       ;; check to see whether filename ends in '.el'
       ;; and if so, add its name to a list.
       ((equal ".el" (substring (car (car current-directory-list)) -3))
        (setq el-files-list
              (cons (car (car current-directory-list)) el-files-list)))
       ;; check whether filename is that of a directory
       ((eq t (car (cdr (car current-directory-list))))
        ;; decide whether to skip or recurse
        (if
            (equal "."
                   (substring (car (car current-directory-list)) -1))
            ;; then do nothing since filename is that of
            ;;   current directory or parent, "." or ".."
            ()
          ;; else descend into the directory and repeat the process
          (setq el-files-list
                (append
                 (files-in-below-directory
                  (car (car current-directory-list)))
                 el-files-list)))))
      ;; move to the next filename in the list; this also
      ;; shortens the list so the while loop eventually comes to an end
      (setq current-directory-list (cdr current-directory-list)))
    ;; return the filenames
    el-files-list))
```

The `files-in-below-directory` directory-files function takes one argument, the name of a directory.

Thus, on my system,

```
(length
 (files-in-below-directory "/usr/local/share/emacs/22.1.1/lisp/"))
```

tells me that in and below my Lisp sources directory are 1031 '.el' files.

`files-in-below-directory` returns a list in reverse alphabetical order. An expression to sort the list in alphabetical order looks like this:

```
(sort
 (files-in-below-directory "/usr/local/share/emacs/22.1.1/lisp/")
 'string-lessp)
```

14.9.3 Counting function definitions

Our immediate goal is to generate a list that tells us how many function definitions contain fewer than 10 words and symbols, how many contain between 10 and 19 words and symbols, how many contain between 20 and 29 words and symbols, and so on.

With a sorted list of numbers, this is easy: count how many elements of the list are smaller than 10, then, after moving past the numbers just counted, count how many are smaller than 20, then, after moving past the numbers just counted, count how many are smaller than 30, and so on. Each of the numbers, 10, 20, 30, 40, and the like, is one larger than the top of that range. We can call the list of such numbers the `top-of-ranges` list.

If we wished, we could generate this list automatically, but it is simpler to write a list manually. Here it is:

```
(defvar top-of-ranges
 '(10   20   30   40   50
   60   70   80   90  100
  110  120  130  140  150
  160  170  180  190  200
  210  220  230  240  250
  260  270  280  290  300)
 "List specifying ranges for `defuns-per-range'.")
```

To change the ranges, we edit this list.

Next, we need to write the function that creates the list of the number of definitions within each range. Clearly, this function must take the `sorted-lengths` and the `top-of-ranges` lists as arguments.

The `defuns-per-range` function must do two things again and again: it must count the number of definitions within a range specified by the current top-of-range value; and it must shift to the next higher value in the `top-of-ranges` list after counting the number of definitions in the current range. Since each of these actions is repetitive, we can use `while` loops for the job. One loop counts the number of definitions in the range defined by the current top-of-range value, and the other loop selects each of the top-of-range values in turn.

Several entries of the `sorted-lengths` list are counted for each range; this means that the loop for the `sorted-lengths` list will be inside the loop for the `top-of-ranges` list, like a small gear inside a big gear.

The inner loop counts the number of definitions within the range. It is a simple counting loop of the type we have seen before. (See Section 11.1.3 "A loop with an incrementing counter", page 108.) The true-or-false test of the loop tests whether the value from the `sorted-lengths` list is smaller than the current value of the top of the range. If it is, the function increments the counter and tests the next value from the `sorted-lengths` list.

The inner loop looks like this:

```
(while length-element-smaller-than-top-of-range
  (setq number-within-range (1+ number-within-range))
  (setq sorted-lengths (cdr sorted-lengths)))
```

The outer loop must start with the lowest value of the `top-of-ranges` list, and then be set to each of the succeeding higher values in turn. This can be done with a loop like this:

```
(while top-of-ranges
  body-of-loop...
  (setq top-of-ranges (cdr top-of-ranges)))
```

Put together, the two loops look like this:

```
(while top-of-ranges

  ;; Count the number of elements within the current range.
  (while length-element-smaller-than-top-of-range
    (setq number-within-range (1+ number-within-range))
    (setq sorted-lengths (cdr sorted-lengths)))

  ;; Move to next range.
  (setq top-of-ranges (cdr top-of-ranges)))
```

In addition, in each circuit of the outer loop, Emacs should record the number of definitions within that range (the value of `number-within-range`) in a list. We can use `cons` for this purpose. (See Section 7.2 "cons", page 72.)

The `cons` function works fine, except that the list it constructs will contain the number of definitions for the highest range at its beginning and the number of definitions for the lowest range at its end. This is because `cons` attaches new elements of the list to the beginning of the list, and since the two loops are working their way through the lengths' list from the lower end first, the `defuns-per-range-list` will end up largest number first. But we will want to print our graph with smallest values first and the larger later. The solution is to reverse the order of the `defuns-per-range-list`. We can do this using the `nreverse` function, which reverses the order of a list.

For example,

```
(nreverse '(1 2 3 4))
```

produces:

```
(4 3 2 1)
```

Note that the `nreverse` function is destructive—that is, it changes the list to which it is applied; this contrasts with the `car` and `cdr` functions, which are nondestructive. In this case, we do not want the original `defuns-per-range-list`, so it does not matter that it is destroyed. (The `reverse` function provides a reversed copy of a list, leaving the original list as is.)

Put all together, the `defuns-per-range` looks like this:

```
(defun defuns-per-range (sorted-lengths top-of-ranges)
  "SORTED-LENGTHS defuns in each TOP-OF-RANGES range."
  (let ((top-of-range (car top-of-ranges))
        (number-within-range 0)
        defuns-per-range-list)

    ;; Outer loop.
    (while top-of-ranges

      ;; Inner loop.
      (while (and
              ;; Need number for numeric test.
              (car sorted-lengths)
              (< (car sorted-lengths) top-of-range))

        ;; Count number of definitions within current range.
        (setq number-within-range (1+ number-within-range))
        (setq sorted-lengths (cdr sorted-lengths)))

      ;; Exit inner loop but remain within outer loop.

      (setq defuns-per-range-list
            (cons number-within-range defuns-per-range-list))
      (setq number-within-range 0)        ; Reset count to zero.

      ;; Move to next range.
      (setq top-of-ranges (cdr top-of-ranges))
      ;; Specify next top of range value.
      (setq top-of-range (car top-of-ranges)))

    ;; Exit outer loop and count the number of defuns larger than
    ;;   the largest top-of-range value.
    (setq defuns-per-range-list
          (cons
            (length sorted-lengths)
            defuns-per-range-list))

    ;; Return a list of the number of definitions within each range,
    ;;   smallest to largest.
    (nreverse defuns-per-range-list)))
```

The function is straightforward except for one subtle feature. The true-or-false test of the inner loop looks like this:

```
(and (car sorted-lengths)
     (< (car sorted-lengths) top-of-range))
```

instead of like this:

```
(< (car sorted-lengths) top-of-range)
```

The purpose of the test is to determine whether the first item in the `sorted-lengths` list is less than the value of the top of the range.

The simple version of the test works fine unless the `sorted-lengths` list has a `nil` value. In that case, the `(car sorted-lengths)` expression function returns `nil`. The `<` function cannot compare a number to `nil`, which is an empty list, so Emacs signals an error and stops the function from attempting to continue to execute.

The `sorted-lengths` list always becomes `nil` when the counter reaches the end of the list. This means that any attempt to use the `defuns-per-range` function with the simple version of the test will fail.

We solve the problem by using the `(car sorted-lengths)` expression in conjunction with the `and` expression. The `(car sorted-lengths)` expression returns a non-`nil` value so long as the list has at least one number within it, but returns `nil` if the list is empty. The `and` expression first evaluates the `(car sorted-lengths)` expression, and if it is `nil`, returns false *without* evaluating the `<` expression. But if the `(car sorted-lengths)` expression returns a non-`nil` value, the `and` expression evaluates the `<` expression, and returns that value as the value of the `and` expression.

This way, we avoid an error. (For information about `and`, see "The `kill-new` function", page 89.)

Here is a short test of the `defuns-per-range` function. First, evaluate the expression that binds (a shortened) `top-of-ranges` list to the list of values, then evaluate the expression for binding the `sorted-lengths` list, and then evaluate the `defuns-per-range` function.

```
;; (Shorter list than we will use later.)
(setq top-of-ranges
 '(110 120 130 140 150
   160 170 180 190 200))

(setq sorted-lengths
      '(85 86 110 116 122 129 154 176 179 200 265 300 300))

(defuns-per-range sorted-lengths top-of-ranges)
```
The list returned looks like this:
```
(2 2 2 0 0 1 0 2 0 0 4)
```
Indeed, there are two elements of the `sorted-lengths` list smaller than 110, two elements between 110 and 119, two elements between 120 and 129, and so on. There are four elements with a value of 200 or larger.

15 Readying a Graph

Our goal is to construct a graph showing the numbers of function definitions of various lengths in the Emacs lisp sources.

As a practical matter, if you were creating a graph, you would probably use a program such as `gnuplot` to do the job. (`gnuplot` is nicely integrated into GNU Emacs.) In this case, however, we create one from scratch, and in the process we will re-acquaint ourselves with some of what we learned before and learn more.

In this chapter, we will first write a simple graph printing function. This first definition will be a *prototype*, a rapidly written function that enables us to reconnoiter this unknown graph-making territory. We will discover dragons, or find that they are myth. After scouting the terrain, we will feel more confident and enhance the function to label the axes automatically.

Since Emacs is designed to be flexible and work with all kinds of terminals, including character-only terminals, the graph will need to be made from one of the typewriter symbols. An asterisk will do; as we enhance the graph-printing function, we can make the choice of symbol a user option.

We can call this function `graph-body-print`; it will take a `numbers-list` as its only argument. At this stage, we will not label the graph, but only print its body.

The `graph-body-print` function inserts a vertical column of asterisks for each element in the `numbers-list`. The height of each line is determined by the value of that element of the `numbers-list`.

Inserting columns is a repetitive act; that means that this function can be written either with a `while` loop or recursively.

Our first challenge is to discover how to print a column of asterisks. Usually, in Emacs, we print characters onto a screen horizontally, line by line, by typing. We have two routes we can follow: write our own column-insertion function or discover whether one exists in Emacs.

To see whether there is one in Emacs, we can use the *M-x apropos* command. This command is like the *C-h a* (`command-apropos`) command, except that the latter finds only those functions that are commands. The *M-x apropos* command lists all symbols that match a regular expression, including functions that are not interactive.

What we want to look for is some command that prints or inserts columns. Very likely, the name of the function will contain either the word "print" or the word "insert" or the word "column". Therefore, we can simply type *M-x apropos RET print\|insert\|column RET* and look at the result. On my system, this command once took quite some time, and then produced a list of 79 functions and variables. Now it does not take much time at all and produces a list of 211 functions and variables. Scanning down the list, the only function that looks as if it might do the job is `insert-rectangle`.

Indeed, this is the function we want; its documentation says:

```
insert-rectangle:
Insert text of RECTANGLE with upper left corner at point.
RECTANGLE's first line is inserted at point,
its second line is inserted at a point vertically under point, etc.
RECTANGLE should be a list of strings.
After this command, the mark is at the upper left corner
and point is at the lower right corner.
```

We can run a quick test, to make sure it does what we expect of it.

Here is the result of placing the cursor after the `insert-rectangle` expression and typing *C-u C-x C-e* (eval-last-sexp). The function inserts the strings '"first"', '"second"', and '"third"' at and below point. Also the function returns `nil`.

```
(insert-rectangle '("first" "second" "third"))first
                                               second
                                               thirdnil
```

Of course, we won't be inserting the text of the `insert-rectangle` expression itself into the buffer in which we are making the graph, but will call the function from our program. We shall, however, have to make sure that point is in the buffer at the place where the `insert-rectangle` function will insert its column of strings.

If you are reading this in Info, you can see how this works by switching to another buffer, such as the `*scratch*` buffer, placing point somewhere in the buffer, typing *M-:*, typing the `insert-rectangle` expression into the minibuffer at the prompt, and then typing RET. This causes Emacs to evaluate the expression in the minibuffer, but to use as the value of point the position of point in the `*scratch*` buffer. (*M-:* is the keybinding for `eval-expression`. Also, `nil` does not appear in the `*scratch*` buffer since the expression is evaluated in the minibuffer.)

We find when we do this that point ends up at the end of the last inserted line—that is to say, this function moves point as a side-effect. If we were to repeat the command, with point at this position, the next insertion would be below and to the right of the previous insertion. We don't want this! If we are going to make a bar graph, the columns need to be beside each other.

So we discover that each cycle of the column-inserting `while` loop must reposition point to the place we want it, and that place will be at the top, not the bottom, of the column. Moreover, we remember that when we print a graph, we do not expect all the columns to be the same height. This means that the top of each column may be at a different height from the previous one. We cannot simply reposition point to the same line each time, but moved over to the right—or perhaps we can...

We are planning to make the columns of the bar graph out of asterisks. The number of asterisks in the column is the number specified by the current element of the `numbers-list`. We need to construct a list of asterisks of the right length for each call to `insert-rectangle`. If this list consists solely of the requisite number of asterisks, then we will have to position point the right number of lines above the base for the graph to print correctly. This could be difficult.

Alternatively, if we can figure out some way to pass `insert-rectangle` a list of the same length each time, then we can place point on the same line each time, but move it over one column to the right for each new column. If we do this, however, some of the entries in the list passed to `insert-rectangle` must be blanks rather than asterisks. For example, if the maximum height of the graph is 5, but the height of the column is 3, then `insert-rectangle` requires an argument that looks like this:

```
(" " " " "*" "*" "*")
```

This last proposal is not so difficult, so long as we can determine the column height. There are two ways for us to specify the column height: we can arbitrarily state what it will be, which would work fine for graphs of that height; or we can search through the list of numbers and use the maximum height of the list as the maximum height of the graph. If the latter operation were difficult, then the former procedure would be easiest, but there is a function built into Emacs that determines the maximum of its arguments. We can use that function. The function is called `max` and it returns the largest of all its arguments, which must be numbers. Thus, for example,

```
(max  3 4 6 5 7 3)
```

returns 7. (A corresponding function called `min` returns the smallest of all its arguments.)

However, we cannot simply call `max` on the `numbers-list`; the `max` function expects numbers as its argument, not a list of numbers. Thus, the following expression,

```
(max  '(3 4 6 5 7 3))
```

produces the following error message;

```
Wrong type of argument:  number-or-marker-p, (3 4 6 5 7 3)
```

We need a function that passes a list of arguments to a function. This function is `apply`. This function applies its first argument (a function) to its remaining arguments, the last of which may be a list.

For example,

```
(apply 'max 3 4 7 3 '(4 8 5))
```

returns 8.

(Incidentally, I don't know how you would learn of this function without a book such as this. It is possible to discover other functions, like `search-forward` or `insert-rectangle`, by guessing at a part of their names and then using `apropos`. Even though its base in metaphor is clear—apply its first argument to the rest—I doubt a novice would come up with that particular word when using `apropos` or other aid. Of course, I could be wrong; after all, the function was first named by someone who had to invent it.)

The second and subsequent arguments to `apply` are optional, so we can use `apply` to call a function and pass the elements of a list to it, like this, which also returns 8:

```
(apply 'max '(4 8 5))
```

This latter way is how we will use `apply`. The `recursive-lengths-list-many-files` function returns a numbers' list to which we can apply `max` (we could also apply `max` to the sorted numbers' list; it does not matter whether the list is sorted or not.)

Hence, the operation for finding the maximum height of the graph is this:

```
(setq max-graph-height (apply 'max numbers-list))
```

Now we can return to the question of how to create a list of strings for a column of the graph. Told the maximum height of the graph and the number of asterisks that should appear in the column, the function should return a list of strings for the `insert-rectangle` command to insert.

Each column is made up of asterisks or blanks. Since the function is passed the value of the height of the column and the number of asterisks in the column, the number of blanks can be found by subtracting the number of asterisks from the height of the column. Given the number of blanks and the number of asterisks, two `while` loops can be used to construct the list:

```
;;; First version.
(defun column-of-graph (max-graph-height actual-height)
  "Return list of strings that is one column of a graph."
  (let ((insert-list nil)
        (number-of-top-blanks
         (- max-graph-height actual-height)))

    ;; Fill in asterisks.
    (while (> actual-height 0)
      (setq insert-list (cons "*" insert-list))
      (setq actual-height (1- actual-height)))

    ;; Fill in blanks.
    (while (> number-of-top-blanks 0)
      (setq insert-list (cons " " insert-list))
      (setq number-of-top-blanks
            (1- number-of-top-blanks)))

    ;; Return whole list.
    insert-list))
```

If you install this function and then evaluate the following expression you will see that it returns the list as desired:

```
(column-of-graph 5 3)
```
returns
```
(" " " " "*" "*" "*")
```

As written, `column-of-graph` contains a major flaw: the symbols used for the blank and for the marked entries in the column are hard-coded as a space and asterisk. This is fine for a prototype, but you, or another user, may wish to use other symbols. For example, in testing the graph function, you may want to use a period in place of the space, to make sure the point is being repositioned properly each time the `insert-rectangle` function is called; or you might want to substitute a '+' sign or other symbol for the asterisk. You might even want to make a graph-column that is more than one display column wide. The program should be more flexible. The way to do that is to replace the blank and the asterisk with two variables that we can call `graph-blank` and `graph-symbol` and define those variables separately.

Also, the documentation is not well written. These considerations lead us to the second version of the function:

```
(defvar graph-symbol "*"
  "String used as symbol in graph, usually an asterisk.")

(defvar graph-blank " "
  "String used as blank in graph, usually a blank space.
graph-blank must be the same number of columns wide
as graph-symbol.")
```

(For an explanation of `defvar`, see Section 8.5 "Initializing a Variable with `defvar`", page 95.)

```
;;; Second version.
(defun column-of-graph (max-graph-height actual-height)
  "Return MAX-GRAPH-HEIGHT strings; ACTUAL-HEIGHT are graph-symbols.

The graph-symbols are contiguous entries at the end
of the list.
The list will be inserted as one column of a graph.
The strings are either graph-blank or graph-symbol."

  (let ((insert-list nil)
        (number-of-top-blanks
         (- max-graph-height actual-height)))

    ;; Fill in graph-symbols.
    (while (> actual-height 0)
      (setq insert-list (cons graph-symbol insert-list))
      (setq actual-height (1- actual-height)))

    ;; Fill in graph-blanks.
    (while (> number-of-top-blanks 0)
      (setq insert-list (cons graph-blank insert-list))
      (setq number-of-top-blanks
            (1- number-of-top-blanks)))

    ;; Return whole list.
    insert-list))
```

If we wished, we could rewrite `column-of-graph` a third time to provide optionally for a line graph as well as for a bar graph. This would not be hard to do. One way to think of a line graph is that it is no more than a bar graph in which the part of each bar that is below the top is blank. To construct a column for a line graph, the function first constructs a list of blanks that is one shorter than the value, then it uses `cons` to attach a graph symbol to the list; then it uses `cons` again to attach the top blanks to the list.

It is easy to see how to write such a function, but since we don't need it, we will not do it. But the job could be done, and if it were done, it would be done with `column-of-graph`. Even more important, it is worth noting that few changes would have to be made anywhere else. The enhancement, if we ever wish to make it, is simple.

Now, finally, we come to our first actual graph printing function. This prints the body of a graph, not the labels for the vertical and horizontal axes, so we can call this `graph-body-print`.

15.1 The `graph-body-print` Function

After our preparation in the preceding section, the `graph-body-print` function is straightforward. The function will print column after column of asterisks and blanks, using the elements of a numbers' list to specify the number of asterisks in each column. This is a repetitive act, which means we can use a decrementing `while` loop or recursive function for the job. In this section, we will write the definition using a `while` loop.

The `column-of-graph` function requires the height of the graph as an argument, so we should determine and record that as a local variable.

This leads us to the following template for the `while` loop version of this function:

```
(defun graph-body-print (numbers-list)
  "documentation..."
  (let ((height  ...
         ...))

    (while numbers-list
      insert-columns-and-reposition-point
      (setq numbers-list (cdr numbers-list)))))
```

We need to fill in the slots of the template.

Clearly, we can use the `(apply 'max numbers-list)` expression to determine the height of the graph.

The `while` loop will cycle through the `numbers-list` one element at a time. As it is shortened by the `(setq numbers-list (cdr numbers-list))` expression, the CAR of each instance of the list is the value of the argument for `column-of-graph`.

At each cycle of the `while` loop, the `insert-rectangle` function inserts the list returned by `column-of-graph`. Since the `insert-rectangle` function moves point to the lower right of the inserted rectangle, we need to save the location of point at the time the rectangle is inserted, move back to that position after the rectangle is inserted, and then move horizontally to the next place from which `insert-rectangle` is called.

If the inserted columns are one character wide, as they will be if single blanks and asterisks are used, the repositioning command is simply `(forward-char 1)`; however, the width of a column may be greater than one. This means that the repositioning command should be written `(forward-char symbol-width)`. The `symbol-width` itself is the length of a `graph-blank` and can be found using the expression `(length graph-blank)`. The best place to bind the `symbol-width` variable to the value of the width of graph column is in the varlist of the `let` expression.

These considerations lead to the following function definition:

```
(defun graph-body-print (numbers-list)
  "Print a bar graph of the NUMBERS-LIST.
The numbers-list consists of the Y-axis values."

  (let ((height (apply 'max numbers-list))
        (symbol-width (length graph-blank))
        from-position)

    (while numbers-list
      (setq from-position (point))
      (insert-rectangle
       (column-of-graph height (car numbers-list)))
      (goto-char from-position)
      (forward-char symbol-width)
      ;; Draw graph column by column.
      (sit-for 0)
      (setq numbers-list (cdr numbers-list)))
    ;; Place point for X axis labels.
    (forward-line height)
    (insert "\n")
    ))
```

The one unexpected expression in this function is the (`sit-for 0`) expression in the `while` loop. This expression makes the graph printing operation more interesting to watch than it would be otherwise. The expression causes Emacs to *sit* or do nothing for a zero length of time and then redraw the screen. Placed here, it causes Emacs to redraw the screen column by column. Without it, Emacs would not redraw the screen until the function exits.

We can test `graph-body-print` with a short list of numbers.

1. Install `graph-symbol`, `graph-blank`, `column-of-graph`, which are in Chapter 15 "Readying a Graph", page 173, and `graph-body-print`.

2. Copy the following expression:

       (graph-body-print '(1 2 3 4 6 4 3 5 7 6 5 2 3))

3. Switch to the `*scratch*` buffer and place the cursor where you want the graph to start.

4. Type *M-*: (eval-expression).

5. Yank the `graph-body-print` expression into the minibuffer with *C-y* (yank).

6. Press RET to evaluate the `graph-body-print` expression.

Emacs will print a graph like this:

15.2 The `recursive-graph-body-print` Function

The `graph-body-print` function may also be written recursively. The recursive solution is divided into two parts: an outside wrapper that uses a `let` expression to determine the values of several variables that need only be found once, such as the maximum height of the graph, and an inside function that is called recursively to print the graph.

The wrapper is uncomplicated:

```
(defun recursive-graph-body-print (numbers-list)
  "Print a bar graph of the NUMBERS-LIST.
The numbers-list consists of the Y-axis values."
  (let ((height (apply 'max numbers-list))
        (symbol-width (length graph-blank))
        from-position)
    (recursive-graph-body-print-internal
     numbers-list
     height
     symbol-width)))
```

The recursive function is a little more difficult. It has four parts: the do-again-test, the printing code, the recursive call, and the next-step-expression. The do-again-test is a `when` expression that determines whether the `numbers-list` contains any remaining elements; if it does, the function prints one column of the graph using the printing code and calls itself again. The function calls itself again according to the value produced by the next-step-expression which causes the call to act on a shorter version of the `numbers-list`.

```
(defun recursive-graph-body-print-internal
  (numbers-list height symbol-width)
  "Print a bar graph.
Used within recursive-graph-body-print function."

  (when numbers-list
        (setq from-position (point))
        (insert-rectangle
         (column-of-graph height (car numbers-list)))
        (goto-char from-position)
        (forward-char symbol-width)
        (sit-for 0)        ; Draw graph column by column.
        (recursive-graph-body-print-internal
         (cdr numbers-list) height symbol-width)))
```

After installation, this expression can be tested; here is a sample:

```
(recursive-graph-body-print '(3 2 5 6 7 5 3 4 6 4 3 2 1))
```

Here is what `recursive-graph-body-print` produces:

```
              *
        **    *
        ****  *
        **** ***
      * ********
      ***********
      ************
```

Either of these two functions, `graph-body-print` or `recursive-graph-body-print`, create the body of a graph.

15.3 Need for Printed Axes

A graph needs printed axes, so you can orient yourself. For a do-once project, it may be reasonable to draw the axes by hand using Emacs's Picture mode; but a graph drawing function may be used more than once.

For this reason, I have written enhancements to the basic `print-graph-body` function that automatically print labels for the horizontal and vertical axes. Since the label printing functions do not contain much new material, I have placed their description in an appendix. See Appendix C "A Graph with Labeled Axes", page 218.

15.4 Exercise

Write a line graph version of the graph printing functions.

16 Your `.emacs` File

"You don't have to like Emacs to like it"—this seemingly paradoxical statement is the secret of GNU Emacs. The plain, out-of-the-box Emacs is a generic tool. Most people who use it customize it to suit themselves.

GNU Emacs is mostly written in Emacs Lisp; this means that by writing expressions in Emacs Lisp you can change or extend Emacs.

There are those who appreciate Emacs's default configuration. After all, Emacs starts you in C mode when you edit a C file, starts you in Fortran mode when you edit a Fortran file, and starts you in Fundamental mode when you edit an unadorned file. This all makes sense, if you do not know who is going to use Emacs. Who knows what a person hopes to do with an unadorned file? Fundamental mode is the right default for such a file, just as C mode is the right default for editing C code. (Enough programming languages have syntaxes that enable them to share or nearly share features, so C mode is now provided by CC mode, the C Collection.)

But when you do know who is going to use Emacs—you, yourself—then it makes sense to customize Emacs.

For example, I seldom want Fundamental mode when I edit an otherwise undistinguished file; I want Text mode. This is why I customize Emacs: so it suits me.

You can customize and extend Emacs by writing or adapting a `~/.emacs` file. This is your personal initialization file; its contents, written in Emacs Lisp, tell Emacs what to do.[1]

A `~/.emacs` file contains Emacs Lisp code. You can write this code yourself; or you can use Emacs's `customize` feature to write the code for you. You can combine your own expressions and auto-written Customize expressions in your `.emacs` file.

(I myself prefer to write my own expressions, except for those, particularly fonts, that I find easier to manipulate using the `customize` command. I combine the two methods.)

Most of this chapter is about writing expressions yourself. It describes a simple `.emacs` file; for more information, see Section "The Init File" in *The GNU Emacs Manual*, and Section "The Init File" in *The GNU Emacs Lisp Reference Manual*.

16.1 Site-wide Initialization Files

In addition to your personal initialization file, Emacs automatically loads various site-wide initialization files, if they exist. These have the same form as your `.emacs` file, but are loaded by everyone.

Two site-wide initialization files, `site-load.el` and `site-init.el`, are loaded into Emacs and then dumped if a dumped version of Emacs is created, as is most common. (Dumped copies of Emacs load more quickly. However, once a file is

---

[1]   You may also add `.el` to `~/.emacs` and call it a `~/.emacs.el` file. In the past, you were forbidden to type the extra keystrokes that the name `~/.emacs.el` requires, but now you may. The new format is consistent with the Emacs Lisp file naming conventions; the old format saves typing.

loaded and dumped, a change to it does not lead to a change in Emacs unless you load it yourself or re-dump Emacs. See Section "Building Emacs" in *The GNU Emacs Lisp Reference Manual*, and the `INSTALL` file.)

Three other site-wide initialization files are loaded automatically each time you start Emacs, if they exist. These are `site-start.el`, which is loaded *before* your `.emacs` file, and `default.el`, and the terminal type file, which are both loaded *after* your `.emacs` file.

Settings and definitions in your `.emacs` file will overwrite conflicting settings and definitions in a `site-start.el` file, if it exists; but the settings and definitions in a `default.el` or terminal type file will overwrite those in your `.emacs` file. (You can prevent interference from a terminal type file by setting `term-file-prefix` to `nil`. See Section 16.11 "A Simple Extension", page 192.)

The `INSTALL` file that comes in the distribution contains descriptions of the `site-init.el` and `site-load.el` files.

The `loadup.el`, `startup.el`, and `loaddefs.el` files control loading. These files are in the `lisp` directory of the Emacs distribution and are worth perusing.

The `loaddefs.el` file contains a good many suggestions as to what to put into your own `.emacs` file, or into a site-wide initialization file.

16.2 Specifying Variables using `defcustom`

You can specify variables using `defcustom` so that you and others can then use Emacs's `customize` feature to set their values. (You cannot use `customize` to write function definitions; but you can write `defuns` in your `.emacs` file. Indeed, you can write any Lisp expression in your `.emacs` file.)

The `customize` feature depends on the `defcustom` macro. Although you can use `defvar` or `setq` for variables that users set, the `defcustom` macro is designed for the job.

You can use your knowledge of `defvar` for writing the first three arguments for `defcustom`. The first argument to `defcustom` is the name of the variable. The second argument is the variable's initial value, if any; and this value is set only if the value has not already been set. The third argument is the documentation.

The fourth and subsequent arguments to `defcustom` specify types and options; these are not featured in `defvar`. (These arguments are optional.)

Each of these arguments consists of a keyword followed by a value. Each keyword starts with the colon character ':'.

For example, the customizable user option variable `text-mode-hook` looks like this:

```
(defcustom text-mode-hook nil
  "Normal hook run when entering Text mode and many related modes."
  :type 'hook
  :options '(turn-on-auto-fill flyspell-mode)
  :group 'wp)
```

The name of the variable is `text-mode-hook`; it has no default value; and its documentation string tells you what it does.

The `:type` keyword tells Emacs the kind of data to which `text-mode-hook` should be set and how to display the value in a Customization buffer.

The `:options` keyword specifies a suggested list of values for the variable. Usually, `:options` applies to a hook. The list is only a suggestion; it is not exclusive; a person who sets the variable may set it to other values; the list shown following the `:options` keyword is intended to offer convenient choices to a user.

Finally, the `:group` keyword tells the Emacs Customization command in which group the variable is located. This tells where to find it.

The `defcustom` macro recognizes more than a dozen keywords. For more information, see Section "Writing Customization Definitions" in *The GNU Emacs Lisp Reference Manual*.

Consider `text-mode-hook` as an example.

There are two ways to customize this variable. You can use the customization command or write the appropriate expressions yourself.

Using the customization command, you can type:

```
M-x customize
```

and find that the group for editing files of text is called "Text". Enter that group. Text Mode Hook is the first member. You can click on its various options, such as `turn-on-auto-fill`, to set the values. After you click on the button to

```
Save for Future Sessions
```

Emacs will write an expression into your `.emacs` file. It will look like this:

```
(custom-set-variables
  ;; custom-set-variables was added by Custom.
  ;; If you edit it by hand, you could mess it up, so be careful.
  ;; Your init file should contain only one such instance.
  ;; If there is more than one, they won't work right.
 '(text-mode-hook (quote (turn-on-auto-fill text-mode-hook-identify))))
```

(The `text-mode-hook-identify` function tells `toggle-text-mode-auto-fill` which buffers are in Text mode. It comes on automatically.)

The `custom-set-variables` function works somewhat differently than a `setq`. While I have never learned the differences, I modify the `custom-set-variables` expressions in my `.emacs` file by hand: I make the changes in what appears to me to be a reasonable manner and have not had any problems. Others prefer to use the Customization command and let Emacs do the work for them.

Another `custom-set-...` function is `custom-set-faces`. This function sets the various font faces. Over time, I have set a considerable number of faces. Some of the time, I re-set them using `customize`; other times, I simply edit the `custom-set-faces` expression in my `.emacs` file itself.

The second way to customize your `text-mode-hook` is to set it yourself in your `.emacs` file using code that has nothing to do with the `custom-set-...` functions.

When you do this, and later use `customize`, you will see a message that says

`CHANGED outside Customize; operating on it here may be unreliable.`

This message is only a warning. If you click on the button to

`Save for Future Sessions`

Emacs will write a `custom-set-...` expression near the end of your `.emacs` file that will be evaluated after your hand-written expression. It will, therefore, overrule your hand-written expression. No harm will be done. When you do this, however, be careful to remember which expression is active; if you forget, you may confuse yourself.

So long as you remember where the values are set, you will have no trouble. In any event, the values are always set in your initialization file, which is usually called `.emacs`.

I myself use `customize` for hardly anything. Mostly, I write expressions myself.

Incidentally, to be more complete concerning defines: `defsubst` defines an inline function. The syntax is just like that of `defun`. `defconst` defines a symbol as a constant. The intent is that neither programs nor users should ever change a value set by `defconst`. (You can change it; the value set is a variable; but please do not.)

16.3 Beginning a `.emacs` File

When you start Emacs, it loads your `.emacs` file unless you tell it not to by specifying '-q' on the command line. (The `emacs -q` command gives you a plain, out-of-the-box Emacs.)

A `.emacs` file contains Lisp expressions. Often, these are no more than expressions to set values; sometimes they are function definitions.

See Section "The Init File `~/.emacs`" in *The GNU Emacs Manual*, for a short description of initialization files.

This chapter goes over some of the same ground, but is a walk among extracts from a complete, long-used `.emacs` file—my own.

The first part of the file consists of comments: reminders to myself. By now, of course, I remember these things, but when I started, I did not.

```
;;;; Bob's .emacs file
; Robert J. Chassell
; 26 September 1985
```

Look at that date! I started this file a long time ago. I have been adding to it ever since.

```
; Each section in this file is introduced by a
; line beginning with four semicolons; and each
; entry is introduced by a line beginning with
; three semicolons.
```

This describes the usual conventions for comments in Emacs Lisp. Everything on a line that follows a semicolon is a comment. Two, three, and four semicolons are used as subsection and section markers. (See Section "Comments" in *The GNU Emacs Lisp Reference Manual*, for more about comments.)

```
;;;; The Help Key
; Control-h is the help key;
; after typing control-h, type a letter to
; indicate the subject about which you want help.
; For an explanation of the help facility,
; type control-h two times in a row.
```

Just remember: type *C-h* two times for help.

```
; To find out about any mode, type control-h m
; while in that mode.  For example, to find out
; about mail mode, enter mail mode and then type
; control-h m.
```

"Mode help", as I call this, is very helpful. Usually, it tells you all you need to know.

Of course, you don't need to include comments like these in your .emacs file. I included them in mine because I kept forgetting about Mode help or the conventions for comments—but I was able to remember to look here to remind myself.

16.4 Text and Auto Fill Mode

Now we come to the part that turns on Text mode and Auto Fill mode.

```
;;; Text mode and Auto Fill mode
;; The next two lines put Emacs into Text mode
;; and Auto Fill mode, and are for writers who
;; want to start writing prose rather than code.
(setq-default major-mode 'text-mode)
(add-hook 'text-mode-hook 'turn-on-auto-fill)
```

Here is the first part of this .emacs file that does something besides remind a forgetful human!

The first of the two lines in parentheses tells Emacs to turn on Text mode when you find a file, *unless* that file should go into some other mode, such as C mode.

When Emacs reads a file, it looks at the extension to the file name, if any. (The extension is the part that comes after a '.'.) If the file ends with a '.c' or '.h' extension then Emacs turns on C mode. Also, Emacs looks at first nonblank line of the file; if the line says '-*- C -*-', Emacs turns on C mode. Emacs possesses a list of extensions and specifications that it uses automatically. In addition, Emacs looks near the last page for a per-buffer, local variables list, if any.

See sections "How Major Modes are Chosen" and "Local Variables in Files" in *The GNU Emacs Manual*.

Now, back to the .emacs file.

Here is the line again; how does it work?

```
(setq major-mode 'text-mode)
```

This line is a short, but complete Emacs Lisp expression.

We are already familiar with `setq`. It sets the following variable, `major-mode`, to the subsequent value, which is `text-mode`. The single-quote before `text-mode` tells Emacs to deal directly with the `text-mode` symbol, not with whatever it might stand for. See Section 1.9 "Setting the Value of a Variable", page 16, for a reminder of how `setq` works. The main point is that there is no difference between the procedure you use to set a value in your `.emacs` file and the procedure you use anywhere else in Emacs.

Here is the next line:

```
(add-hook 'text-mode-hook 'turn-on-auto-fill)
```

In this line, the `add-hook` command adds `turn-on-auto-fill` to the variable.

`turn-on-auto-fill` is the name of a program, that, you guessed it!, turns on Auto Fill mode.

Every time Emacs turns on Text mode, Emacs runs the commands hooked onto Text mode. So every time Emacs turns on Text mode, Emacs also turns on Auto Fill mode.

In brief, the first line causes Emacs to enter Text mode when you edit a file, unless the file name extension, a first non-blank line, or local variables to tell Emacs otherwise.

Text mode among other actions, sets the syntax table to work conveniently for writers. In Text mode, Emacs considers an apostrophe as part of a word like a letter; but Emacs does not consider a period or a space as part of a word. Thus, *M-f* moves you over 'it's'. On the other hand, in C mode, *M-f* stops just after the 't' of 'it's'.

The second line causes Emacs to turn on Auto Fill mode when it turns on Text mode. In Auto Fill mode, Emacs automatically breaks a line that is too wide and brings the excessively wide part of the line down to the next line. Emacs breaks lines between words, not within them.

When Auto Fill mode is turned off, lines continue to the right as you type them. Depending on how you set the value of `truncate-lines`, the words you type either disappear off the right side of the screen, or else are shown, in a rather ugly and unreadable manner, as a continuation line on the screen.

In addition, in this part of my `.emacs` file, I tell the Emacs fill commands to insert two spaces after a colon:

```
(setq colon-double-space t)
```

16.5 Mail Aliases

Here is a `setq` that turns on mail aliases, along with more reminders.

```
;;; Mail mode
; To enter mail mode, type 'C-x m'
; To enter RMAIL (for reading mail),
; type 'M-x rmail'
(setq mail-aliases t)
```

This `setq` command sets the value of the variable `mail-aliases` to `t`. Since `t` means true, the line says, in effect, "Yes, use mail aliases."

Mail aliases are convenient short names for long email addresses or for lists of email addresses. The file where you keep your aliases is `~/.mailrc`. You write an alias like this:

```
alias geo george@foobar.wiz.edu
```

When you write a message to George, address it to 'geo'; the mailer will automatically expand 'geo' to the full address.

16.6 Indent Tabs Mode

By default, Emacs inserts tabs in place of multiple spaces when it formats a region. (For example, you might indent many lines of text all at once with the `indent-region` command.) Tabs look fine on a terminal or with ordinary printing, but they produce badly indented output when you use TeX or Texinfo since TeX ignores tabs.

The following turns off Indent Tabs mode:

```
;;; Prevent Extraneous Tabs
(setq-default indent-tabs-mode nil)
```

Note that this line uses `setq-default` rather than the `setq` command that we have seen before. The `setq-default` command sets values only in buffers that do not have their own local values for the variable.

See sections "Tabs vs. Spaces" and "Local Variables in Files" in *The GNU Emacs Manual*.

16.7 Some Keybindings

Now for some personal keybindings:

```
;;; Compare windows
(global-set-key "\C-cw" 'compare-windows)
```

`compare-windows` is a nifty command that compares the text in your current window with text in the next window. It makes the comparison by starting at point in each window, moving over text in each window as far as they match. I use this command all the time.

This also shows how to set a key globally, for all modes.

The command is `global-set-key`. It is followed by the keybinding. In a `.emacs` file, the keybinding is written as shown: \C-c stands for Control-C, which means to press the control key and the `c` key at the same time. The `w` means to press the `w` key. The keybinding is surrounded by double quotation marks. In documentation, you would write this as *C-c w*. (If you were binding a META key, such as *M-c*, rather than a CTRL key, you would write \M-c in your `.emacs` file. See Section "Rebinding Keys in Your Init File" in *The GNU Emacs Manual*, for details.)

The command invoked by the keys is `compare-windows`. Note that `compare-windows` is preceded by a single-quote; otherwise, Emacs would first try to evaluate the symbol to determine its value.

These three things, the double quotation marks, the backslash before the 'C', and the single-quote are necessary parts of keybinding that I tend to forget. Fortunately, I have come to remember that I should look at my existing `.emacs` file, and adapt what is there.

As for the keybinding itself: *C-c w*. This combines the prefix key, *C-c*, with a single character, in this case, *w*. This set of keys, *C-c* followed by a single character, is strictly reserved for individuals' own use. (I call these *own* keys, since these are for my own use.) You should always be able to create such a keybinding for your own use without stomping on someone else's keybinding. If you ever write an extension to Emacs, please avoid taking any of these keys for public use. Create a key like *C-c C-w* instead. Otherwise, we will run out of own keys.

Here is another keybinding, with a comment:

```
;;; Keybinding for 'occur'
; I use occur a lot, so let's bind it to a key:
(global-set-key "\C-co" 'occur)
```

The `occur` command shows all the lines in the current buffer that contain a match for a regular expression. Matching lines are shown in a buffer called `*Occur*`. That buffer serves as a menu to jump to occurrences.

Here is how to unbind a key, so it does not work:

```
;;; Unbind 'C-x f'
(global-unset-key "\C-xf")
```

There is a reason for this unbinding: I found I inadvertently typed *C-x f* when I meant to type *C-x C-f*. Rather than find a file, as I intended, I accidentally set the width for filled text, almost always to a width I did not want. Since I hardly ever reset my default width, I simply unbound the key.

The following rebinds an existing key:

```
;;; Rebind 'C-x C-b' for 'buffer-menu'
(global-set-key "\C-x\C-b" 'buffer-menu)
```

By default, *C-x C-b* runs the `list-buffers` command. This command lists your buffers in *another* window. Since I almost always want to do something in that window, I prefer the `buffer-menu` command, which not only lists the buffers, but moves point into that window.

16.8 Keymaps

Emacs uses *keymaps* to record which keys call which commands. When you use `global-set-key` to set the keybinding for a single command in all parts of Emacs, you are specifying the keybinding in `current-global-map`.

Specific modes, such as C mode or Text mode, have their own keymaps; the mode-specific keymaps override the global map that is shared by all buffers.

The `global-set-key` function binds, or rebinds, the global keymap. For example, the following binds the key *C-x C-b* to the function `buffer-menu`:

```
(global-set-key "\C-x\C-b" 'buffer-menu)
```

Mode-specific keymaps are bound using the `define-key` function, which takes a specific keymap as an argument, as well as the key and the command. For example, my `.emacs` file contains the following expression to bind the `texinfo-insert-@group` command to *C-c C-c g*:

```
(define-key texinfo-mode-map "\C-c\C-cg" 'texinfo-insert-@group)
```

The `texinfo-insert-@group` function itself is a little extension to Texinfo mode that inserts '@group' into a Texinfo file. I use this command all the time and prefer to type the three strokes *C-c C-c g* rather than the six strokes *@ g r o u p*. ('@group' and its matching '@end group' are commands that keep all enclosed text together on one page; many multi-line examples in this book are surrounded by '@group ... @end group'.)

Here is the `texinfo-insert-@group` function definition:

```
(defun texinfo-insert-@group ()
  "Insert the string @group in a Texinfo buffer."
  (interactive)
  (beginning-of-line)
  (insert "@group\n"))
```

(Of course, I could have used Abbrev mode to save typing, rather than write a function to insert a word; but I prefer key strokes consistent with other Texinfo mode key bindings.)

You will see numerous `define-key` expressions in `loaddefs.el` as well as in the various mode libraries, such as `cc-mode.el` and `lisp-mode.el`.

See Section "Customizing Key Bindings" in *The GNU Emacs Manual*, and Section "Keymaps" in *The GNU Emacs Lisp Reference Manual*, for more information about keymaps.

16.9 Loading Files

Many people in the GNU Emacs community have written extensions to Emacs. As time goes by, these extensions are often included in new releases. For example, the Calendar and Diary packages are now part of the standard GNU Emacs, as is Calc.

You can use a `load` command to evaluate a complete file and thereby install all the functions and variables in the file into Emacs. For example:

```
(load "~/emacs/slowsplit")
```

This evaluates, i.e., loads, the `slowsplit.el` file or if it exists, the faster, byte compiled `slowsplit.elc` file from the `emacs` sub-directory of your home directory. The file contains the function `split-window-quietly`, which John Robinson wrote in 1989.

The `split-window-quietly` function splits a window with the minimum of redisplay. I installed it in 1989 because it worked well with the slow 1200 baud terminals I was then using. Nowadays, I only occasionally come across such a slow connection, but I continue to use the function because I like the way it leaves the bottom half of a buffer in the lower of the new windows and the top half in the upper window.

To replace the key binding for the default `split-window-vertically`, you must also unset that key and bind the keys to `split-window-quietly`, like this:

```
(global-unset-key "\C-x2")
(global-set-key "\C-x2" 'split-window-quietly)
```

If you load many extensions, as I do, then instead of specifying the exact location of the extension file, as shown above, you can specify that directory as part of Emacs's `load-path`. Then, when Emacs loads a file, it will search that directory as well as its default list of directories. (The default list is specified in `paths.h` when Emacs is built.)

The following command adds your `~/emacs` directory to the existing load path:

```
;;; Emacs Load Path
(setq load-path (cons "~/emacs" load-path))
```

Incidentally, `load-library` is an interactive interface to the `load` function. The complete function looks like this:

```
(defun load-library (library)
  "Load the Emacs Lisp library named LIBRARY.
This is an interface to the function `load'.  LIBRARY is searched
for in `load-path', both with and without `load-suffixes' (as
well as `load-file-rep-suffixes').

See Info node `(emacs)Lisp Libraries' for more details.
See `load-file' for a different interface to `load'."
  (interactive
   (list (completing-read "Load library: "
                          (apply-partially 'locate-file-completion-table
                                           load-path
                                           (get-load-suffixes)))))
  (load library))
```

The name of the function, `load-library`, comes from the use of "library" as a conventional synonym for "file". The source for the `load-library` command is in the `files.el` library.

Another interactive command that does a slightly different job is `load-file`. See Section "Libraries of Lisp Code for Emacs" in *The GNU Emacs Manual*, for information on the distinction between `load-library` and this command.

16.10 Autoloading

Instead of installing a function by loading the file that contains it, or by evaluating the function definition, you can make the function available but not actually install it until it is first called. This is called *autoloading*.

When you execute an autoloaded function, Emacs automatically evaluates the file that contains the definition, and then calls the function.

Emacs starts quicker with autoloaded functions, since their libraries are not loaded right away; but you need to wait a moment when you first use such a function, while its containing file is evaluated.

Rarely used functions are frequently autoloaded. The `loaddefs.el` library contains thousands of autoloaded functions, from `5x5` to `zone`. Of course, you may come to use a rare function frequently. When you do, you should load that function's file with a `load` expression in your `.emacs` file.

In my `.emacs` file, I load 14 libraries that contain functions that would otherwise be autoloaded. (Actually, it would have been better to include these files in my dumped Emacs, but I forgot. See Section "Building Emacs" in *The GNU Emacs Lisp Reference Manual*, and the `INSTALL` file for more about dumping.)

You may also want to include autoloaded expressions in your `.emacs` file. `autoload` is a built-in function that takes up to five arguments, the final three of which are optional. The first argument is the name of the function to be autoloaded; the second is the name of the file to be loaded. The third argument is documentation for the function, and the fourth tells whether the function can be called interactively. The fifth argument tells what type of object—autoload can handle a keymap or macro as well as a function (the default is a function).

Here is a typical example:

```
(autoload 'html-helper-mode
  "html-helper-mode" "Edit HTML documents" t)
```

(html-helper-mode is an older alternative to html-mode, which is a standard part of the distribution.)

This expression autoloads the html-helper-mode function. It takes it from the html-helper-mode.el file (or from the byte compiled version html-helper-mode.elc, if that exists.) The file must be located in a directory specified by load-path. The documentation says that this is a mode to help you edit documents written in the HyperText Markup Language. You can call this mode interactively by typing *M-x html-helper-mode*. (You need to duplicate the function's regular documentation in the autoload expression because the regular function is not yet loaded, so its documentation is not available.)

See Section "Autoload" in *The GNU Emacs Lisp Reference Manual*, for more information.

16.11 A Simple Extension: line-to-top-of-window

Here is a simple extension to Emacs that moves the line point is on to the top of the window. I use this all the time, to make text easier to read.

You can put the following code into a separate file and then load it from your .emacs file, or you can include it within your .emacs file.

Here is the definition:

```
;;; Line to top of window;
;;; replace three keystroke sequence  C-u 0 C-l
(defun line-to-top-of-window ()
  "Move the line point is on to top of window."
  (interactive)
  (recenter 0))
```

Now for the keybinding.

Nowadays, function keys as well as mouse button events and non-ASCII characters are written within square brackets, without quotation marks. (In Emacs version 18 and before, you had to write different function key bindings for each different make of terminal.)

I bind line-to-top-of-window to my F6 function key like this:

```
(global-set-key [f6] 'line-to-top-of-window)
```

For more information, see Section "Rebinding Keys in Your Init File" in *The GNU Emacs Manual*.

If you run two versions of GNU Emacs, such as versions 22 and 23, and use one .emacs file, you can select which code to evaluate with the following conditional:

```
(cond
 ((= 22 emacs-major-version)
  ;; evaluate version 22 code
  ( ... ))
 ((= 23 emacs-major-version)
  ;; evaluate version 23 code
  ( ... )))
```

For example, recent versions blink their cursors by default. I hate such blinking, as well as other features, so I placed the following in my .emacs file[2]:

```
(when (>= emacs-major-version 21)
  (blink-cursor-mode 0)
  ;; Insert newline when you press 'C-n' (next-line)
  ;; at the end of the buffer
  (setq next-line-add-newlines t)
  ;; Turn on image viewing
  (auto-image-file-mode t)
  ;; Turn on menu bar (this bar has text)
  ;; (Use numeric argument to turn on)
  (menu-bar-mode 1)
  ;; Turn off tool bar (this bar has icons)
  ;; (Use numeric argument to turn on)
  (tool-bar-mode nil)
  ;; Turn off tooltip mode for tool bar
  ;; (This mode causes icon explanations to pop up)
  ;; (Use numeric argument to turn on)
  (tooltip-mode nil)
  ;; If tooltips turned on, make tips appear promptly
  (setq tooltip-delay 0.1)  ; default is 0.7 second
  )
```

16.12 X11 Colors

You can specify colors when you use Emacs with the MIT X Windowing system.

I dislike the default colors and specify my own.

---

[2] When I start instances of Emacs that do not load my .emacs file or any site file, I also turn off blinking:

```
emacs -q --no-site-file -eval '(blink-cursor-mode nil)'
```

Or nowadays, using an even more sophisticated set of options,

```
emacs -Q -D
```

Here are the expressions in my `.emacs` file that set values:

```
;; Set cursor color
(set-cursor-color "white")

;; Set mouse color
(set-mouse-color "white")

;; Set foreground and background
(set-foreground-color "white")
(set-background-color "darkblue")

;;; Set highlighting colors for isearch and drag
(set-face-foreground 'highlight "white")
(set-face-background 'highlight "blue")

(set-face-foreground 'region "cyan")
(set-face-background 'region "blue")

(set-face-foreground 'secondary-selection "skyblue")
(set-face-background 'secondary-selection "darkblue")

;; Set calendar highlighting colors
(add-hook 'calendar-load-hook
      (lambda ()
        (set-face-foreground 'diary-face   "skyblue")
        (set-face-background 'holiday-face "slate blue")
        (set-face-foreground 'holiday-face "white")))
```

The various shades of blue soothe my eye and prevent me from seeing the screen flicker.

Alternatively, I could have set my specifications in various X initialization files. For example, I could set the foreground, background, cursor, and pointer (i.e., mouse) colors in my `~/.Xresources` file like this:

```
Emacs*foreground:   white
Emacs*background:   darkblue
Emacs*cursorColor:  white
Emacs*pointerColor: white
```

In any event, since it is not part of Emacs, I set the root color of my X window in my `~/.xinitrc` file, like this[3]:

```
xsetroot -solid Navy -fg white &
```

---

[3] I also run more modern window managers, such as Enlightenment, Gnome, or KDE; in those cases, I often specify an image rather than a plain color.

16.13 Miscellaneous Settings for a .emacs File

Here are a few miscellaneous settings:

— Set the shape and color of the mouse cursor:

```
; Cursor shapes are defined in
; '/usr/include/X11/cursorfont.h';
; for example, the 'target' cursor is number 128;
; the 'top_left_arrow' cursor is number 132.

(let ((mpointer (x-get-resource "*mpointer"
                                "*emacs*mpointer")))
  ;; If you have not set your mouse pointer
  ;;     then set it, otherwise leave as is:
  (if (eq mpointer nil)
      (setq mpointer "132")) ; top_left_arrow
  (setq x-pointer-shape (string-to-int mpointer))
  (set-mouse-color "white"))
```

— Or you can set the values of a variety of features in an alist, like this:

```
(setq-default
 default-frame-alist
 '((cursor-color . "white")
   (mouse-color . "white")
   (foreground-color . "white")
   (background-color . "DodgerBlue4")
   ;; (cursor-type . bar)
   (cursor-type . box)
   (tool-bar-lines . 0)
   (menu-bar-lines . 1)
   (width . 80)
   (height . 58)
   (font .
         "-Misc-Fixed-Medium-R-Normal--20-200-75-75-C-100-ISO8859-1")
   ))
```

— Convert *CTRL-h* into DEL and DEL into *CTRL-h*.
(Some older keyboards needed this, although I have not seen the problem recently.)

```
;; Translate 'C-h' to <DEL>.
; (keyboard-translate ?\C-h ?\C-?)

;; Translate <DEL> to 'C-h'.
(keyboard-translate ?\C-? ?\C-h)
```

— Turn off a blinking cursor!

```
(if (fboundp 'blink-cursor-mode)
    (blink-cursor-mode -1))
```

or start GNU Emacs with the command emacs -nbc.

— When using `grep`
  '-i' Ignore case distinctions
  '-n' Prefix each line of output with line number
  '-H' Print the filename for each match.
  '-e' Protect patterns beginning with a hyphen character, '-'

    ```
    (setq grep-command "grep -i -nH -e ")
    ```

— Find an existing buffer, even if it has a different name
  This avoids problems with symbolic links.

    ```
    (setq find-file-existing-other-name t)
    ```

— Set your language environment and default input method

    ```
    (set-language-environment "latin-1")
    ;; Remember you can enable or disable multilingual text input
    ;; with the toggle-input-method' (C-\) command
    (setq default-input-method "latin-1-prefix")
    ```

  If you want to write with Chinese GB characters, set this instead:

    ```
    (set-language-environment "Chinese-GB")
    (setq default-input-method "chinese-tonepy")
    ```

Fixing Unpleasant Key Bindings

Some systems bind keys unpleasantly. Sometimes, for example, the CTRL key appears in an awkward spot rather than at the far left of the home row.

Usually, when people fix these sorts of keybindings, they do not change their `~/.emacs` file. Instead, they bind the proper keys on their consoles with the `loadkeys` or `install-keymap` commands in their boot script and then include `xmodmap` commands in their `.xinitrc` or `.Xsession` file for X Windows.

For a boot script:

    ```
    loadkeys /usr/share/keymaps/i386/qwerty/emacs2.kmap.gz
    ```

or

    ```
    install-keymap emacs2
    ```

For a `.xinitrc` or `.Xsession` file when the Caps Lock key is at the far left of the home row:

    ```
    # Bind the key labeled 'Caps Lock' to 'Control'
    # (Such a broken user interface suggests that keyboard manufacturers
    # think that computers are typewriters from 1885.)

    xmodmap -e "clear Lock"
    xmodmap -e "add Control = Caps_Lock"
    ```

In a `.xinitrc` or `.Xsession` file, to convert an `ALT` key to a `META` key:

```
# Some ill designed keyboards have a key labeled ALT and no Meta
xmodmap -e "keysym Alt_L = Meta_L Alt_L"
```

16.14 A Modified Mode Line

Finally, a feature I really like: a modified mode line.

When I work over a network, I forget which machine I am using. Also, I tend to I lose track of where I am, and which line point is on.

So I reset my mode line to look like this:

```
-:-- foo.texi   rattlesnake:/home/bob/  Line 1  (Texinfo Fill) Top
```

I am visiting a file called `foo.texi`, on my machine `rattlesnake` in my `/home/bob` buffer. I am on line 1, in Texinfo mode, and am at the top of the buffer.

My `.emacs` file has a section that looks like this:

```
;; Set a Mode Line that tells me which machine, which directory,
;; and which line I am on, plus the other customary information.
(setq-default mode-line-format
 (quote
  (#("-" 0 1
     (help-echo
      "mouse-1: select window, mouse-2: delete others ..."))
   mode-line-mule-info
   mode-line-modified
   mode-line-frame-identification
   "    "
   mode-line-buffer-identification
   "    "
   (:eval (substring
           (system-name) 0 (string-match "\\..+" (system-name))))
   ":"
   default-directory
   #(" " 0 1
     (help-echo
      "mouse-1: select window, mouse-2: delete others ..."))
   (line-number-mode " Line %l ")
   global-mode-string
   #("   %[(" 0 6
     (help-echo
      "mouse-1: select window, mouse-2: delete others ..."))
   (:eval (mode-line-mode-name))
   mode-line-process
   minor-mode-alist
   #("%n" 0 2 (help-echo "mouse-2: widen" local-map (keymap ...)))
   ")%] "
   (-3 . "%P")
   ;;    "-%-"
   )))
```

Here, I redefine the default mode line. Most of the parts are from the original; but I make a few changes. I set the *default* mode line format so as to permit various modes, such as Info, to override it.

Many elements in the list are self-explanatory: `mode-line-modified` is a variable that tells whether the buffer has been modified, `mode-name` tells the name of the mode, and so on. However, the format looks complicated because of two features we have not discussed.

The first string in the mode line is a dash or hyphen, '-'. In the old days, it would have been specified simply as `"-"`. But nowadays, Emacs can add properties to a string, such as highlighting or, as in this case, a help feature. If you place your mouse cursor over the hyphen, some help information appears (By default, you must wait seven-tenths of a second before the information appears. You can change that timing by changing the value of `tooltip-delay`.)

The new string format has a special syntax:

```
#("-" 0 1 (help-echo "mouse-1: select window, ..."))
```

The `#(` begins a list. The first element of the list is the string itself, just one '-'. The second and third elements specify the range over which the fourth element applies. A range starts *after* a character, so a zero means the range starts just before the first character; a 1 means that the range ends just after the first character. The third element is the property for the range. It consists of a property list, a property name, in this case, '`help-echo`', followed by a value, in this case, a string. The second, third, and fourth elements of this new string format can be repeated.

See Section "Text Properties" in *The GNU Emacs Lisp Reference Manual*, and see Section "Mode Line Format" in *The GNU Emacs Lisp Reference Manual*, for more information.

`mode-line-buffer-identification` displays the current buffer name. It is a list beginning `(#("%12b" 0 4 ....` The `#(` begins the list.

The '`"%12b"`' displays the current buffer name, using the `buffer-name` function with which we are familiar; the '`12`' specifies the maximum number of characters that will be displayed. When a name has fewer characters, whitespace is added to fill out to this number. (Buffer names can and often should be longer than 12 characters; this length works well in a typical 80 column wide window.)

`:eval` says to evaluate the following form and use the result as a string to display. In this case, the expression displays the first component of the full system name. The end of the first component is a '`.`' (period), so I use the `string-match` function to tell me the length of the first component. The substring from the zeroth character to that length is the name of the machine.

This is the expression:

```
(:eval (substring
         (system-name) 0 (string-match "\\..+" (system-name))))
```

'`%[`' and '`%]`' cause a pair of square brackets to appear for each recursive editing level. '`%n`' says "Narrow" when narrowing is in effect. '`%P`' tells you the percentage of the buffer that is above the bottom of the window, or "Top", "Bottom", or "All". (A lower case '`p`' tell you the percentage above the *top* of the window.) '`%-`' inserts enough dashes to fill out the line.

Remember, you don't have to like Emacs to like it—your own Emacs can have different colors, different commands, and different keys than a default Emacs.

On the other hand, if you want to bring up a plain out-of-the-box Emacs, with no customization, type:

```
emacs -q
```

This will start an Emacs that does *not* load your `~/.emacs` initialization file. A plain, default Emacs. Nothing more.

17 Debugging

GNU Emacs has two debuggers, `debug` and `edebug`. The first is built into the internals of Emacs and is always with you; the second requires that you instrument a function before you can use it.

Both debuggers are described extensively in Section "Debugging Lisp Programs" in *The GNU Emacs Lisp Reference Manual*. In this chapter, I will walk through a short example of each.

17.1 debug

Suppose you have written a function definition that is intended to return the sum of the numbers 1 through a given number. (This is the `triangle` function discussed earlier. See "Example with Decrementing Counter", page 112, for a discussion.)

However, your function definition has a bug. You have mistyped '1=' for '1-'. Here is the broken definition:

```
(defun triangle-bugged (number)
  "Return sum of numbers 1 through NUMBER inclusive."
  (let ((total 0))
    (while (> number 0)
      (setq total (+ total number))
      (setq number (1= number)))       ; Error here.
    total))
```

If you are reading this in Info, you can evaluate this definition in the normal fashion. You will see `triangle-bugged` appear in the echo area.

Now evaluate the `triangle-bugged` function with an argument of 4:

```
(triangle-bugged 4)
```

In a recent GNU Emacs, you will create and enter a `*Backtrace*` buffer that says:

```
---------- Buffer: *Backtrace* ----------
Debugger entered--Lisp error: (void-function 1=)
  (1= number)
  (setq number (1= number))
  (while (> number 0) (setq total (+ total number))
        (setq number (1= number)))
  (let ((total 0)) (while (> number 0) (setq total ...)
    (setq number ...)) total)
  triangle-bugged(4)
  eval((triangle-bugged 4))
  eval-last-sexp-1(nil)
  eval-last-sexp(nil)
  call-interactively(eval-last-sexp)
---------- Buffer: *Backtrace* ----------
```

(I have reformatted this example slightly; the debugger does not fold long lines. As usual, you can quit the debugger by typing *q* in the `*Backtrace*` buffer.)

In practice, for a bug as simple as this, the Lisp error line will tell you what you need to know to correct the definition. The function `1=` is void.

However, suppose you are not quite certain what is going on? You can read the complete backtrace.

In this case, you need to run a recent GNU Emacs, which automatically starts the debugger that puts you in the *Backtrace* buffer; or else, you need to start the debugger manually as described below.

Read the *Backtrace* buffer from the bottom up; it tells you what Emacs did that led to the error. Emacs made an interactive call to `C-x C-e` (`eval-last-sexp`), which led to the evaluation of the `triangle-bugged` expression. Each line above tells you what the Lisp interpreter evaluated next.

The third line from the top of the buffer is

```
(setq number (1= number))
```

Emacs tried to evaluate this expression; in order to do so, it tried to evaluate the inner expression shown on the second line from the top:

```
(1= number)
```

This is where the error occurred; as the top line says:

```
Debugger entered--Lisp error: (void-function 1=)
```

You can correct the mistake, re-evaluate the function definition, and then run your test again.

17.2 `debug-on-entry`

A recent GNU Emacs starts the debugger automatically when your function has an error.

Incidentally, you can start the debugger manually for all versions of Emacs; the advantage is that the debugger runs even if you do not have a bug in your code. Sometimes your code will be free of bugs!

You can enter the debugger when you call the function by calling `debug-on-entry`.

Type:

```
M-x debug-on-entry RET triangle-bugged RET
```

Now, evaluate the following:

```
(triangle-bugged 5)
```

All versions of Emacs will create a *Backtrace* buffer and tell you that it is beginning to evaluate the `triangle-bugged` function:

```
---------- Buffer: *Backtrace* ----------
Debugger entered--entering a function:
* triangle-bugged(5)
  eval((triangle-bugged 5))
  eval-last-sexp-1(nil)
  eval-last-sexp(nil)
  call-interactively(eval-last-sexp)
---------- Buffer: *Backtrace* ----------
```

In the *Backtrace* buffer, type *d*. Emacs will evaluate the first expression in `triangle-bugged`; the buffer will look like this:

```
---------- Buffer: *Backtrace* ----------
Debugger entered--beginning evaluation of function call form:
* (let ((total 0)) (while (> number 0) (setq total ...)
        (setq number ...)) total)
* triangle-bugged(5)
  eval((triangle-bugged 5))
  eval-last-sexp-1(nil)
  eval-last-sexp(nil)
  call-interactively(eval-last-sexp)
---------- Buffer: *Backtrace* ----------
```

Now, type *d* again, eight times, slowly. Each time you type *d*, Emacs will evaluate another expression in the function definition.

Eventually, the buffer will look like this:

```
---------- Buffer: *Backtrace* ----------
Debugger entered--beginning evaluation of function call form:
* (setq number (1= number))
* (while (> number 0) (setq total (+ total number))
        (setq number (1= number)))

* (let ((total 0)) (while (> number 0) (setq total ...)
        (setq number ...)) total)
* triangle-bugged(5)
  eval((triangle-bugged 5))

  eval-last-sexp-1(nil)
  eval-last-sexp(nil)
  call-interactively(eval-last-sexp)
---------- Buffer: *Backtrace* ----------
```

Finally, after you type *d* two more times, Emacs will reach the error, and the top two lines of the *Backtrace* buffer will look like this:

```
---------- Buffer: *Backtrace* ----------
Debugger entered--Lisp error: (void-function 1=)
* (1= number)
  ...
---------- Buffer: *Backtrace* ----------
```

By typing *d*, you were able to step through the function.

You can quit a *Backtrace* buffer by typing *q* in it; this quits the trace, but does not cancel debug-on-entry.

To cancel the effect of debug-on-entry, call cancel-debug-on-entry and the name of the function, like this:

```
M-x cancel-debug-on-entry RET triangle-bugged RET
```

(If you are reading this in Info, cancel debug-on-entry now.)

17.3 debug-on-quit and (debug)

In addition to setting debug-on-error or calling debug-on-entry, there are two other ways to start debug.

You can start debug whenever you type *C-g* (keyboard-quit) by setting the variable debug-on-quit to t. This is useful for debugging infinite loops.

Or, you can insert a line that says (`debug`) into your code where you want the debugger to start, like this:

```
(defun triangle-bugged (number)
  "Return sum of numbers 1 through NUMBER inclusive."
  (let ((total 0))
    (while (> number 0)
      (setq total (+ total number))
      (debug)                          ; Start debugger.
      (setq number (1= number)))       ; Error here.
    total))
```

The `debug` function is described in detail in Section "The Lisp Debugger" in *The GNU Emacs Lisp Reference Manual*.

17.4 The `edebug` Source Level Debugger

Edebug is a source level debugger. Edebug normally displays the source of the code you are debugging, with an arrow at the left that shows which line you are currently executing.

You can walk through the execution of a function, line by line, or run quickly until reaching a *breakpoint* where execution stops.

Edebug is described in Section "Edebug" in *The GNU Emacs Lisp Reference Manual*.

Here is a bugged function definition for `triangle-recursively`. See Section 11.3.4 "Recursion in place of a counter", page 119, for a review of it.

```
(defun triangle-recursively-bugged (number)
  "Return sum of numbers 1 through NUMBER inclusive.
Uses recursion."
  (if (= number 1)
      1
    (+ number
       (triangle-recursively-bugged
        (1= number)))))              ; Error here.
```

Normally, you would install this definition by positioning your cursor after the function's closing parenthesis and typing `C-x C-e` (`eval-last-sexp`) or else by positioning your cursor within the definition and typing `C-M-x` (`eval-defun`). (By default, the `eval-defun` command works only in Emacs Lisp mode or in Lisp Interaction mode.)

However, to prepare this function definition for Edebug, you must first *instrument* the code using a different command. You can do this by positioning your cursor within or just after the definition and typing

```
M-x edebug-defun RET
```

This will cause Emacs to load Edebug automatically if it is not already loaded, and properly instrument the function.

After instrumenting the function, place your cursor after the following expression and type `C-x C-e` (`eval-last-sexp`):

```
(triangle-recursively-bugged 3)
```

You will be jumped back to the source for `triangle-recursively-bugged` and the cursor positioned at the beginning of the `if` line of the function. Also, you will see an arrowhead at the left hand side of that line. The arrowhead marks the line where the function is executing. (In the following examples, we show the arrowhead with '=>'; in a windowing system, you may see the arrowhead as a solid triangle in the window fringe.)

```
=>*(if (= number 1)
```

In the example, the location of point is displayed with a star, '*' (in Info, it is displayed as '-!-').

If you now press SPC, point will move to the next expression to be executed; the line will look like this:

```
=>(if *(= number 1)
```

As you continue to press SPC, point will move from expression to expression. At the same time, whenever an expression returns a value, that value will be displayed in the echo area. For example, after you move point past `number`, you will see the following:

```
Result: 3 (#o3, #x3, ?\C-c)
```

This means the value of `number` is 3, which is octal three, hexadecimal three, and ASCII Control-C (the third letter of the alphabet, in case you need to know this information).

You can continue moving through the code until you reach the line with the error. Before evaluation, that line looks like this:

```
=>         *(1= number)))))                          ; Error here.
```

When you press SPC once again, you will produce an error message that says:

```
Symbol's function definition is void: 1=
```

This is the bug.

Press *q* to quit Edebug.

To remove instrumentation from a function definition, simply re-evaluate it with a command that does not instrument it. For example, you could place your cursor after the definition's closing parenthesis and type *C-x C-e*.

Edebug does a great deal more than walk with you through a function. You can set it so it races through on its own, stopping only at an error or at specified stopping points; you can cause it to display the changing values of various expressions; you can find out how many times a function is called, and more.

Edebug is described in Section "Edebug" in *The GNU Emacs Lisp Reference Manual*.

17.5 Debugging Exercises

- Install the `count-words-example` function and then cause it to enter the built-in debugger when you call it. Run the command on a region containing two words. You will need to press *d* a remarkable number of times. On your system, is a hook called after the command finishes? (For information on hooks, see Section "Command Loop Overview" in *The GNU Emacs Lisp Reference Manual*.)

- Copy `count-words-example` into the `*scratch*` buffer, instrument the function for Edebug, and walk through its execution. The function does not need to have a bug, although you can introduce one if you wish. If the function lacks a bug, the walk-through completes without problems.

- While running Edebug, type *?* to see a list of all the Edebug commands. (The `global-edebug-prefix` is usually *C-x X*, i.e., *CTRL-x* followed by an upper case *X*; use this prefix for commands made outside of the Edebug debugging buffer.)

- In the Edebug debugging buffer, use the *p* (`edebug-bounce-point`) command to see where in the region the `count-words-example` is working.

- Move point to some spot further down the function and then type the *h* (`edebug-goto-here`) command to jump to that location.

- Use the *t* (`edebug-trace-mode`) command to cause Edebug to walk through the function on its own; use an upper case *T* for `edebug-Trace-fast-mode`.

- Set a breakpoint, then run Edebug in Trace mode until it reaches the stopping point.

18 Conclusion

We have now reached the end of this Introduction. You have now learned enough about programming in Emacs Lisp to set values, to write simple `.emacs` files for yourself and your friends, and write simple customizations and extensions to Emacs.

This is a place to stop. Or, if you wish, you can now go onward, and teach yourself.

You have learned some of the basic nuts and bolts of programming. But only some. There are a great many more brackets and hinges that are easy to use that we have not touched.

A path you can follow right now lies among the sources to GNU Emacs and in *The GNU Emacs Lisp Reference Manual*.

The Emacs Lisp sources are an adventure. When you read the sources and come across a function or expression that is unfamiliar, you need to figure out or find out what it does.

Go to the Reference Manual. It is a thorough, complete, and fairly easy-to-read description of Emacs Lisp. It is written not only for experts, but for people who know what you know. (The *Reference Manual* comes with the standard GNU Emacs distribution. Like this introduction, it comes as a Texinfo source file, so you can read it on your computer and as a typeset, printed book.)

Go to the other built-in help that is part of GNU Emacs: the built-in documentation for all functions and variables, and `find-tag`, the program that takes you to sources.

Here is an example of how I explore the sources. Because of its name, `simple.el` is the file I looked at first, a long time ago. As it happens some of the functions in `simple.el` are complicated, or at least look complicated at first sight. The `open-line` function, for example, looks complicated.

You may want to walk through this function slowly, as we did with the `forward-sentence` function. (See Section 12.3 "forward-sentence", page 131.) Or you may want to skip that function and look at another, such as `split-line`. You don't need to read all the functions. According to `count-words-in-defun`, the `split-line` function contains 102 words and symbols.

Even though it is short, `split-line` contains expressions we have not studied: `skip-chars-forward`, `indent-to`, `current-column` and `insert-and-inherit`.

Consider the `skip-chars-forward` function. In GNU Emacs, you can find out more about `skip-chars-forward` by typing *C-h f* (`describe-function`) and the name of the function. This gives you the function documentation.

You may be able to guess what is done by a well named function such as `indent-to`; or you can look it up, too. Incidentally, the `describe-function` function itself is in `help.el`; it is one of those long, but decipherable functions. You can look up `describe-function` using the *C-h f* command!

In this instance, since the code is Lisp, the `*Help*` buffer contains the name of the library containing the function's source. You can put point over the name of the library and press the RET key, which in this situation is bound to `help-follow`, and be taken directly to the source, in the same way as *M-.* (`find-tag`).

The definition for `describe-function` illustrates how to customize the `interactive` expression without using the standard character codes; and it shows how to create a temporary buffer.

(The `indent-to` function is written in C rather than Emacs Lisp; it is a built-in function. `help-follow` takes you to its source as does `find-tag`, when properly set up.)

You can look at a function's source using `find-tag`, which is bound to `M-.`. Finally, you can find out what the Reference Manual has to say by visiting the manual in Info, and typing `i` (`Info-index`) and the name of the function, or by looking up the function in the index to a printed copy of the manual.

Similarly, you can find out what is meant by `insert-and-inherit`.

Other interesting source files include `paragraphs.el`, `loaddefs.el`, and `loadup.el`. The `paragraphs.el` file includes short, easily understood functions as well as longer ones. The `loaddefs.el` file contains the many standard autoloads and many keymaps. I have never looked at it all; only at parts. `loadup.el` is the file that loads the standard parts of Emacs; it tells you a great deal about how Emacs is built. (See Section "Building Emacs" in *The GNU Emacs Lisp Reference Manual*, for more about building.)

As I said, you have learned some nuts and bolts; however, and very importantly, we have hardly touched major aspects of programming; I have said nothing about how to sort information, except to use the predefined `sort` function; I have said nothing about how to store information, except to use variables and lists; I have said nothing about how to write programs that write programs. These are topics for another, and different kind of book, a different kind of learning.

What you have done is learn enough for much practical work with GNU Emacs. What you have done is get started. This is the end of a beginning.

Appendix A The the-the Function

Sometimes when you you write text, you duplicate words—as with "you you" near the beginning of this sentence. I find that most frequently, I duplicate "the"; hence, I call the function for detecting duplicated words, the-the.

As a first step, you could use the following regular expression to search for duplicates:

```
\\(\\w+[ \t\n]+\\)\\1
```

This regexp matches one or more word-constituent characters followed by one or more spaces, tabs, or newlines. However, it does not detect duplicated words on different lines, since the ending of the first word, the end of the line, is different from the ending of the second word, a space. (For more information about regular expressions, see Chapter 12 "Regular Expression Searches", page 129, as well as Section "Syntax of Regular Expressions" in *The GNU Emacs Manual*, and Section "Regular Expressions" in *The GNU Emacs Lisp Reference Manual*.)

You might try searching just for duplicated word-constituent characters but that does not work since the pattern detects doubles such as the two occurrences of "th" in "with the".

Another possible regexp searches for word-constituent characters followed by non-word-constituent characters, reduplicated. Here, '\\w+' matches one or more word-constituent characters and '\\W*' matches zero or more non-word-constituent characters.

```
\\(\\(\\w+\\)\\W*\\)\\1
```

Again, not useful.

Here is the pattern that I use. It is not perfect, but good enough. '\\b' matches the empty string, provided it is at the beginning or end of a word; '[^@ \n\t]+' matches one or more occurrences of any characters that are *not* an @-sign, space, newline, or tab.

```
\\b\\([^@ \n\t]+\\)[ \n\t]+\\1\\b
```

One can write more complicated expressions, but I found that this expression is good enough, so I use it.

Here is the the-the function, as I include it in my .emacs file, along with a handy global key binding:

```
(defun the-the ()
  "Search forward for for a duplicated word."
  (interactive)
  (message "Searching for for duplicated words ...")
  (push-mark)
  ;; This regexp is not perfect
  ;; but is fairly good over all:
  (if (re-search-forward
        "\\b\\([^@ \n\t]+\\)[ \n\t]+\\1\\b" nil 'move)
      (message "Found duplicated word.")
    (message "End of buffer")))

;; Bind 'the-the' to  C-c \
(global-set-key "\C-c\\" 'the-the)
```

Here is test text:
```
one two two three four five
five six seven
```
You can substitute the other regular expressions shown above in the function definition and try each of them on this list.

Appendix B Handling the Kill Ring

The kill ring is a list that is transformed into a ring by the workings of the `current-kill` function. The `yank` and `yank-pop` commands use the `current-kill` function.

This appendix describes the `current-kill` function as well as both the `yank` and the `yank-pop` commands, but first, consider the workings of the kill ring.

The kill ring has a default maximum length of sixty items; this number is too large for an explanation. Instead, set it to four. Please evaluate the following:

```
(setq old-kill-ring-max kill-ring-max)
(setq kill-ring-max 4)
```

Then, please copy each line of the following indented example into the kill ring. You may kill each line with *C-k* or mark it and copy it with *M-w*.

(In a read-only buffer, such as the *info* buffer, the kill command, *C-k* (`kill-line`), will not remove the text, merely copy it to the kill ring. However, your machine may beep at you. Alternatively, for silence, you may copy the region of each line with the *M-w* (`kill-ring-save`) command. You must mark each line for this command to succeed, but it does not matter at which end you put point or mark.)

Please invoke the calls in order, so that five elements attempt to fill the kill ring:

```
first some text
second piece of text
third line
fourth line of text
fifth bit of text
```

Then find the value of `kill-ring` by evaluating

```
kill-ring
```

It is:

```
("fifth bit of text" "fourth line of text"
"third line" "second piece of text")
```

The first element, '`first some text`', was dropped.

To return to the old value for the length of the kill ring, evaluate:

```
(setq kill-ring-max old-kill-ring-max)
```

B.1 The `current-kill` Function

The `current-kill` function changes the element in the kill ring to which `kill-ring-yank-pointer` points. (Also, the `kill-new` function sets `kill-ring-yank-pointer` to point to the latest element of the kill ring. The `kill-new` function is used directly or indirectly by `kill-append`, `copy-region-as-kill`, `kill-ring-save`, `kill-line`, and `kill-region`.)

The `current-kill` function is used by `yank` and by `yank-pop`. Here is the code for `current-kill`:

```
(defun current-kill (n &optional do-not-move)
  "Rotate the yanking point by N places, and then return that kill.
If N is zero and `interprogram-paste-function' is set to a
function that returns a string or a list of strings, and if that
function doesn't return nil, then that string (or list) is added
to the front of the kill ring and the string (or first string in
the list) is returned as the latest kill.
If N is not zero, and if `yank-pop-change-selection' is
non-nil, use `interprogram-cut-function' to transfer the
kill at the new yank point into the window system selection.
If optional arg DO-NOT-MOVE is non-nil, then don't actually
move the yanking point; just return the Nth kill forward."

  (let ((interprogram-paste (and (= n 0)
                                 interprogram-paste-function
                                 (funcall interprogram-paste-function))))
    (if interprogram-paste
        (progn
          ;; Disable the interprogram cut function when we add the new
          ;; text to the kill ring, so Emacs doesn't try to own the
          ;; selection, with identical text.
          (let ((interprogram-cut-function nil))
            (if (listp interprogram-paste)
                (mapc 'kill-new (nreverse interprogram-paste))
              (kill-new interprogram-paste)))
          (car kill-ring))
      (or kill-ring (error "Kill ring is empty"))
      (let ((ARGth-kill-element
             (nthcdr (mod (- n (length kill-ring-yank-pointer))
                          (length kill-ring))
                     kill-ring)))
        (unless do-not-move
          (setq kill-ring-yank-pointer ARGth-kill-element)
          (when (and yank-pop-change-selection
                     (> n 0)
                     interprogram-cut-function)
            (funcall interprogram-cut-function (car ARGth-kill-element))))
        (car ARGth-kill-element)))))
```

Remember also that the `kill-new` function sets `kill-ring-yank-pointer` to the latest element of the kill ring, which means that all the functions that call it set the value indirectly: `kill-append`, `copy-region-as-kill`, `kill-ring-save`, `kill-line`, and `kill-region`.

Here is the line in `kill-new`, which is explained in "The `kill-new` function",
page 89.

```
(setq kill-ring-yank-pointer kill-ring)
```

The `current-kill` function looks complex, but as usual, it can be understood
by taking it apart piece by piece. First look at it in skeletal form:

```
(defun current-kill (n &optional do-not-move)
  "Rotate the yanking point by N places, and then return that kill."
  (let varlist
    body...)
```

This function takes two arguments, one of which is optional. It has a documentation string. It is *not* interactive.

The body of the function definition is a `let` expression, which itself has a body
as well as a *varlist*.

The `let` expression declares a variable that will be only usable within the bounds
of this function. This variable is called `interprogram-paste` and is for copying to
another program. It is not for copying within this instance of GNU Emacs. Most
window systems provide a facility for interprogram pasting. Sadly, that facility usually provides only for the last element. Most windowing systems have not adopted
a ring of many possibilities, even though Emacs has provided it for decades.

The `if` expression has two parts, one if there exists `interprogram-paste` and
one if not.

Let us consider the else-part of the `current-kill` function. (The then-part
uses the `kill-new` function, which we have already described. See "The `kill-new`
function", page 89.)

```
(or kill-ring (error "Kill ring is empty"))
(let ((ARGth-kill-element
       (nthcdr (mod (- n (length kill-ring-yank-pointer))
                    (length kill-ring))
               kill-ring)))
  (or do-not-move
      (setq kill-ring-yank-pointer ARGth-kill-element))
  (car ARGth-kill-element))
```

The code first checks whether the kill ring has content; otherwise it signals an error.

Note that the `or` expression is very similar to testing length with an `if`:

```
(if (zerop (length kill-ring))          ; if-part
    (error "Kill ring is empty"))        ; then-part
  ;; No else-part
```

If there is not anything in the kill ring, its length must be zero and an error message
sent to the user: 'Kill ring is empty'. The `current-kill` function uses an `or`
expression which is simpler. But an `if` expression reminds us what goes on.

This `if` expression uses the function `zerop` which returns true if the value it
is testing is zero. When `zerop` tests true, the then-part of the `if` is evaluated.
The then-part is a list starting with the function `error`, which is a function that
is similar to the `message` function (see Section 1.8.5 "The `message` Function",
page 14) in that it prints a one-line message in the echo area. However, in addition
to printing a message, `error` also stops evaluation of the function within which it

is embedded. This means that the rest of the function will not be evaluated if the length of the kill ring is zero.

Then the `current-kill` function selects the element to return. The selection depends on the number of places that `current-kill` rotates and on where `kill-ring-yank-pointer` points.

Next, either the optional `do-not-move` argument is true or the current value of `kill-ring-yank-pointer` is set to point to the list. Finally, another expression returns the first element of the list even if the `do-not-move` argument is true.

In my opinion, it is slightly misleading, at least to humans, to use the term "error" as the name of the `error` function. A better term would be "cancel". Strictly speaking, of course, you cannot point to, much less rotate a pointer to a list that has no length, so from the point of view of the computer, the word "error" is correct. But a human expects to attempt this sort of thing, if only to find out whether the kill ring is full or empty. This is an act of exploration.

From the human point of view, the act of exploration and discovery is not necessarily an error, and therefore should not be labeled as one, even in the bowels of a computer. As it is, the code in Emacs implies that a human who is acting virtuously, by exploring his or her environment, is making an error. This is bad. Even though the computer takes the same steps as it does when there is an error, a term such as "cancel" would have a clearer connotation.

Among other actions, the else-part of the `if` expression sets the value of `kill-ring-yank-pointer` to `ARGth-kill-element` when the kill ring has something in it and the value of `do-not-move` is `nil`.

The code looks like this:

```
(nthcdr (mod (- n (length kill-ring-yank-pointer))
             (length kill-ring))
        kill-ring)))
```

This needs some examination. Unless it is not supposed to move the pointer, the `current-kill` function changes where `kill-ring-yank-pointer` points. That is what the `(setq kill-ring-yank-pointer ARGth-kill-element))` expression does. Also, clearly, `ARGth-kill-element` is being set to be equal to some CDR of the kill ring, using the `nthcdr` function that is described in an earlier section. (See Section 8.3 "copy-region-as-kill", page 86.) How does it do this?

As we have seen before (see Section 7.3 "nthcdr", page 74), the `nthcdr` function works by repeatedly taking the CDR of a list—it takes the CDR of the CDR of the CDR . . .

The two following expressions produce the same result:

```
(setq kill-ring-yank-pointer (cdr kill-ring))
```

```
(setq kill-ring-yank-pointer (nthcdr 1 kill-ring))
```

However, the `nthcdr` expression is more complicated. It uses the `mod` function to determine which CDR to select.

(You will remember to look at inner functions first; indeed, we will have to go inside the `mod`.)

The `mod` function returns the value of its first argument modulo the second; that is to say, it returns the remainder after dividing the first argument by the second. The value returned has the same sign as the second argument.

Thus,

```
(mod 12 4)
   ⇒ 0   ;; because there is no remainder
(mod 13 4)
   ⇒ 1
```

In this case, the first argument is often smaller than the second. That is fine.

```
(mod 0 4)
   ⇒ 0
(mod 1 4)
   ⇒ 1
```

We can guess what the - function does. It is like + but subtracts instead of adds; the - function subtracts its second argument from its first. Also, we already know what the `length` function does (see Section 7.2.1 "length", page 73). It returns the length of a list.

And `n` is the name of the required argument to the `current-kill` function.

So when the first argument to `nthcdr` is zero, the `nthcdr` expression returns the whole list, as you can see by evaluating the following:

```
;; kill-ring-yank-pointer and kill-ring have a length of four
;; and (mod (- 0 4) 4) ⇒ 0
(nthcdr (mod (- 0 4) 4)
        '("fourth line of text"
          "third line"
          "second piece of text"
          "first some text"))
```

When the first argument to the `current-kill` function is one, the `nthcdr` expression returns the list without its first element.

```
(nthcdr (mod (- 1 4) 4)
        '("fourth line of text"
          "third line"
          "second piece of text"
          "first some text"))
```

Incidentally, both `kill-ring` and `kill-ring-yank-pointer` are *global variables*. That means that any expression in Emacs Lisp can access them. They are not like the local variables set by `let` or like the symbols in an argument list. Local variables can only be accessed within the `let` that defines them or the function that specifies them in an argument list (and within expressions called by them).

B.2 yank

After learning about `current-kill`, the code for the `yank` function is almost easy.

The `yank` function does not use the `kill-ring-yank-pointer` variable directly. It calls `insert-for-yank` which calls `current-kill` which sets the `kill-ring-yank-pointer` variable.

The code looks like this:

```
(defun yank (&optional arg)
  "Reinsert (\"paste\") the last stretch of killed text.
More precisely, reinsert the stretch of killed text most recently
killed OR yanked.  Put point at end, and set mark at beginning.
With just \\[universal-argument] as argument, same but put point at begin-
ning (and mark at end).
With argument N, reinsert the Nth most recently killed stretch of killed
text.

When this command inserts killed text into the buffer, it honors
`yank-excluded-properties' and `yank-handler' as described in the
doc string for `insert-for-yank-1', which see.

See also the command `yank-pop' (\\[yank-pop])."
  (interactive "*P")
  (setq yank-window-start (window-start))
  ;; If we don't get all the way thru, make last-command indicate that
  ;; for the following command.
  (setq this-command t)
  (push-mark (point))
  (insert-for-yank (current-kill (cond
                                  ((listp arg) 0)
                                  ((eq arg '-) -2)
                                  (t (1- arg)))))
  (if (consp arg)
      ;; This is like exchange-point-and-mark, but doesn't activate the mark.
      ;; It is cleaner to avoid activation, even though the command
      ;; loop would deactivate the mark because we inserted text.
      (goto-char (prog1 (mark t)
                   (set-marker (mark-marker) (point) (current-buffer)))))
  ;; If we do get all the way thru, make this-command indicate that.
  (if (eq this-command t)
      (setq this-command 'yank))
  nil)
```

The key expression is `insert-for-yank`, which inserts the string returned by `current-kill`, but removes some text properties from it.

However, before getting to that expression, the function sets the value of `yank-window-start` to the position returned by the `(window-start)` expression, the position at which the display currently starts. The `yank` function also sets `this-command` and pushes the mark.

After it yanks the appropriate element, if the optional argument is a CONS rather than a number or nothing, it puts point at beginning of the yanked text and mark at its end.

(The `prog1` function is like `progn` but returns the value of its first argument rather than the value of its last argument. Its first argument is forced to return the buffer's mark as an integer. You can see the documentation for these functions by placing point over them in this buffer and then typing `C-h f` (`describe-function`) followed by a `RET`; the default is the function.)

The last part of the function tells what to do when it succeeds.

B.3 yank-pop

After understanding yank and current-kill, you know how to approach the
yank-pop function. Leaving out the documentation to save space, it looks like
this:

```
(defun yank-pop (&optional arg)
  "..."
  (interactive "*p")
  (if (not (eq last-command 'yank))
      (error "Previous command was not a yank"))
  (setq this-command 'yank)
  (unless arg (setq arg 1))
  (let ((inhibit-read-only t)
        (before (< (point) (mark t))))
    (if before
        (funcall (or yank-undo-function 'delete-region) (point) (mark t))
      (funcall (or yank-undo-function 'delete-region) (mark t) (point)))
    (setq yank-undo-function nil)
    (set-marker (mark-marker) (point) (current-buffer))
    (insert-for-yank (current-kill arg))
    ;; Set the window start back where it was in the yank command,
    ;; if possible.
    (set-window-start (selected-window) yank-window-start t)
    (if before
        ;; This is like exchange-point-and-mark,
        ;;    but doesn't activate the mark.
        ;; It is cleaner to avoid activation, even though the command
        ;; loop would deactivate the mark because we inserted text.
        (goto-char (prog1 (mark t)
                     (set-marker (mark-marker)
                                 (point)
                                 (current-buffer)))))))
  nil)
```

The function is interactive with a small 'p' so the prefix argument is processed
and passed to the function. The command can only be used after a previous yank;
otherwise an error message is sent. This check uses the variable last-command which
is set by yank and is discussed elsewhere. (See Section 8.3 "copy-region-as-kill",
page 86.)

The let clause sets the variable before to true or false depending whether point
is before or after mark and then the region between point and mark is deleted. This
is the region that was just inserted by the previous yank and it is this text that will
be replaced.

funcall calls its first argument as a function, passing remaining arguments to
it. The first argument is whatever the or expression returns. The two remaining
arguments are the positions of point and mark set by the preceding yank command.

There is more, but that is the hardest part.

B.4 The `ring.el` File

Interestingly, GNU Emacs posses a file called `ring.el` that provides many of the features we just discussed. But functions such as `kill-ring-yank-pointer` do not use this library, possibly because they were written earlier.

Appendix C A Graph with Labeled Axes

Printed axes help you understand a graph. They convey scale. In an earlier chapter (see Chapter 15 "Readying a Graph", page 173), we wrote the code to print the body of a graph. Here we write the code for printing and labeling vertical and horizontal axes, along with the body itself.

Since insertions fill a buffer to the right and below point, the new graph printing function should first print the Y or vertical axis, then the body of the graph, and finally the X or horizontal axis. This sequence lays out for us the contents of the function:

1. Set up code.

2. Print Y axis.

3. Print body of graph.

4. Print X axis.

Here is an example of how a finished graph should look:

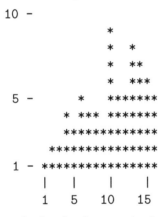

In this graph, both the vertical and the horizontal axes are labeled with numbers. However, in some graphs, the horizontal axis is time and would be better labeled with months, like this:

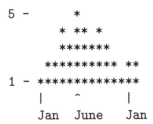

Indeed, with a little thought, we can easily come up with a variety of vertical and horizontal labeling schemes. Our task could become complicated. But complications breed confusion. Rather than permit this, it is better choose a simple labeling scheme for our first effort, and to modify or replace it later.

These considerations suggest the following outline for the `print-graph` function:

```
(defun print-graph (numbers-list)
  "documentation..."
  (let ((height  ...
         ...))
    (print-Y-axis height ... )
    (graph-body-print numbers-list)
    (print-X-axis ... )))
```

We can work on each part of the `print-graph` function definition in turn.

C.1 The `print-graph` Varlist

In writing the `print-graph` function, the first task is to write the varlist in the `let` expression. (We will leave aside for the moment any thoughts about making the function interactive or about the contents of its documentation string.)

The varlist should set several values. Clearly, the top of the label for the vertical axis must be at least the height of the graph, which means that we must obtain this information here. Note that the `print-graph-body` function also requires this information. There is no reason to calculate the height of the graph in two different places, so we should change `print-graph-body` from the way we defined it earlier to take advantage of the calculation.

Similarly, both the function for printing the X axis labels and the `print-graph-body` function need to learn the value of the width of each symbol. We can perform the calculation here and change the definition for `print-graph-body` from the way we defined it in the previous chapter.

The length of the label for the horizontal axis must be at least as long as the graph. However, this information is used only in the function that prints the horizontal axis, so it does not need to be calculated here.

These thoughts lead us directly to the following form for the varlist in the `let` for `print-graph`:

```
(let ((height (apply 'max numbers-list)) ; First version.
      (symbol-width (length graph-blank)))
```

As we shall see, this expression is not quite right.

C.2 The `print-Y-axis` Function

The job of the `print-Y-axis` function is to print a label for the vertical axis that looks like this:

```
10 -




 5 -




 1 -
```

The function should be passed the height of the graph, and then should construct and insert the appropriate numbers and marks.

It is easy enough to see in the figure what the Y axis label should look like; but to say in words, and then to write a function definition to do the job is another matter. It is not quite true to say that we want a number and a tic every five lines: there are only three lines between the '1' and the '5' (lines 2, 3, and 4), but four lines between the '5' and the '10' (lines 6, 7, 8, and 9). It is better to say that we want a number and a tic mark on the base line (number 1) and then that we want a number and a tic on the fifth line from the bottom and on every line that is a multiple of five.

The next issue is what height the label should be? Suppose the maximum height of tallest column of the graph is seven. Should the highest label on the Y axis be '5 -', and should the graph stick up above the label? Or should the highest label be '7 -', and mark the peak of the graph? Or should the highest label be 10 -, which is a multiple of five, and be higher than the topmost value of the graph?

The latter form is preferred. Most graphs are drawn within rectangles whose sides are an integral number of steps long—5, 10, 15, and so on for a step distance of five. But as soon as we decide to use a step height for the vertical axis, we discover that the simple expression in the varlist for computing the height is wrong. The expression is `(apply 'max numbers-list)`. This returns the precise height, not the maximum height plus whatever is necessary to round up to the nearest multiple of five. A more complex expression is required.

As usual in cases like this, a complex problem becomes simpler if it is divided into several smaller problems.

First, consider the case when the highest value of the graph is an integral multiple of five—when it is 5, 10, 15, or some higher multiple of five. We can use this value as the Y axis height.

A fairly simply way to determine whether a number is a multiple of five is to divide it by five and see if the division results in a remainder. If there is no remainder, the number is a multiple of five. Thus, seven divided by five has a remainder of two, and seven is not an integral multiple of five. Put in slightly different language, more reminiscent of the classroom, five goes into seven once, with a remainder of two. However, five goes into ten twice, with no remainder: ten is an integral multiple of five.

C.2.1 Side Trip: Compute a Remainder

In Lisp, the function for computing a remainder is `%`. The function returns the remainder of its first argument divided by its second argument. As it happens, `%` is a function in Emacs Lisp that you cannot discover using `apropos`: you find nothing if you type `M-x apropos RET remainder RET`. The only way to learn of the existence of `%` is to read about it in a book such as this or in the Emacs Lisp sources.

You can try the `%` function by evaluating the following two expressions:

```
(% 7 5)
```

```
(% 10 5)
```

The first expression returns 2 and the second expression returns 0.

To test whether the returned value is zero or some other number, we can use the `zerop` function. This function returns `t` if its argument, which must be a number, is zero.

```
(zerop (% 7 5))
     ⇒ nil

(zerop (% 10 5))
     ⇒ t
```

Thus, the following expression will return `t` if the height of the graph is evenly divisible by five:

```
(zerop (% height 5))
```

(The value of `height`, of course, can be found from (`apply 'max numbers-list`).)

On the other hand, if the value of `height` is not a multiple of five, we want to reset the value to the next higher multiple of five. This is straightforward arithmetic using functions with which we are already familiar. First, we divide the value of `height` by five to determine how many times five goes into the number. Thus, five goes into twelve twice. If we add one to this quotient and multiply by five, we will obtain the value of the next multiple of five that is larger than the height. Five goes into twelve twice. Add one to two, and multiply by five; the result is fifteen, which is the next multiple of five that is higher than twelve. The Lisp expression for this is:

```
(* (1+ (/ height 5)) 5)
```

For example, if you evaluate the following, the result is 15:

```
(* (1+ (/ 12 5)) 5)
```

All through this discussion, we have been using 5 as the value for spacing labels on the Y axis; but we may want to use some other value. For generality, we should replace 5 with a variable to which we can assign a value. The best name I can think of for this variable is `Y-axis-label-spacing`.

Using this term, and an `if` expression, we produce the following:

```
(if (zerop (% height Y-axis-label-spacing))
    height
  ;; else
  (* (1+ (/ height Y-axis-label-spacing))
     Y-axis-label-spacing))
```

This expression returns the value of `height` itself if the height is an even multiple of the value of the `Y-axis-label-spacing` or else it computes and returns a value of `height` that is equal to the next higher multiple of the value of the `Y-axis-label-spacing`.

We can now include this expression in the `let` expression of the `print-graph` function (after first setting the value of `Y-axis-label-spacing`):

```
(defvar Y-axis-label-spacing 5
  "Number of lines from one Y axis label to next.")
```

```
      ...
     (let* ((height (apply 'max numbers-list))
            (height-of-top-line
              (if (zerop (% height Y-axis-label-spacing))
                  height
                ;; else
                (* (1+ (/ height Y-axis-label-spacing))
                   Y-axis-label-spacing)))
            (symbol-width (length graph-blank))))
      ...
```

(Note use of the `let*` function: the initial value of height is computed once by the
(`apply 'max numbers-list`) expression and then the resulting value of **height** is
used to compute its final value. See "The `let*` expression", page 135, for more
about `let*`.)

C.2.2 Construct a Y Axis Element

When we print the vertical axis, we want to insert strings such as '5 -' and '10 - '
every five lines. Moreover, we want the numbers and dashes to line up, so shorter
numbers must be padded with leading spaces. If some of the strings use two digit
numbers, the strings with single digit numbers must include a leading blank space
before the number.

To figure out the length of the number, the `length` function is used. But the
`length` function works only with a string, not with a number. So the number has
to be converted from being a number to being a string. This is done with the
`number-to-string` function. For example,

```
    (length (number-to-string 35))
        ⇒ 2


    (length (number-to-string 100))
        ⇒ 3
```

(`number-to-string` is also called `int-to-string`; you will see this alternative name
in various sources.)

In addition, in each label, each number is followed by a string such as ' - ', which
we will call the `Y-axis-tic` marker. This variable is defined with `defvar`:

```
    (defvar Y-axis-tic " - "
       "String that follows number in a Y axis label.")
```

The length of the Y label is the sum of the length of the Y axis tic mark and
the length of the number of the top of the graph.

```
    (length (concat (number-to-string height) Y-axis-tic)))
```

This value will be calculated by the `print-graph` function in its varlist as
`full-Y-label-width` and passed on. (Note that we did not think to include this
in the varlist when we first proposed it.)

To make a complete vertical axis label, a tic mark is concatenated with a number;
and the two together may be preceded by one or more spaces depending on how
long the number is. The label consists of three parts: the (optional) leading spaces,
the number, and the tic mark. The function is passed the value of the number for

the specific row, and the value of the width of the top line, which is calculated (just once) by `print-graph`.

```
(defun Y-axis-element (number full-Y-label-width)
  "Construct a NUMBERed label element.
A numbered element looks like this ` 5 - ',
and is padded as needed so all line up with
the element for the largest number."
  (let* ((leading-spaces
          (- full-Y-label-width
             (length
              (concat (number-to-string number)
                      Y-axis-tic)))))
    (concat
     (make-string leading-spaces ? )
     (number-to-string number)
     Y-axis-tic)))
```

The `Y-axis-element` function concatenates together the leading spaces, if any; the number, as a string; and the tic mark.

To figure out how many leading spaces the label will need, the function subtracts the actual length of the label—the length of the number plus the length of the tic mark—from the desired label width.

Blank spaces are inserted using the `make-string` function. This function takes two arguments: the first tells it how long the string will be and the second is a symbol for the character to insert, in a special format. The format is a question mark followed by a blank space, like this, '? '. See Section "Character Type" in *The GNU Emacs Lisp Reference Manual*, for a description of the syntax for characters. (Of course, you might want to replace the blank space by some other character ... You know what to do.)

The `number-to-string` function is used in the concatenation expression, to convert the number to a string that is concatenated with the leading spaces and the tic mark.

C.2.3 Create a Y Axis Column

The preceding functions provide all the tools needed to construct a function that generates a list of numbered and blank strings to insert as the label for the vertical axis:

```
(defun Y-axis-column (height width-of-label)
  "Construct list of Y axis labels and blank strings.
For HEIGHT of line above base and WIDTH-OF-LABEL."
  (let (Y-axis)

    (while (> height 1)
      (if (zerop (% height Y-axis-label-spacing))
          ;; Insert label.
          (setq Y-axis
                (cons
                 (Y-axis-element height width-of-label)
                 Y-axis))

        ;; Else, insert blanks.
        (setq Y-axis
              (cons
               (make-string width-of-label ? )
               Y-axis)))
      (setq height (1- height)))
    ;; Insert base line.
    (setq Y-axis
          (cons (Y-axis-element 1 width-of-label) Y-axis))
    (nreverse Y-axis)))
```

In this function, we start with the value of **height** and repetitively subtract one from its value. After each subtraction, we test to see whether the value is an integral multiple of the **Y-axis-label-spacing**. If it is, we construct a numbered label using the **Y-axis-element** function; if not, we construct a blank label using the **make-string** function. The base line consists of the number one followed by a tic mark.

C.2.4 The Not Quite Final Version of print-Y-axis

The list constructed by the **Y-axis-column** function is passed to the **print-Y-axis** function, which inserts the list as a column.

```
(defun print-Y-axis (height full-Y-label-width)
  "Insert Y axis using HEIGHT and FULL-Y-LABEL-WIDTH.
Height must be the maximum height of the graph.
Full width is the width of the highest label element."
;; Value of height and full-Y-label-width
;; are passed by print-graph.
  (let ((start (point)))
    (insert-rectangle
     (Y-axis-column height full-Y-label-width))
    ;; Place point ready for inserting graph.
    (goto-char start)
    ;; Move point forward by value of full-Y-label-width
    (forward-char full-Y-label-width)))
```

The **print-Y-axis** uses the **insert-rectangle** function to insert the Y axis labels created by the **Y-axis-column** function. In addition, it places point at the correct position for printing the body of the graph.

You can test **print-Y-axis**:

1. Install

   ```
   Y-axis-label-spacing
   Y-axis-tic
   Y-axis-element
   Y-axis-column
   print-Y-axis
   ```

2. Copy the following expression:

   ```
   (print-Y-axis 12 5)
   ```

3. Switch to the `*scratch*` buffer and place the cursor where you want the axis labels to start.

4. Type *M-:* (eval-expression).

5. Yank the `graph-body-print` expression into the minibuffer with *C-y* (yank).

6. Press RET to evaluate the expression.

Emacs will print labels vertically, the top one being '10 - '. (The `print-graph` function will pass the value of `height-of-top-line`, which in this case will end up as 15, thereby getting rid of what might appear as a bug.)

C.3 The `print-X-axis` Function

X axis labels are much like Y axis labels, except that the ticks are on a line above the numbers. Labels should look like this:

```
 |   |    |    |
 1   5   10   15
```

The first tic is under the first column of the graph and is preceded by several blank spaces. These spaces provide room in rows above for the Y axis labels. The second, third, fourth, and subsequent ticks are all spaced equally, according to the value of `X-axis-label-spacing`.

The second row of the X axis consists of numbers, preceded by several blank spaces and also separated according to the value of the variable `X-axis-label-spacing`.

The value of the variable `X-axis-label-spacing` should itself be measured in units of `symbol-width`, since you may want to change the width of the symbols that you are using to print the body of the graph without changing the ways the graph is labeled.

The `print-X-axis` function is constructed in more or less the same fashion as the `print-Y-axis` function except that it has two lines: the line of tic marks and the numbers. We will write a separate function to print each line and then combine them within the `print-X-axis` function.

This is a three step process:

1. Write a function to print the X axis tic marks, `print-X-axis-tic-line`.

2. Write a function to print the X numbers, `print-X-axis-numbered-line`.

3. Write a function to print both lines, the `print-X-axis` function, using `print-X-axis-tic-line` and `print-X-axis-numbered-line`.

C.3.1 X Axis Tic Marks

The first function should print the X axis tic marks. We must specify the tic marks
themselves and their spacing:

```
(defvar X-axis-label-spacing
  (if (boundp 'graph-blank)
      (* 5 (length graph-blank)) 5)
  "Number of units from one X axis label to next.")
```

(Note that the value of `graph-blank` is set by another `defvar`. The `boundp` predicate checks whether it has already been set; `boundp` returns `nil` if it has not. If
`graph-blank` were unbound and we did not use this conditional construction, in a
recent GNU Emacs, we would enter the debugger and see an error message saying
'`Debugger entered--Lisp error: (void-variable graph-blank)`'.)

Here is the `defvar` for `X-axis-tic-symbol`:

```
(defvar X-axis-tic-symbol "|"
  "String to insert to point to a column in X axis.")
```

The goal is to make a line that looks like this:

```
            |    |     |      |
```

The first tic is indented so that it is under the first column, which is indented
to provide space for the Y axis labels.

A tic element consists of the blank spaces that stretch from one tic to the next
plus a tic symbol. The number of blanks is determined by the width of the tic
symbol and the `X-axis-label-spacing`.

The code looks like this:

```
;;; X-axis-tic-element
...
(concat
 (make-string
  ;; Make a string of blanks.
  (-  (* symbol-width X-axis-label-spacing)
      (length X-axis-tic-symbol))
  ? )
 ;; Concatenate blanks with tic symbol.
 X-axis-tic-symbol)
...
```

Next, we determine how many blanks are needed to indent the first tic mark to
the first column of the graph. This uses the value of `full-Y-label-width` passed
it by the `print-graph` function.

The code to make `X-axis-leading-spaces` looks like this:

```
;; X-axis-leading-spaces
...
(make-string full-Y-label-width ? )
...
```

We also need to determine the length of the horizontal axis, which is the length
of the numbers list, and the number of ticks in the horizontal axis:

```
;; X-length
...
(length numbers-list)
```

```
;; tic-width
...
(* symbol-width X-axis-label-spacing)

;; number-of-X-ticks
(if (zerop (% (X-length tic-width)))
    (/ (X-length tic-width))
  (1+ (/ (X-length tic-width)))))
```

All this leads us directly to the function for printing the X axis tic line:

```
(defun print-X-axis-tic-line
  (number-of-X-tics X-axis-leading-spaces X-axis-tic-element)
  "Print ticks for X axis."
  (insert X-axis-leading-spaces)
  (insert X-axis-tic-symbol)   ; Under first column.
  ;; Insert second tic in the right spot.
  (insert (concat
            (make-string
             (-  (* symbol-width X-axis-label-spacing)
                 ;; Insert white space up to second tic symbol.
                 (* 2 (length X-axis-tic-symbol)))
             ? )
            X-axis-tic-symbol))
  ;; Insert remaining ticks.
  (while (> number-of-X-tics 1)
    (insert X-axis-tic-element)
    (setq number-of-X-tics (1- number-of-X-tics)))))
```

The line of numbers is equally straightforward:

First, we create a numbered element with blank spaces before each number:

```
(defun X-axis-element (number)
  "Construct a numbered X axis element."
  (let ((leading-spaces
         (-  (* symbol-width X-axis-label-spacing)
             (length (number-to-string number)))))
    (concat (make-string leading-spaces ? )
            (number-to-string number))))
```

Next, we create the function to print the numbered line, starting with the number 1 under the first column:

```
(defun print-X-axis-numbered-line
  (number-of-X-tics X-axis-leading-spaces)
  "Print line of X-axis numbers"
  (let ((number X-axis-label-spacing))
    (insert X-axis-leading-spaces)
    (insert "1")
    (insert (concat
              (make-string
               ;; Insert white space up to next number.
               (-  (* symbol-width X-axis-label-spacing) 2)
               ? )
              (number-to-string number)))
```

```
;; Insert remaining numbers.
(setq number (+ number X-axis-label-spacing))
(while (> number-of-X-tics 1)
  (insert (X-axis-element number))
  (setq number (+ number X-axis-label-spacing))
  (setq number-of-X-tics (1- number-of-X-tics)))))
```

Finally, we need to write the `print-X-axis` that uses `print-X-axis-tic-line` and `print-X-axis-numbered-line`.

The function must determine the local values of the variables used by both `print-X-axis-tic-line` and `print-X-axis-numbered-line`, and then it must call them. Also, it must print the carriage return that separates the two lines.

The function consists of a varlist that specifies five local variables, and calls to each of the two line printing functions:

```
(defun print-X-axis (numbers-list)
  "Print X axis labels to length of NUMBERS-LIST."
  (let* ((leading-spaces
          (make-string full-Y-label-width ? ))
         ;; symbol-width is provided by graph-body-print
         (tic-width (* symbol-width X-axis-label-spacing))
         (X-length (length numbers-list))
         (X-tic
          (concat
           (make-string
            ;; Make a string of blanks.
            (-  (* symbol-width X-axis-label-spacing)
                (length X-axis-tic-symbol))
            ? )
           ;; Concatenate blanks with tic symbol.
           X-axis-tic-symbol))
         (tic-number
          (if (zerop (% X-length tic-width))
              (/ X-length tic-width)
            (1+ (/ X-length tic-width)))))
    (print-X-axis-tic-line tic-number leading-spaces X-tic)
    (insert "\n")
    (print-X-axis-numbered-line tic-number leading-spaces)))
```

You can test `print-X-axis`:

1. Install `X-axis-tic-symbol`, `X-axis-label-spacing`, `print-X-axis-tic-line`, as well as `X-axis-element`, `print-X-axis-numbered-line`, and `print-X-axis`.

2. Copy the following expression:

```
(progn
  (let ((full-Y-label-width 5)
        (symbol-width 1))
    (print-X-axis
     '(1 2 3 4 5 6 7 8 9 10 11 12 13 14 15 16))))
```

3. Switch to the *scratch* buffer and place the cursor where you want the axis labels to start.

4. Type *M-:* (eval-expression).

5. Yank the test expression into the minibuffer with *C-y* (yank).

6. Press RET to evaluate the expression.

Emacs will print the horizontal axis like this:

```
|   |    |    |    |
1   5   10   15   20
```

C.4 Printing the Whole Graph

Now we are nearly ready to print the whole graph.

The function to print the graph with the proper labels follows the outline we created earlier (see Appendix C "A Graph with Labeled Axes", page 218), but with additions.

Here is the outline:

```
(defun print-graph (numbers-list)
  "documentation..."
  (let ((height  ...
         ...))
    (print-Y-axis height ... )
    (graph-body-print numbers-list)
    (print-X-axis ... )))
```

The final version is different from what we planned in two ways: first, it contains additional values calculated once in the varlist; second, it carries an option to specify the labels' increment per row. This latter feature turns out to be essential; otherwise, a graph may have more rows than fit on a display or on a sheet of paper.

This new feature requires a change to the Y-axis-column function, to add vertical-step to it. The function looks like this:

```
;;; Final version.
(defun Y-axis-column
  (height width-of-label &optional vertical-step)
  "Construct list of labels for Y axis.
HEIGHT is maximum height of graph.
WIDTH-OF-LABEL is maximum width of label.
VERTICAL-STEP, an option, is a positive integer
that specifies how much a Y axis label increments
for each line.  For example, a step of 5 means
that each line is five units of the graph."
  (let (Y-axis
        (number-per-line (or vertical-step 1)))
    (while (> height 1)
      (if (zerop (% height Y-axis-label-spacing))
          ;; Insert label.
          (setq Y-axis
                (cons
                 (Y-axis-element
                  (* height number-per-line)
                  width-of-label)
                 Y-axis))
```

```
;; Else, insert blanks.
(setq Y-axis
      (cons
       (make-string width-of-label ? )
       Y-axis)))
  (setq height (1- height)))
;; Insert base line.
(setq Y-axis (cons (Y-axis-element
                    (or vertical-step 1)
                    width-of-label)
                   Y-axis))
(nreverse Y-axis)))
```

The values for the maximum height of graph and the width of a symbol are computed by `print-graph` in its `let` expression; so `graph-body-print` must be changed to accept them.

```
;;; Final version.
(defun graph-body-print (numbers-list height symbol-width)
  "Print a bar graph of the NUMBERS-LIST.
The numbers-list consists of the Y-axis values.
HEIGHT is maximum height of graph.
SYMBOL-WIDTH is number of each column."
  (let (from-position)
    (while numbers-list
      (setq from-position (point))
      (insert-rectangle
       (column-of-graph height (car numbers-list)))
      (goto-char from-position)
      (forward-char symbol-width)
      ;; Draw graph column by column.
      (sit-for 0)
      (setq numbers-list (cdr numbers-list)))
    ;; Place point for X axis labels.
    (forward-line height)
    (insert "\n")))
```

Finally, the code for the `print-graph` function:

```
;;; Final version.
(defun print-graph
    (numbers-list &optional vertical-step)
  "Print labeled bar graph of the NUMBERS-LIST.
The numbers-list consists of the Y-axis values.

Optionally, VERTICAL-STEP, a positive integer,
specifies how much a Y axis label increments for
each line.  For example, a step of 5 means that
each row is five units."
  (let* ((symbol-width (length graph-blank))
         ;; height is both the largest number
         ;; and the number with the most digits.
         (height (apply 'max numbers-list))
```

```
      (height-of-top-line
       (if (zerop (% height Y-axis-label-spacing))
           height
         ;; else
         (* (1+ (/ height Y-axis-label-spacing))
            Y-axis-label-spacing)))
      (vertical-step (or vertical-step 1))
      (full-Y-label-width
       (length
        (concat
         (number-to-string
          (* height-of-top-line vertical-step))
         Y-axis-tic)))))

 (print-Y-axis
  height-of-top-line full-Y-label-width vertical-step)
 (graph-body-print
  numbers-list height-of-top-line symbol-width)
 (print-X-axis numbers-list)))
```

C.4.1 Testing `print-graph`

We can test the `print-graph` function with a short list of numbers:

1. Install the final versions of `Y-axis-column`, `graph-body-print`, and `print-graph` (in addition to the rest of the code.)

2. Copy the following expression:

   ```
   (print-graph '(3 2 5 6 7 5 3 4 6 4 3 2 1))
   ```

3. Switch to the `*scratch*` buffer and place the cursor where you want the axis labels to start.

4. Type *M-:* (eval-expression).

5. Yank the test expression into the minibuffer with *C-y* (`yank`).

6. Press `RET` to evaluate the expression.

Emacs will print a graph that looks like this:

```
10 -



        *
        **    *
 5 -    ****  *
        **** ***
      * ********
      ***********
 1 -  ***********

      |   |   |   |
      1   5  10  15
```

On the other hand, if you pass `print-graph` a `vertical-step` value of 2, by evaluating this expression:

```
(print-graph '(3 2 5 6 7 5 3 4 6 4 3 2 1) 2)
```

The graph looks like this:

```
20 -



          *
         **    *
10 -    ****   *
        **** ***
       * ********
       ***********
 2 -   ************


       |   |    |    |
       1   5   10   15
```

(A question: is the '2' on the bottom of the vertical axis a bug or a feature? If you think it is a bug, and should be a '1' instead, (or even a '0'), you can modify the sources.)

C.4.2 Graphing Numbers of Words and Symbols

Now for the graph for which all this code was written: a graph that shows how many function definitions contain fewer than 10 words and symbols, how many contain between 10 and 19 words and symbols, how many contain between 20 and 29 words and symbols, and so on.

This is a multi-step process. First make sure you have loaded all the requisite code.

It is a good idea to reset the value of `top-of-ranges` in case you have set it to some different value. You can evaluate the following:

```
(setq top-of-ranges
 '(10   20   30   40   50
   60   70   80   90  100
  110  120  130  140  150
  160  170  180  190  200
  210  220  230  240  250
  260  270  280  290  300)
```

Next create a list of the number of words and symbols in each range.

Evaluate the following:

```
(setq list-for-graph
       (defuns-per-range
         (sort
          (recursive-lengths-list-many-files
           (directory-files "/usr/local/emacs/lisp"
                            t ".+el$"))
          '<)
        top-of-ranges))
```

On my old machine, this took about an hour. It looked though 303 Lisp files in my copy of Emacs version 19.23. After all that computing, the `list-for-graph` had this value:

```
(537 1027 955 785 594 483 349 292 224 199 166 120 116 99
  90 80 67 48 52 45 41 33 28 26 25 20 12 28 11 13 220)
```

This means that my copy of Emacs had 537 function definitions with fewer than 10 words or symbols in them, 1,027 function definitions with 10 to 19 words or symbols in them, 955 function definitions with 20 to 29 words or symbols in them, and so on.

Clearly, just by looking at this list we can see that most function definitions contain ten to thirty words and symbols.

Now for printing. We do *not* want to print a graph that is 1,030 lines high . . . Instead, we should print a graph that is fewer than twenty-five lines high. A graph that height can be displayed on almost any monitor, and easily printed on a sheet of paper.

This means that each value in `list-for-graph` must be reduced to one-fiftieth its present value.

Here is a short function to do just that, using two functions we have not yet seen, `mapcar` and `lambda`.

```
(defun one-fiftieth (full-range)
  "Return list, each number one-fiftieth of previous."
(mapcar (lambda (arg) (/ arg 50)) full-range))
```

C.4.3 A `lambda` Expression: Useful Anonymity

`lambda` is the symbol for an anonymous function, a function without a name. Every time you use an anonymous function, you need to include its whole body.
Thus,

```
(lambda (arg) (/ arg 50))
```

is a function that returns the value resulting from dividing whatever is passed to it as `arg` by 50.

Earlier, for example, we had a function `multiply-by-seven`; it multiplied its argument by 7. This function is similar, except it divides its argument by 50; and, it has no name. The anonymous equivalent of `multiply-by-seven` is:

```
(lambda (number) (* 7 number))
```

(See Section 3.1 "The `defun` Macro", page 26.)
If we want to multiply 3 by 7, we can write:

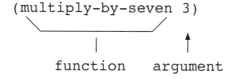

This expression returns 21.

Similarly, we can write:

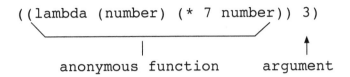

If we want to divide 100 by 50, we can write:

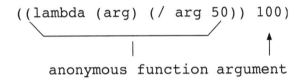

This expression returns 2. The 100 is passed to the function, which divides that number by 50.

See Section "Lambda Expressions" in *The GNU Emacs Lisp Reference Manual*, for more about `lambda`. Lisp and lambda expressions derive from the Lambda Calculus.

C.4.4 The `mapcar` Function

`mapcar` is a function that calls its first argument with each element of its second argument, in turn. The second argument must be a sequence.

The 'map' part of the name comes from the mathematical phrase, "mapping over a domain", meaning to apply a function to each of the elements in a domain. The mathematical phrase is based on the metaphor of a surveyor walking, one step at a time, over an area he is mapping. And 'car', of course, comes from the Lisp notion of the first of a list.

For example,

```
(mapcar '1+ '(2 4 6))
     ⇒ (3 5 7)
```

The function `1+` which adds one to its argument, is executed on *each* element of the list, and a new list is returned.

Contrast this with `apply`, which applies its first argument to all the remaining. (See Chapter 15 "Readying a Graph", page 173, for a explanation of `apply`.)

In the definition of `one-fiftieth`, the first argument is the anonymous function:

```
(lambda (arg) (/ arg 50))
```

and the second argument is `full-range`, which will be bound to `list-for-graph`.

The whole expression looks like this:

```
(mapcar (lambda (arg) (/ arg 50)) full-range))
```

See Section "Mapping Functions" in *The GNU Emacs Lisp Reference Manual*, for more about `mapcar`.

Using the `one-fiftieth` function, we can generate a list in which each element is one-fiftieth the size of the corresponding element in `list-for-graph`.

```
(setq fiftieth-list-for-graph
      (one-fiftieth list-for-graph))
```

The resulting list looks like this:

```
(10 20 19 15 11 9 6 5 4 3 3 2 2
1 1 1 1 0 1 0 0 0 0 0 0 0 0 0 0 4)
```

This, we are almost ready to print! (We also notice the loss of information: many of the higher ranges are 0, meaning that fewer than 50 defuns had that many words or symbols—but not necessarily meaning that none had that many words or symbols.)

C.4.5 Another Bug ... Most Insidious

I said "almost ready to print"! Of course, there is a bug in the `print-graph` function ... It has a `vertical-step` option, but not a `horizontal-step` option. The `top-of-range` scale goes from 10 to 300 by tens. But the `print-graph` function will print only by ones.

This is a classic example of what some consider the most insidious type of bug, the bug of omission. This is not the kind of bug you can find by studying the code, for it is not in the code; it is an omitted feature. Your best actions are to try your program early and often; and try to arrange, as much as you can, to write code that is easy to understand and easy to change. Try to be aware, whenever you can, that whatever you have written, *will* be rewritten, if not soon, eventually. A hard maxim to follow.

It is the `print-X-axis-numbered-line` function that needs the work; and then the `print-X-axis` and the `print-graph` functions need to be adapted. Not much needs to be done; there is one nicety: the numbers ought to line up under the tic marks. This takes a little thought.

Here is the corrected `print-X-axis-numbered-line`:

```
(defun print-X-axis-numbered-line
  (number-of-X-tics X-axis-leading-spaces
   &optional horizontal-step)
  "Print line of X-axis numbers"
  (let ((number X-axis-label-spacing)
        (horizontal-step (or horizontal-step 1)))
```

```
(insert X-axis-leading-spaces)
;; Delete extra leading spaces.
(delete-char
 (- (1-
     (length (number-to-string horizontal-step)))))
(insert (concat
          (make-string
           ;; Insert white space.
           (- (* symbol-width
                 X-axis-label-spacing)
              (1-
               (length
                (number-to-string horizontal-step)))
              2)
           ? )
          (number-to-string
           (* number horizontal-step))))
;; Insert remaining numbers.
(setq number (+ number X-axis-label-spacing))
(while (> number-of-X-tics 1)
  (insert (X-axis-element
            (* number horizontal-step)))
  (setq number (+ number X-axis-label-spacing))
  (setq number-of-X-tics (1- number-of-X-tics)))))
```

If you are reading this in Info, you can see the new versions of `print-X-axis` `print-graph` and evaluate them. If you are reading this in a printed book, you can see the changed lines here (the full text is too much to print).

```
(defun print-X-axis (numbers-list horizontal-step)
   ...
    (print-X-axis-numbered-line
     tic-number leading-spaces horizontal-step))
(defun print-graph
  (numbers-list
   &optional vertical-step horizontal-step)
   ...
    (print-X-axis numbers-list horizontal-step))
```

C.4.6 The Printed Graph

When made and installed, you can call the `print-graph` command like this:

```
(print-graph fiftieth-list-for-graph 50 10)
```

Here is the graph:

```
1000 -   *
         **
         **
         **
         **
 750 -   ***
         ***
         ***
         ***
         ****
 500 - *****
       ******
       ******
       ******
       *******
 250 - ********
       ********                       *
       **********                     *
       ************                   *
  50 - ****************  *             *
        |    |     |     |     |     |     |     |
        10   50   100   150   200   250   300   350
```

The largest group of functions contain 10–19 words and symbols each.

Appendix D Free Software and Free Manuals

by Richard M. Stallman

The biggest deficiency in free operating systems is not in the software—it is the lack of good free manuals that we can include in these systems. Many of our most important programs do not come with full manuals. Documentation is an essential part of any software package; when an important free software package does not come with a free manual, that is a major gap. We have many such gaps today.

Once upon a time, many years ago, I thought I would learn Perl. I got a copy of a free manual, but I found it hard to read. When I asked Perl users about alternatives, they told me that there were better introductory manuals—but those were not free.

Why was this? The authors of the good manuals had written them for O'Reilly Associates, which published them with restrictive terms—no copying, no modification, source files not available—which exclude them from the free software community.

That wasn't the first time this sort of thing has happened, and (to our community's great loss) it was far from the last. Proprietary manual publishers have enticed a great many authors to restrict their manuals since then. Many times I have heard a GNU user eagerly tell me about a manual that he is writing, with which he expects to help the GNU project—and then had my hopes dashed, as he proceeded to explain that he had signed a contract with a publisher that would restrict it so that we cannot use it.

Given that writing good English is a rare skill among programmers, we can ill afford to lose manuals this way.

Free documentation, like free software, is a matter of freedom, not price. The problem with these manuals was not that O'Reilly Associates charged a price for printed copies—that in itself is fine. The Free Software Foundation sells printed copies (`http://shop.fsf.org`) of free GNU manuals (`http://www.gnu.org/doc/doc.html`), too. But GNU manuals are available in source code form, while these manuals are available only on paper. GNU manuals come with permission to copy and modify; the Perl manuals do not. These restrictions are the problems.

The criterion for a free manual is pretty much the same as for free software: it is a matter of giving all users certain freedoms. Redistribution (including commercial redistribution) must be permitted, so that the manual can accompany every copy of the program, on-line or on paper. Permission for modification is crucial too.

As a general rule, I don't believe that it is essential for people to have permission to modify all sorts of articles and books. The issues for writings are not necessarily the same as those for software. For example, I don't think you or I are obliged to give permission to modify articles like this one, which describe our actions and our views.

But there is a particular reason why the freedom to modify is crucial for documentation for free software. When people exercise their right to modify the software, and add or change its features, if they are conscientious they will change the manual too—so they can provide accurate and usable documentation with the modified program. A manual which forbids programmers to be conscientious and finish the job, or more precisely requires them to write a new manual from scratch if they change the program, does not fill our community's needs.

While a blanket prohibition on modification is unacceptable, some kinds of limits on the method of modification pose no problem. For example, requirements to preserve the original author's copyright notice, the distribution terms, or the list of authors, are ok. It is also no problem to require modified versions to include notice that they were modified, even to have entire sections that may not be deleted or changed, as long as these sections deal with nontechnical topics. (Some GNU manuals have them.)

These kinds of restrictions are not a problem because, as a practical matter, they don't stop the conscientious programmer from adapting the manual to fit the modified program. In other words, they don't block the free software community from making full use of the manual.

However, it must be possible to modify all the technical content of the manual, and then distribute the result in all the usual media, through all the usual channels; otherwise, the restrictions do block the community, the manual is not free, and so we need another manual.

Unfortunately, it is often hard to find someone to write another manual when a proprietary manual exists. The obstacle is that many users think that a proprietary manual is good enough—so they don't see the need to write a free manual. They do not see that the free operating system has a gap that needs filling.

Why do users think that proprietary manuals are good enough? Some have not considered the issue. I hope this article will do something to change that.

Other users consider proprietary manuals acceptable for the same reason so many people consider proprietary software acceptable: they judge in purely practical terms, not using freedom as a criterion. These people are entitled to their opinions, but since those opinions spring from values which do not include freedom, they are no guide for those of us who do value freedom.

Please spread the word about this issue. We continue to lose manuals to proprietary publishing. If we spread the word that proprietary manuals are not sufficient, perhaps the next person who wants to help GNU by writing documentation will realize, before it is too late, that he must above all make it free.

We can also encourage commercial publishers to sell free, copylefted manuals instead of proprietary ones. One way you can help this is to check the distribution terms of a manual before you buy it, and prefer copylefted manuals to non-copylefted ones.

Note: The Free Software Foundation maintains a page on its Web site that lists free books available from other publishers:
`http://www.gnu.org/doc/other-free-books.html`

Appendix E GNU Free Documentation License

Version 1.3, 3 November 2008

Copyright © 2000, 2001, 2002, 2007, 2008 Free Software Foundation, Inc.
http://fsf.org/

Everyone is permitted to copy and distribute verbatim copies
of this license document, but changing it is not allowed.

0. PREAMBLE

The purpose of this License is to make a manual, textbook, or other functional
and useful document *free* in the sense of freedom: to assure everyone the
effective freedom to copy and redistribute it, with or without modifying it,
either commercially or noncommercially. Secondarily, this License preserves
for the author and publisher a way to get credit for their work, while not being
considered responsible for modifications made by others.

This License is a kind of "copyleft", which means that derivative works of the
document must themselves be free in the same sense. It complements the GNU
General Public License, which is a copyleft license designed for free software.

We have designed this License in order to use it for manuals for free software,
because free software needs free documentation: a free program should come
with manuals providing the same freedoms that the software does. But this
License is not limited to software manuals; it can be used for any textual work,
regardless of subject matter or whether it is published as a printed book. We
recommend this License principally for works whose purpose is instruction or
reference.

1. APPLICABILITY AND DEFINITIONS

This License applies to any manual or other work, in any medium, that contains
a notice placed by the copyright holder saying it can be distributed under the
terms of this License. Such a notice grants a world-wide, royalty-free license,
unlimited in duration, to use that work under the conditions stated herein.
The "Document", below, refers to any such manual or work. Any member of
the public is a licensee, and is addressed as "you". You accept the license if
you copy, modify or distribute the work in a way requiring permission under
copyright law.

A "Modified Version" of the Document means any work containing the Document
or a portion of it, either copied verbatim, or with modifications and/or
translated into another language.

A "Secondary Section" is a named appendix or a front-matter section of the
Document that deals exclusively with the relationship of the publishers or authors of the Document to the Document's overall subject (or to related matters) and contains nothing that could fall directly within that overall subject.
(Thus, if the Document is in part a textbook of mathematics, a Secondary Section may not explain any mathematics.) The relationship could be a matter
of historical connection with the subject or with related matters, or of legal,
commercial, philosophical, ethical or political position regarding them.

The "Invariant Sections" are certain Secondary Sections whose titles are designated, as being those of Invariant Sections, in the notice that says that the Document is released under this License. If a section does not fit the above definition of Secondary then it is not allowed to be designated as Invariant. The Document may contain zero Invariant Sections. If the Document does not identify any Invariant Sections then there are none.

The "Cover Texts" are certain short passages of text that are listed, as Front-Cover Texts or Back-Cover Texts, in the notice that says that the Document is released under this License. A Front-Cover Text may be at most 5 words, and a Back-Cover Text may be at most 25 words.

A "Transparent" copy of the Document means a machine-readable copy, represented in a format whose specification is available to the general public, that is suitable for revising the document straightforwardly with generic text editors or (for images composed of pixels) generic paint programs or (for drawings) some widely available drawing editor, and that is suitable for input to text formatters or for automatic translation to a variety of formats suitable for input to text formatters. A copy made in an otherwise Transparent file format whose markup, or absence of markup, has been arranged to thwart or discourage subsequent modification by readers is not Transparent. An image format is not Transparent if used for any substantial amount of text. A copy that is not "Transparent" is called "Opaque".

Examples of suitable formats for Transparent copies include plain ASCII without markup, Texinfo input format, LaTeX input format, SGML or XML using a publicly available DTD, and standard-conforming simple HTML, PostScript or PDF designed for human modification. Examples of transparent image formats include PNG, XCF and JPG. Opaque formats include proprietary formats that can be read and edited only by proprietary word processors, SGML or XML for which the DTD and/or processing tools are not generally available, and the machine-generated HTML, PostScript or PDF produced by some word processors for output purposes only.

The "Title Page" means, for a printed book, the title page itself, plus such following pages as are needed to hold, legibly, the material this License requires to appear in the title page. For works in formats which do not have any title page as such, "Title Page" means the text near the most prominent appearance of the work's title, preceding the beginning of the body of the text.

The "publisher" means any person or entity that distributes copies of the Document to the public.

A section "Entitled XYZ" means a named subunit of the Document whose title either is precisely XYZ or contains XYZ in parentheses following text that translates XYZ in another language. (Here XYZ stands for a specific section name mentioned below, such as "Acknowledgements", "Dedications", "Endorsements", or "History".) To "Preserve the Title" of such a section when you modify the Document means that it remains a section "Entitled XYZ" according to this definition.

The Document may include Warranty Disclaimers next to the notice which states that this License applies to the Document. These Warranty Disclaimers are considered to be included by reference in this License, but only as regards disclaiming warranties: any other implication that these Warranty Disclaimers may have is void and has no effect on the meaning of this License.

2. VERBATIM COPYING

You may copy and distribute the Document in any medium, either commercially or noncommercially, provided that this License, the copyright notices, and the license notice saying this License applies to the Document are reproduced in all copies, and that you add no other conditions whatsoever to those of this License. You may not use technical measures to obstruct or control the reading or further copying of the copies you make or distribute. However, you may accept compensation in exchange for copies. If you distribute a large enough number of copies you must also follow the conditions in section 3.

You may also lend copies, under the same conditions stated above, and you may publicly display copies.

3. COPYING IN QUANTITY

If you publish printed copies (or copies in media that commonly have printed covers) of the Document, numbering more than 100, and the Document's license notice requires Cover Texts, you must enclose the copies in covers that carry, clearly and legibly, all these Cover Texts: Front-Cover Texts on the front cover, and Back-Cover Texts on the back cover. Both covers must also clearly and legibly identify you as the publisher of these copies. The front cover must present the full title with all words of the title equally prominent and visible. You may add other material on the covers in addition. Copying with changes limited to the covers, as long as they preserve the title of the Document and satisfy these conditions, can be treated as verbatim copying in other respects.

If the required texts for either cover are too voluminous to fit legibly, you should put the first ones listed (as many as fit reasonably) on the actual cover, and continue the rest onto adjacent pages.

If you publish or distribute Opaque copies of the Document numbering more than 100, you must either include a machine-readable Transparent copy along with each Opaque copy, or state in or with each Opaque copy a computer-network location from which the general network-using public has access to download using public-standard network protocols a complete Transparent copy of the Document, free of added material. If you use the latter option, you must take reasonably prudent steps, when you begin distribution of Opaque copies in quantity, to ensure that this Transparent copy will remain thus accessible at the stated location until at least one year after the last time you distribute an Opaque copy (directly or through your agents or retailers) of that edition to the public.

It is requested, but not required, that you contact the authors of the Document well before redistributing any large number of copies, to give them a chance to provide you with an updated version of the Document.

4. MODIFICATIONS

You may copy and distribute a Modified Version of the Document under the conditions of sections 2 and 3 above, provided that you release the Modified Version under precisely this License, with the Modified Version filling the role of the Document, thus licensing distribution and modification of the Modified Version to whoever possesses a copy of it. In addition, you must do these things in the Modified Version:

A. Use in the Title Page (and on the covers, if any) a title distinct from that of the Document, and from those of previous versions (which should, if there were any, be listed in the History section of the Document). You may use the same title as a previous version if the original publisher of that version gives permission.

B. List on the Title Page, as authors, one or more persons or entities responsible for authorship of the modifications in the Modified Version, together with at least five of the principal authors of the Document (all of its principal authors, if it has fewer than five), unless they release you from this requirement.

C. State on the Title page the name of the publisher of the Modified Version, as the publisher.

D. Preserve all the copyright notices of the Document.

E. Add an appropriate copyright notice for your modifications adjacent to the other copyright notices.

F. Include, immediately after the copyright notices, a license notice giving the public permission to use the Modified Version under the terms of this License, in the form shown in the Addendum below.

G. Preserve in that license notice the full lists of Invariant Sections and required Cover Texts given in the Document's license notice.

H. Include an unaltered copy of this License.

I. Preserve the section Entitled "History", Preserve its Title, and add to it an item stating at least the title, year, new authors, and publisher of the Modified Version as given on the Title Page. If there is no section Entitled "History" in the Document, create one stating the title, year, authors, and publisher of the Document as given on its Title Page, then add an item describing the Modified Version as stated in the previous sentence.

J. Preserve the network location, if any, given in the Document for public access to a Transparent copy of the Document, and likewise the network locations given in the Document for previous versions it was based on. These may be placed in the "History" section. You may omit a network location for a work that was published at least four years before the Document itself, or if the original publisher of the version it refers to gives permission.

K. For any section Entitled "Acknowledgements" or "Dedications", Preserve the Title of the section, and preserve in the section all the substance and tone of each of the contributor acknowledgements and/or dedications given therein.

L. Preserve all the Invariant Sections of the Document, unaltered in their text and in their titles. Section numbers or the equivalent are not considered part of the section titles.

M. Delete any section Entitled "Endorsements". Such a section may not be included in the Modified Version.

N. Do not retitle any existing section to be Entitled "Endorsements" or to conflict in title with any Invariant Section.

O. Preserve any Warranty Disclaimers.

If the Modified Version includes new front-matter sections or appendices that qualify as Secondary Sections and contain no material copied from the Document, you may at your option designate some or all of these sections as invariant. To do this, add their titles to the list of Invariant Sections in the Modified Version's license notice. These titles must be distinct from any other section titles.

You may add a section Entitled "Endorsements", provided it contains nothing but endorsements of your Modified Version by various parties—for example, statements of peer review or that the text has been approved by an organization as the authoritative definition of a standard.

You may add a passage of up to five words as a Front-Cover Text, and a passage of up to 25 words as a Back-Cover Text, to the end of the list of Cover Texts in the Modified Version. Only one passage of Front-Cover Text and one of Back-Cover Text may be added by (or through arrangements made by) any one entity. If the Document already includes a cover text for the same cover, previously added by you or by arrangement made by the same entity you are acting on behalf of, you may not add another; but you may replace the old one, on explicit permission from the previous publisher that added the old one.

The author(s) and publisher(s) of the Document do not by this License give permission to use their names for publicity for or to assert or imply endorsement of any Modified Version.

5. COMBINING DOCUMENTS

You may combine the Document with other documents released under this License, under the terms defined in section 4 above for modified versions, provided that you include in the combination all of the Invariant Sections of all of the original documents, unmodified, and list them all as Invariant Sections of your combined work in its license notice, and that you preserve all their Warranty Disclaimers.

The combined work need only contain one copy of this License, and multiple identical Invariant Sections may be replaced with a single copy. If there are multiple Invariant Sections with the same name but different contents, make the title of each such section unique by adding at the end of it, in parentheses, the name of the original author or publisher of that section if known, or else a unique number. Make the same adjustment to the section titles in the list of Invariant Sections in the license notice of the combined work.

In the combination, you must combine any sections Entitled "History" in the various original documents, forming one section Entitled "History"; likewise combine any sections Entitled "Acknowledgements", and any sections Entitled "Dedications". You must delete all sections Entitled "Endorsements."

6. COLLECTIONS OF DOCUMENTS

You may make a collection consisting of the Document and other documents released under this License, and replace the individual copies of this License in the various documents with a single copy that is included in the collection, provided that you follow the rules of this License for verbatim copying of each of the documents in all other respects.

You may extract a single document from such a collection, and distribute it individually under this License, provided you insert a copy of this License into the extracted document, and follow this License in all other respects regarding verbatim copying of that document.

7. AGGREGATION WITH INDEPENDENT WORKS

A compilation of the Document or its derivatives with other separate and independent documents or works, in or on a volume of a storage or distribution medium, is called an "aggregate" if the copyright resulting from the compilation is not used to limit the legal rights of the compilation's users beyond what the individual works permit. When the Document is included in an aggregate, this License does not apply to the other works in the aggregate which are not themselves derivative works of the Document.

If the Cover Text requirement of section 3 is applicable to these copies of the Document, then if the Document is less than one half of the entire aggregate, the Document's Cover Texts may be placed on covers that bracket the Document within the aggregate, or the electronic equivalent of covers if the Document is in electronic form. Otherwise they must appear on printed covers that bracket the whole aggregate.

8. TRANSLATION

Translation is considered a kind of modification, so you may distribute translations of the Document under the terms of section 4. Replacing Invariant Sections with translations requires special permission from their copyright holders, but you may include translations of some or all Invariant Sections in addition to the original versions of these Invariant Sections. You may include a translation of this License, and all the license notices in the Document, and any Warranty Disclaimers, provided that you also include the original English version of this License and the original versions of those notices and disclaimers. In case of a disagreement between the translation and the original version of this License or a notice or disclaimer, the original version will prevail.

If a section in the Document is Entitled "Acknowledgements", "Dedications", or "History", the requirement (section 4) to Preserve its Title (section 1) will typically require changing the actual title.

9. TERMINATION

You may not copy, modify, sublicense, or distribute the Document except as expressly provided under this License. Any attempt otherwise to copy, modify, sublicense, or distribute it is void, and will automatically terminate your rights under this License.

However, if you cease all violation of this License, then your license from a particular copyright holder is reinstated (a) provisionally, unless and until the copyright holder explicitly and finally terminates your license, and (b) permanently, if the copyright holder fails to notify you of the violation by some reasonable means prior to 60 days after the cessation.

Moreover, your license from a particular copyright holder is reinstated permanently if the copyright holder notifies you of the violation by some reasonable means, this is the first time you have received notice of violation of this License (for any work) from that copyright holder, and you cure the violation prior to 30 days after your receipt of the notice.

Termination of your rights under this section does not terminate the licenses of parties who have received copies or rights from you under this License. If your rights have been terminated and not permanently reinstated, receipt of a copy of some or all of the same material does not give you any rights to use it.

10. FUTURE REVISIONS OF THIS LICENSE

The Free Software Foundation may publish new, revised versions of the GNU Free Documentation License from time to time. Such new versions will be similar in spirit to the present version, but may differ in detail to address new problems or concerns. See `http://www.gnu.org/copyleft/`.

Each version of the License is given a distinguishing version number. If the Document specifies that a particular numbered version of this License "or any later version" applies to it, you have the option of following the terms and conditions either of that specified version or of any later version that has been published (not as a draft) by the Free Software Foundation. If the Document does not specify a version number of this License, you may choose any version ever published (not as a draft) by the Free Software Foundation. If the Document specifies that a proxy can decide which future versions of this License can be used, that proxy's public statement of acceptance of a version permanently authorizes you to choose that version for the Document.

11. RELICENSING

"Massive Multiauthor Collaboration Site" (or "MMC Site") means any World Wide Web server that publishes copyrightable works and also provides prominent facilities for anybody to edit those works. A public wiki that anybody can edit is an example of such a server. A "Massive Multiauthor Collaboration" (or "MMC") contained in the site means any set of copyrightable works thus published on the MMC site.

"CC-BY-SA" means the Creative Commons Attribution-Share Alike 3.0 license published by Creative Commons Corporation, a not-for-profit corporation with a principal place of business in San Francisco, California, as well as future copyleft versions of that license published by that same organization.

"Incorporate" means to publish or republish a Document, in whole or in part, as part of another Document.

An MMC is "eligible for relicensing" if it is licensed under this License, and if all works that were first published under this License somewhere other than this MMC, and subsequently incorporated in whole or in part into the MMC, (1) had no cover texts or invariant sections, and (2) were thus incorporated prior to November 1, 2008.

The operator of an MMC Site may republish an MMC contained in the site under CC-BY-SA on the same site at any time before August 1, 2009, provided the MMC is eligible for relicensing.

ADDENDUM: How to use this License for your documents

To use this License in a document you have written, include a copy of the License in the document and put the following copyright and license notices just after the title page:

```
Copyright (C)  year  your name.
Permission is granted to copy, distribute and/or modify this document
under the terms of the GNU Free Documentation License, Version 1.3
or any later version published by the Free Software Foundation;
with no Invariant Sections, no Front-Cover Texts, and no Back-Cover
Texts.  A copy of the license is included in the section entitled ``GNU
Free Documentation License''.
```

If you have Invariant Sections, Front-Cover Texts and Back-Cover Texts, replace the "with...Texts." line with this:

```
with the Invariant Sections being list their titles, with
the Front-Cover Texts being list, and with the Back-Cover Texts
being list.
```

If you have Invariant Sections without Cover Texts, or some other combination of the three, merge those two alternatives to suit the situation.

If your document contains nontrivial examples of program code, we recommend releasing these examples in parallel under your choice of free software license, such as the GNU General Public License, to permit their use in free software.

Index

About the Author

Robert J. Chassell has worked with GNU Emacs since 1985. He writes and edits, teaches Emacs and Emacs Lisp, and speaks throughout the world on software freedom. Chassell was a founding Director and Treasurer of the Free Software Foundation, Inc. He is co-author of the *Texinfo* manual, and has edited more than a dozen other books. He graduated from Cambridge University, in England. He has an abiding interest in social and economic history and flies his own airplane.

CPSIA information can be obtained
at www.ICGtesting.com
Printed in the USA
BVHW011302210120
570078BV00013B/169